D0064999

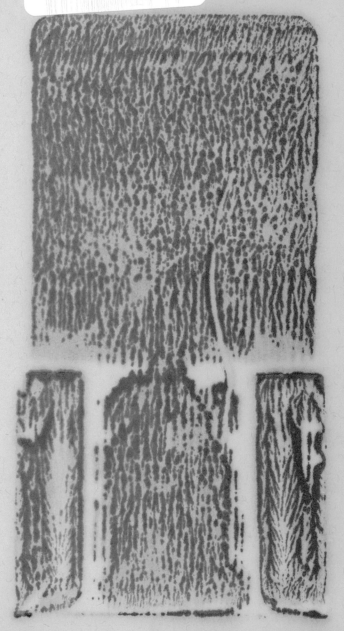

HARVARD

HISTORICAL STUDIES

VOLUME VII.

THE PROVINCIAL GOVERNOR

IN

THE ENGLISH COLONIES OF
NORTH AMERICA

THE PROVINCIAL GOVERNOR

IN

THE ENGLISH COLONIES OF NORTH AMERICA

BY

EVARTS BOUTELL GREENE

NEW YORK / RUSSELL & RUSSELL

1966

POINT PARK COLLEGE LIBRARY

FIRST PUBLISHED IN 1898
REISSUED, 1966, BY RUSSELL & RUSSELL
A DIVISION OF ATHENEUM HOUSE INC.
L.C. CATALOG CARD NO: 66—24700

REPRINTED FROM A COPY IN THE COLLECTIONS OF
THE BROOKLYN COLLEGE LIBRARY

PRINTED IN THE UNITED STATES OF AMERICA

PREFACE.

THIS essay was in its original form presented as a dissertation for the degree of Doctor of Philosophy in Harvard University. It has since been revised and in considerable part rewritten. Though in the process of revision many errors of fact and errors of judgment have been corrected, there are doubtless many which have escaped the author's notice, and which remain to be pointed out by others. It is hoped, however, that the conclusions here set forth may at least serve to provoke discussion and investigation in a comparatively unworked and exceedingly important field of research.

The title and scope of the work require some explanation. The term *Provincial Governor* has been chosen to designate the chief executive of the royal and proprietary colonies. As will be subsequently explained, the internal constitution of the proprietary colony became so nearly like that of the royal province that the two may with advantage be treated together. In the proprietary and in the royal governor alike we have the representative of an externally imposed authority. The elective governors of Rhode Island and Connecticut stood upon an essentially different footing, and do not therefore come within the scope of this work. Two other important limitations must be noted. After a brief introduction on the beginnings of constitutional development, the field is restricted, in the main, to the period between the Revolution of 1688 and the close of the last French war; excluding, therefore, the complications of the revolutionary era, and presenting a simple view of the normal working of the provincial constitution. The field of study is further restricted to those colonies which afterwards became a part of the United States of America, though occasional illustrations have been drawn from the practice of other British provinces.

In the appendices are included, first, a few representative commissions and sets of instructions; secondly, a list of printed commissions and instructions to royal and proprietary governors; and, finally, a list of authorities cited. In citing any provision of the commissions or instructions, the reference in the footnote is to the particular section or page where that provision occurs. The place in which the document is printed may then be found by reference to Appendix B. The commission and instructions to Francis Bernard, which are given in Appendix A, have, so far as possible, been cited in the discussion of particular powers and duties assigned to the governor. In this way many statements made in the text may be conveniently checked by reference to the documentary material in the appendix.

It is impossible to express adequately the author's indebtedness to all those who have aided in the successive stages of this work, and to whom such measure of success as may have been attained is very largely due. The officers of the Harvard University Library have done much by their courtesy and liberal extension of privileges to facilitate both the original labor of investigation and the subsequent task of verification and revision. Special acknowledgments are due to Mr. Philip A. Bruce of the *Virginia Magazine of History and Biography*, Dr. Alexander Brown, and Messrs. Houghton, Mifflin and Company for permission to print documents included in Appendix A; and also to Miss Addie F. Rowe, of Cambridge, for conscientious and intelligent service in preparing the manuscript for the press.

The author desires finally to express his deep sense of obligation to his teachers and friends in the historical department of Harvard University — especially to Professor Edward Channing, under whose guidance the work has been carried on, and Professor Albert Bushnell Hart, to whom he has been indebted throughout for kindly criticism and encouragement.

EVARTS B. GREENE.

Urbana, *September,* 1898.

CONTENTS.

APPENDICES.

THE PROVINCIAL GOVERNOR.

CHAPTER I.

THE EVOLUTION OF THE PROVINCIAL GOVERNMENT.

IN 1763 the royal government was the predominant type in the English colonies which were later to become the United States of America. Of the twelve colonial governments,[1] eight belonged to the class of royal or provincial governments, two were proprietary governments, and two were chartered colonies with elective governors. This condition was, however, the result of very gradual development, inasmuch as the policy of direct control by the crown was finally adopted only after a long period, during which it was the rule to intrust the government, as well as the soil of the colonies, to proprietors or colonizing companies. In no colony was the system of royal government continuous from the beginning. So, too, the form and the powers of the colonial executive were not fixed from the start, but were adopted after various experiments with other forms, and were the result of a gradual limitation of powers at first vague and undefined. The first question to be considered, then, is as to the steps by which the royal government took shape and became the prevailing form in the colonies.

For the earliest indications of royal policy in regard to the government of the colonies, it is necessary to go back to the sixteenth century. In the patent granted to Sir Humphrey Gilbert, in 1578, the right of government was given to the proprietor substantially without limitation as to internal

---

[1] Counting Delaware with Pennsylvania as a single government. These two colonies had separate legislatures, but a common executive.

affairs.[1] In 1584, Sir Walter Raleigh received a charter conferring similar rights, under which the colony on Roanoke
Island was organized.[2] In each of these cases, the government of the colony was left in the hands of the patentee.

The first permanent English colony was that of Virginia,
founded in 1607.[3] Here the king at first retained considerable
control. The charter to the Virginia Company provided that
the governing council in England should be named by the
crown, and reserved to the king the right of making from time
to time such regulations as he saw fit for the government of
the colony. In the exercise of this reserved right, the king
issued in the same year a set of "Articles, Instructions, and
Orders" for the government of Virginia, providing for a resident council which was to be appointed by the superior council
at home.[4] By the second charter, however, the king resigned
these important rights, leaving the governing council to be
elected thenceforth by the company, which was now left quite
free in the organization of the government in Virginia.[5]

The period of independence was, however, of short duration.
In various ways, which need not be recited in detail here, the
company incurred the ill-will of the king, a calamity which
was rendered still more serious by internal dissensions. The
dissentients soon caused serious charges of mismanagement to
be brought against the company. It is true that these were
squarely met, and that the people of the colony, far from join-
ing in the attack, as it was hoped that they might do, declared
in favor of the existing government.[6] Still, the case was pre-
judged. In July, 1623, the attorney-general was directed to
inquire whether the conduct of the Virginia Company did not
furnish ground for annulling the charter, and, as might have

[1] Hazard, *Historical Collections*, i. 24.   [2] *Ibid.*, 33.
[3] Charter in Poore, *Charters and Constitutions*, ii. 1890.
[4] Alexander Brown, *Genesis of the United States*, i. 65.
[5] Charter of 1609 in Poore, *Charters and Constitutions*, ii. 1893 *seq.*
[6] Sainsbury, *Calendar of State Papers, Colonial Series, America and
West Indies*, 1574–1660, pp. 22, 24, 44, 59, 63, 65; *Proceedings of the Virginia Company* (Virginia Historical Society, *Collections*, New Series, vii.–
viii.), i. 63, 77 *seq.*, ii. 146; Stith, *History of Virginia* (1865), 304; Chalmers,
Political Annals, 64.

been expected, the royal law officers gave the opinion desired by the crown.[1] The king then proposed a considerable modification of the old charter, but the company refused to make the concession; whereupon a writ of *quo warranto* was issued against the company, and in 1624 the charter was annulled.[2]

The policy of direct control by the crown was now announced. In August, 1624, King James formally assumed authority by the issue of a special commission to Sir Francis Wyatt and others as the "governor and council" of Virginia.[3] In the following year Charles I. came to the throne, and immediately issued a proclamation declaring his intention of maintaining a direct royal government, a declaration which was soon followed by a commission for the government of Virginia by a royal governor and council.[4] Efforts to secure a renewal of the charter were made without success. As late as 1642 the governor, council, and assembly found it necessary to disavow a petition presented in their names praying for the restoration of the old government;[5] and the king took the occasion to declare emphatically his adherence to the principle of direct royal control. If the brief revolutionary period of the commonwealth be excepted, royal government in Virginia was now permanently established.

Elsewhere, however, direct control by the crown was not to come for half a century.[6] The charter of 1606, which organized the London Company for Virginia, created also the Plymouth Company, which in 1620 was reorganized as the "Council for New England," with rights of government over the territory granted by the charter.[7] This latter corporation,

[1] Sainsbury, as above, pp. 48, 51.

[2] *Ibid.*, 52–54, 63; Stith, *History of Virginia*, 304 *seq.*

[3] Rymer, *Fœdera*, xvii. 618.

[4] Proclamation for settling Virginia, in Chalmers, *Political Annals*, 126; Rymer, *Fœdera*, xviii. 72. Commission in Rymer, *Fœdera*, xviii. 311; cf. Chalmers, *Political Annals*, 111–112.

[5] Sainsbury, *Calendar of State Papers, Colonial Series, America and West Indies*, 1574–1660, pp. 171, 324.

[6] If we except the provisional royal government in Maine (1665–1668). See Winsor, *Narrative and Critical History*, i. 324.

[7] Hazard, *Historical Collections*, i. 103.

however, lasted only fifteen years, surrendering its patent to
the crown in 1635. The Council for New England soon
granted large portions of their territory to individuals or to
groups of individuals, and in some cases the proprietors
of these sections succeeded in securing from the crown
rights of government over the territory thus acquired.[1] Two
of these grants — that of 1621 to the Plymouth Colony,
and that of 1629 to the Massachusetts Bay Company — resulted in the formation of more or less permanent political
establishments.[2]

The charter of the Massachusetts Bay Company created an
organization which was in form very much like that established by the charters to the Virginia Company in 1609 and
1612.[3] By its provisions the governor and company were empowered to make all necessary rules for the administration of
the colony, and to govern either directly or by a resident governor of their appointment. On the face of the document, the
government here, like that in Virginia, seemed to rest in the
hands of a commercial company in England; and for a short
time precisely this state of things did exist. In April, 1629,
at a meeting in London, the company voted to establish "an
absolute government at our plantation," and in accordance
with this resolution chose John Endicott as governor and seven
others as councillors. For the time being, this governor with
his council was invested with full powers of administration
in the colony.[4] The charter of the Massachusetts Bay Company, however, contained no clause restricting the seat of
government of Massachusetts to England. Advantage was
taken of this omission to transplant the principal seat of government to the colony. In this way the settlers of Massachusetts, instead of being ruled by a corporation across the

[1] Winsor, *Narrative and Critical History*, iii. 295–310; Hutchinson,
History of Massachusetts, i. 13; Poore, *Charters and Constitutions*, i. 774,
ii. 1270–1273.

[2] Massachusetts Historical Society, *Collections*, 4th Series, ii. 156;
Hazard, *Historical Collections*, i. 298 (patent of 1630).

[3] See Poore, *Charters and Constitutions*, i. 932.

[4] *Records of Massachusetts Bay*, i. 361.

water, became a self-governing community, and the governor came to be, not an externally imposed ruler, but the agent of the voters. Already in Plymouth a self-governing colony had grown up independently of any royal sanction; and these republican models were followed in the younger colonies of New England. Rhode Island and Providence Plantations, Connecticut and New Haven, existed for years without any legal recognition.[1] After the Restoration, however, the consolidated governments of Connecticut and Rhode Island respectively received charters securing them in the possession of their local liberties.

There were, then, in New England in 1663, after the issue of the Connecticut and Rhode Island charters, three elective governments protected by royal charters, — namely, Massachusetts, Rhode Island, and Connecticut. Plymouth had no such security, but she had not as yet been disturbed. The royal form had not at that time a foothold in New England. The commission issued by the parliamentary council to Coddington in 1650 for the government of Rhode Island was, it is true, an interesting anticipation of the future policy of direct control by the crown;[2] but Coddington's attempt to enforce his claims had proved a complete failure.

In the southern and middle colonies, founded during the Stuart reigns, the policy of direct control which the crown seemed to have announced by its action in Virginia was apparently abandoned. In 1632 came the charter of Maryland; in 1663, the grant to the proprietors of the Carolinas. In 1664, by the grant to the Duke of York, the conquest from the Dutch, New Netherland, passed into the hands of a private

---

[1] For Rhode Island, however, see the parliamentary patent of 1644, *Rhode Island Records*, i. 143. In New Hampshire the proprietors were not strong enough or energetic enough to enforce their claims. At Portsmouth, Exeter, and Dover little independent communities grew up, each with its elected governor or "ruler" at its head, and maintained their positions during the short period which elapsed before their absorption by Massachusetts. See *New Hampshire Provincial Papers*, i. 110, 111, 119, 132–134, 142, 144; Belknap, *History of New Hampshire*, ch. ii.

[2] Sainsbury, *Calendar of State Papers, Colonial Series, America and West Indies*, 1574–1660, p. 354.

proprietor;[1] and by the Duke's releases of the same year the
Jerseys passed into the hands of Berkeley and Carteret.[2]   In
1681, on the security of a royal charter, William Penn founded
the proprietary colony of Pennsylvania, though the crown reserved the right to declare void, within six months after their
delivery in England, legislative acts of the colony inconsistent
with the supreme allegiance due to the crown, and reserved also
the right to take appeals from judgments given in the province.[3]

Until the year 1685, royal governments had been established in but two colonies.   In Virginia the crown maintained
its control until 1652.   The colony was then left largely to
itself, having for a few years an elective government.   In
this period the governor and council were chosen by the assembly, which had become the real source of authority within
the colony.[4]   At the Restoration, however, the old order was
re-established without a struggle, and from that time to the
War of Independence Virginia had a regular succession of
royal governors.   The second royal government was established in New Hampshire by a commission to John Cutts and
others as the "president and council" of the province of New
Hampshire, which went into effect in 1680.[5]

In this brief sketch two general classes of colonial governments which were not under the direct control of the crown
have been distinguished.   First, there was the proprietary
form, in which the governor was nominated by a single man
or by a group of men, usually resident in England, who had
financial interests in the colony.   Such was the government
of Virginia before the revocation of its charter in 1624, and
such were the later governments of Maryland, the Carolinas,
and Pennsylvania.   In the second place, there was the elective
form, sometimes springing up independently, as in Plymouth,
Rhode Island, Providence, Connecticut, and New Haven; and
sometimes secured by royal charter, as was the case in Massa-

---

[1] All these charters are to be found in Poore, *Charters and Constitutions.*
[2] *New Jersey Documents*, i. 8, 10.
[3] Charter in Poore, *Charters and Constitutions*, ii. 1509.
[4] Documents in Hening, *Statutes*, i. 369 *seq.*, and Appendix.
[5] Commission in *New Hampshire Provincial Papers*, i. 373.

chusetts and in the later consolidated governments of Connecticut and Rhode Island.

In a rough way, the line of division was geographical. The proprietary form never took root in New England, though it played an important part in the colonization of the southern and middle States. The elective form, on the other hand, which held the field in New England during the first half-century of colonization, was never firmly established elsewhere, though there were a few interesting experiments with popular government in other colonies. Thus in Virginia during the commonwealth period there was, as has been seen, a practically independent elective government.[1] Some tendency toward a more popular form of administration also appears in the early history of the Carolinas;[2] but by far the most interesting example of elective governments outside of New England is to be found in the history of West Jersey.

In 1676 the province of New Jersey was divided into two parts. East Jersey went to Sir George Carteret, and West Jersey to William Penn and others in trust for one Edward Byllinge, who had acquired the rights of John, Lord Berkeley, one of the two original proprietors.[3] In the following year

[1] The House of Burgesses declared, in 1658, that the governing power resided in such persons "as shall be impowered by the Burgesses (the representatives of the people):" Hening, *Statutes*, i. 499–504.

[2] In 1663 the proprietors of the Carolinas received proposals from certain gentlemen of Barbadoes, who wished to colonize in Carolina on the condition that they might elect their own governors and make their own laws. At about the same time the Cape Fear Company, formed for the purpose of sending settlers to Carolina, wrote to the proprietors, declaring that, as the English in New England had enjoyed the privilege of electing their own governors, it would be difficult to attract them elsewhere unless the same privileges were granted (*North Carolina Records*, i. 36, 39; Hawks, *History of North Carolina*, ii. 23). These representations seem to have had some influence upon the proprietors; for in the same year they issued proposals promising to appoint the governor and council from a list of thirteen named by the planters (see "Proposealls to all yᵗ will plant in Carrolina," in Rivers, *Sketch of the History of South Carolina*, 335). These schemes, however, never went into operation, and the governors were from the start named by the proprietors.

[3] *New Jersey Documents*, i. 205.

the new Quaker proprietors and freeholders issued the so-called "Concessions" of West Jersey, by which all the powers of government were vested in the assembly and a body of elected commissioners.[1] In spite of these provisions, the proprietor, Edward Byllinge, sent out as his deputy-governor one Samuel Jennings; whereupon the assembly drew up a new set of "Fundamentals," on the acceptance of which by the new governor it agreed "to accept and receive him" as deputy-governor.[2] From 1683 to 1685 there were annual elections. In 1685, however, the assembly, "reserving their just rights and privileges," acknowledged the authority of the proprietor's deputy, John Skene, and the brief line of elective governors came to an end.[3]

Of these two classes of governments not under the direct control of the crown, the elective government lies beyond the scope of this work. The proprietary form, on the other hand, approaches so nearly the prevailing type of royal government that the two groups may for most purposes be classed together. It will, therefore, be enough here to note briefly the peculiar features of the proprietary system, those characteristics that distinguish the proprietary governor from his neighbor in the royal province.

In order to understand the position of the proprietary governor, that of the proprietor himself as set forth in the proprietary charter must first be considered. The charter to Lord Baltimore in 1632 granted the territory of Maryland, with all the rights, privileges, and immunities within .that territory which were enjoyed by the Bishop of Durham within the bishopric or county palatine of Durham. Lord Baltimore and his heirs were to hold this palatinate as "true and absolute lords and proprietaries . . . saving always the faith and allegiance and sovereign dominion" due to the crown. The land was to be held in free and common socage, and not

---

[1] *New Jersey Documents*, i. 241.

[2] Smith, *History of New Jersey*, 126–129; Leaming and Spicer, *Grants, Concessions*, etc., 423.

[3] Smith, *History of New Jersey*, 155, 190; Leaming and Spicer, *Grants, Concessions*, etc., 471, 490, 499, 503.

by knight's service. As the expression of his vassal relation to the crown, the proprietor was to make an annual payment of two Indian arrows and one fifth of the gold and silver found within the colony.[1] Similar language is to be found in the Carolina charter.[2] In spite of the exemption from knight's service, the whole phraseology carries us back to the days of feudal society. The principle implied is distinctly feudal, namely, the association of rights in the soil with rights of government; that is, the king parts with a portion of his prerogative, and exempts this particular piece of territory from the ordinary jurisdiction, very much as his predecessors had done when they created the palatinates of Lancaster and Durham.

In the proprietary charters of New York and Pennsylvania, the powers granted to the proprietor were subject to some important limitations. In New York the crown had reserved to itself the right to receive appeals from any judgments given in the province.[3] In Pennsylvania there was the additional requirement that all acts passed by the proprietor and the freemen should be subject to the royal veto for a limited time after their transmission to the crown.[4] In these charters there is no reference to the English palatinate as the measure of the proprietor's powers, but the main principle is the same as in the Maryland and Carolina charters. In each case were created private jurisdictions exempt wholly or in part from the ordinary operation of the royal sovereignty. The proprietary governor was, in a sense, not even a public officer at all, but the agent of a private person or group of persons, intrusted, it is true, with the powers and duties of an officer of State, but charged also with the defence and promotion of distinctly private interests. He had at the start scarcely any organic connection with the royal governmental system.

This is, in essence, the difference between the proprietary

---

[1] Charter translated in Bozman, *History of Maryland*, ii. 9.
[2] Carolina charters of 1663 and 1665 in Poore, *Charters and Constitutions*, ii. 1382, 1390.
[3] Grant to the Duke of York, *Ibid.*, i. 783.
[4] Charter to William Penn, 1681, *Ibid.*, ii. 1509.

governor and the royal governor. Individual governments might have special peculiarities, but the only essential point of difference between the two classes as a whole lay in the fact that in the one the governor received his authority from a quasi-feudal dignitary or body of proprietors, while in the other he received his authority directly from the crown. The form of his office and the extent of his powers were not necessarily altered by a change from the one relation to the other.

As a matter of fact, however, the proprietary governments exhibit greater varieties in form than the royal governments, inasmuch as the ownership of a colony offered peculiar opportunities for political experiment. The extent of these experiments varied. There were not many of them in Maryland and New York, though in the former colony some steps were taken in the direction of a partly feudal organization. In the Carolinas, the Jerseys, and in Pennsylvania, however, there were striking instances of this kind of political experiment; indeed each of these colonies had an abundant crop of original, if not workable, constitutions. In the Carolinas there were, first, the tentative propositions of 1663 looking toward a system of popular government;[1] then the "Concessions" of 1665, which reserved to the proprietors the appointment of the executive, but gave to the assembly an unusual degree of control;[2] and, finally, the various editions of the "Fundamental Constitutions" from 1669 to 1698, with their cumbrous machinery and formidable terminology; their "Palatine's Court," "Grand Council," "Parliament," aristocratic upper house, "landgraves," and "caciques."[3] Two of the Carolina proprietors were also proprietors of the Jerseys, where the same tendencies appeared in a similar set of "Concessions."[4] In this case, the division of the province between two new sets of proprietors gave rise to another set of fundamental documents. From the West Jersey proprietors came the "Concessions" of West Jersey, modified

[1] *North Carolina Records*, i. 43.

[2] *Ibid.*, 79 *seq.*

[3] Poore, *Charters and Constitutions*, ii. 1397; The Two Charters granted by King Charles II., etc.

[4] Issued in 1665. See *New Jersey Documents*, i. 28.

by the "Fundamentals" of the West Jersey assembly, while in the eastern division there was another elaborate paper constitution.

The peculiar tendency toward the making of elaborate constitutional documents, shown in the West Jersey "Concessions" of William Penn and his Quaker associates, appears again in the various frames of government set up in Pennsylvania. In the intricate constitutional mechanism of Penn's first "Frame of Government" for Pennsylvania, we have a fair counterpart of the "Fundamental Constitutions" of Carolina. In all these colonies the elaborate machinery passed away, the paper constitutions died an early and natural death, but the popular tendencies embodied in some of the early documents left their impress on the later constitutional development.

The defects of the proprietary system are not hard to see. The first of these was inherent in the union of the two characters of governor and private proprietor. The proprietor had great landed interests in the colony: he was the landlord, whose financial interests often clashed with those of his tenants. Out of this situation arose the interminable quit-rent controversies, and later the question as to the taxation of proprietary lands, which proved so serious an element of conflict in Pennsylvania and Maryland.[1] The quit-rent troubles were not, it is true, confined to the proprietary colonies. The crown, like the proprietor, had financial interests at variance with those of the colonists, and the royal governor, like the proprietary governor, was bound to become the defender of these interests against the assembly. In the proprietary colonies, however, such conflicts were embittered by a feeling that the strife was obviously one between public and private interests. Then, too, many of the proprietors had undertaken these enterprises as distinctly commercial investments, considering that their right of government was only incidental to their general right of property, and, like that, was to be worked to its full value. Consequently there was a tendency to dispose of colonial offices as purely private property. In Pennsylvania this course was checked by limiting closely the power

[1] See below, p. 13.

of appointment;[1] but in Maryland there seems to have been a regular traffic in minor colonial offices nominally in the gift of the governor. This practice was perhaps at its height in the time of Governor Sharpe, during the French and Indian war. Many appointments were practically taken out of his hands; and offices were sold on peculiar terms, by which the proprietor's relatives and friends received a certain share of the profits.[2]

It would, of course, be unjust to imply that all of the proprietors were influenced by improper motives. The last days of the Virginia Company, the attitude of Penn toward his colony, and the history of Maryland under some of the earlier proprietors furnish conclusive evidence that the possession of proprietary rights and a reasonable desire to protect them were not necessarily inconsistent with some regard for the interests of the colonists. Nevertheless, the proprietors were exposed to peculiar temptations, and the system was one which could work well only under the most favorable conditions.

As the home government came to exercise a closer supervision over the colonies, especially after the development of parliamentary control through the navigation acts, a second element of difficulty was introduced, namely, the conflict between royal and proprietary interests. In Pennsylvania, Maryland, the Carolinas, and the Jerseys, there was often friction between the proprietary governors and the royal revenue and admiralty officers,[3] — such, for example, as that which arose in 1681 in Maryland, where Lord Baltimore was charged with obstructing the collection of the royal·customs, a quarrel which ended in the killing of one of the royal officers.[4] Edward Randolph, the most persistent upholder of the British customs laws, asserted in strong terms that the proprietary governments were particularly remiss in the enforcement of the navigation laws.[5]

[1] See speech of Hamilton in Proud, *History of Pennsylvania*, ii. 217–218.

[2] Sharpe's Correspondence, *Maryland Archives*, vi. 354, ix. 39–40.

[3] Randolph's memorial, 1696, *New Jersey Documents*, ii. 116 *seq.* Cf. Randolph's letter of 1701, *Ibid.*, 358 *seq.*

[4] *Maryland Archives*, v. 274, 286, 305, 428 *seq.*

[5] Randolph's memorial, as above.

A still more serious conflict of interests occurred during the period of the French and Indian wars of the eighteenth century. The assemblies were, of course, frequently called upon for supplies; and when, as in Pennsylvania and Maryland, they passed supply bills which included taxes on the estates of the proprietors, the refusal of the latter to permit such taxes led to prolonged and angry deadlocks.[1] At such times the position of the proprietary governor was peculiarly difficult, compelled, as he often was, to choose between his duty to the crown and his obligations to the proprietor. The royal governor, it is true, was frequently called upon to choose between a refusal of supplies by the assembly and disobedience to his instructions; but the proprietary governor was hampered by an additional set of instructions based, not on constitutional and political grounds, but often on purely selfish interests. How energetic men chafed under such restraints, and how the public interests often suffered, is well illustrated in the correspondence of Governor Sharpe of Maryland. In 1756, in the crisis of the conflict with the French, he wrote impatiently: "If my hands had not been tied up by such Instructions as empty Coffers seem to have dictated I should many Months ago have had a Regiment of Maryland Troops under my Command & in all probability have been enabled to prevent any Incursions of Indians into this Province."[2]

The mere intervention of a third party between the province and the crown seems to have been felt as a grievance. This was true at least in Pennsylvania, where the crown had reserved to itself a veto on legislation,[3] and where the proprietor also had the right of assent or veto. There was no trouble so long as the proprietor was present; but when in his absence he reserved the right of rejecting laws approved by his deputy, there was vigorous opposition. The proprietor was

[1] For Maryland, see Sharpe's Correspondence, *Maryland Archives*, vols. vi., ix. *passim*, especially vi. 384, 424–427. For Pennsylvania, see *Historical Review of the Constitution and Government of Pennsylvania* (1759), 81–84, 232–312, and Appendix.

[2] *Maryland Archives*, vi. 399.

[3] Charter to William Penn, 1681, in Poore, *Charters and Constitutions*, ii. 1509.

finally obliged to yield on this point;[1] but he retaliated by imposing limitations on the governor's power of assent to legislation, clinching them by the requirement of a bond for the due observance of all such instructions.[2]

In Maryland and the Carolinas, where the crown had re-served no veto, there was similar opposition to the exercise of the proprietary veto, inasmuch as the colonists claimed that the acts of an agent bound his principal. In Maryland the assembly regarded it as a serious grievance that there should be no one in the province capable of giving a final assent to legislation, and in 1681 a bill was passed by the lower house, making the governor's assent final in legislation. The bill was thrown out by the council, which defended the proprietary veto as necessary to the security of proprietary rights. The proprietor agreed, however, that during his absence his assent or dissent should be published within eighteen months.[3] The same view as that held in Maryland was taken by the assembly of South Carolina; and when the proprietary government was finally overthrown, the proprietor's right of veto was cited as one of the grievances that justified revolutionary action.[4] The veto by the proprietor was not, it is true, essentially different from that by the crown in the royal governments; but, as the charters gave the right of legislation to the proprietor and the freemen,[5] it was felt that the absence of the proprietor ought not to add a second veto.

[1] Opinion of Attorney-General Northey, 1705, *Statutes at Large of Pennsylvania* (1896), ii. 473.

[2] *Pennsylvania Records*, vi. 525 *seq.*; Proud, *History of Pennsylvania*, ii. 177 *seq.* See also the decision of the council, quoted in *Historical Review of the Constitution and Government of Pennsylvania* (1759), 79: "This [the bond] was first submitted to by *Keith*, and has been a Rule to his Successors, with this Difference, that whereas the Penalty exacted from him was but 1000*l. Sterl.* it has been since raised to 2, or 3000*l.*" Cf. the argument, *Ibid.*, 78.

[3] *Maryland Archives*, i. 31, ii. 174, 470, iii. 50–51, vii. 152, 160, 182, 508.

[4] Rivers, *Sketch of the History of South Carolina*, 433–435; South Carolina Historical Society, *Collections*, i. 170; "Narrative of the Proceedings of the People of South Carolina," in Carroll, *Historical Collections*, ii. 169.

[5] In Maryland, the Carolinas, and Pennsylvania; there was no such clause in the patent to the Duke of York.

In addition to these difficulties of the proprietary system, the proprietors in many cases proved their inability to maintain stable and efficient governments. This circumstance was strikingly true in the Carolinas, where the proprietors seemed almost helpless to deal with the turbulent population. Edward Randolph, for whose partisanship some allowance must perhaps be made, wrote that North Carolina at the end of the seventeenth century was on the verge of anarchy.[1] The people of South Carolina, in their petition for a royal government, urged among other reasons for the change the desire for royal protection from the Spanish and Indian invasions which were then threatening the colony.[2] A similar state of things existed in New Jersey, whither the crown was called upon to send governors capable of enforcing law and order.[3]

Besides all these elements of weakness which worked against the proprietary system, there were other circumstances in the situation which rendered the transition to the royal government peculiarly easy. The various experiments in constitution-making had for the most part proved failures; and as a result there grew up in the proprietary colonies political organizations very similar to those in the royal governments. In all these colonies there was, for example, a governor nominated by the proprietor, with a nominated council and an elective assembly. Thus the only step necessary in the transition from proprietary to royal government was the resumption by the crown of the prerogatives which it had intrusted to the proprietor. The changes in the internal constitution of the colony were very slight.

In the last years of the Stuarts, the policy of direct royal control began to be aggressively pushed. In one case, that of New York, the change came naturally, without a contest; for when James, Duke of York, became king, New York ceased

---

[1] Randolph's memorial, 1696, *New Jersey Documents*, ii. 120.

[2] "Narrative of the Proceedings of the People of South Carolina," in Carroll, *Historical Collections*, ii. 192.

[3] Edward Randolph, "Articles of High Crimes: Misdemeanours Charged upon the Governours in the Severall Proprieties," *New Jersey Documents*, ii. 358; recommendations of the Lords of Trade, *Ibid.*, ii. 420.

to be a proprietary colony and became a royal province. In most cases, however, the new policy included measures much more aggressive, which took shape, now for the first time, in a definite and determined attack upon the charters all along the line. The blow fell first upon Massachusetts.

Massachusetts, almost from the beginning, had been compelled to face attacks, open or secret, upon the charter of 1629. As early as 1634, Gorges had urged the establishment of royal governments in New England.[1] Legal processes had been begun against the charter, and more than once Massachusetts had stood on the verge of a catastrophe from which she had been saved only by skilful diplomacy and a fortunate combination of circumstances.[2] The unfriendly attitude of the crown after the Restoration excited new apprehensions, but for a few years the company held its ground. At last, however, the blow fell. In 1681 the king reinforced his demands for a change in the colonial constitution by threatening to annul the charter;[3] in 1683 a writ of *quo warranto* was issued against it;[4] in the next year the case was transferred to the Court of Chancery; and before the year was over the charter was annulled.[5] For a time, however, the old charter government was allowed to go on, until the new king, James II., by his commission to Joseph Dudley, organized the first royal government in Massachusetts.[6] Dudley's title was that of president, and he was supported by a council also nominated by the crown. Besides Massachusetts Bay, the commission included New Hampshire, Maine, and the King's Province; and in the following year, 1686, Sir Edmund Andros received a new commission, which included also the colony of Plymouth.[7]

---

[1] Sainsbury, *Calendar of State Papers, Colonial Series, America and West Indies,* 1574–1660, pp. 178, 192.

[2] *Ibid.,* 200, 206, 251, 256; Winthrop Papers, in Massachusetts Historical Society, *Collections,* 4th Series, vi. 58; Hutchinson, *History of Massachusetts,* i. Appendix, 442, 460.

[3] Doyle, *English in America,* iii. 280.

[4] *Records of Massachusetts Bay,* v. 421 seq.

[5] Hutchinson, *History of Massachusetts,* i. 305–306, and notes.

[6] *New Hampshire Provincial Papers,* i. 590.

[7] Force, *Tracts,* iv. No. 8.

Proceedings had already been begun against other colonial charters. Rhode Island and Connecticut were brought under royal control, and in 1688 Andros received a commission as governor of New England, which was then defined so as to include New York and the Jerseys.[1] Orders had also been issued for the prosecution of *quo warranto* writs against the governments of Connecticut, Rhode Island, East and West Jersey, Maryland, Carolina, and Delaware.[2] Thus, within two years after the accession of James II., proceedings had been entered upon against all the proprietary and charter governments, with the exception of Pennsylvania. In general, then, it may be said that the new royal policy included two things: first, the substitution of royal for proprietary and charter governments; and, secondly, a process of consolidation, as illustrated by Andros's commission as governor of the greater New England.

The Revolution of 1688 put a stop to these proceedings; but William III. did not altogether abandon the policy of his predecessor. To him, as the head of the great European alliance against Louis XIV., careful organization and concentration of forces in all quarters must have seemed highly desirable. The first period of the great conflict between England and France for the possession of the North American continent was just beginning, and clearly a well-organized system of royal governments was far better adapted to meet such a test than the old aggregation of proprietary and charter colonies. Moreover, the navigation acts could be better enforced by royal governors than by irresponsible proprietary agents. Thus, although Rhode Island, Connecticut, and, for a time, the Jerseys were allowed to retain their independent governments, the establishment of royal governments in Massachusetts and New York was a substantial and permanent result of this first war upon the charters.

The positions of the Maryland and Pennsylvania proprietors were complicated by personal considerations. Lord Baltimore

---

[1] Commission in *New York Documents*, iii. 537.

[2] Order of July, 1685, *Ibid.*, iii. 362. Order of April, 1687, *Maryland Archives*, v. 542; Chalmers, in Carroll, *Historical Collections*, ii. 323.

was a Roman Catholic; and Penn's relations with James II. were such as to arouse suspicion in the minds of the dominant party. In Maryland, an unfortunate emphasis was given to the religious element by the rebellion in that colony, which was conducted on ostensibly anti-Catholic lines.[1] At length, in 1689, the Committee of Trade and Plantations recommended that measures be taken to bring the "proprieties" of Carolina, Maryland, and Pennsylvania "under a nearer dependence on the Crown";[2] and in 1690 the attorney-general was ordered to proceed by *scire facias* against the charter of Maryland.

A new theory was now formulated to justify royal inter-ference. Chief Justice Holt, being called upon to give an opinion, declared that, "it being in a case of necessity," the king might appoint a governor in Maryland, though the pro-prietor could not be deprived of his income from the province[3] except through forfeiture. This theory was more distinctly stated by the law officers of the crown a few years later when the solicitor-general made a report on the charters of Connecticut and New Jersey, giving his opinion "that notwithstanding any thing in the said Charters or Grants, there Majesties by virtue of their Prerogative and Soverainty over those Colonies, which is not granted from the Crown to the Gov.[r] and Company, nor to the proprietors by any of the Chart[rs] may appoint Governors for these places with such Powers, and authorities for the Gov-ernment thereof . . . as their Majesties shall in their great wisdom judge reasonable."[4] A similar opinion was given by the crown law officers some years afterwards, upon complaint made against the governments of Rhode Island and Connecti-cut. They declared that there was nothing in the charters which could "exclude your Majesty (who has a right to govern all your subjects) from naming a Governor on your Majesty's behalf, for those colonies at all times."[5] This statement is one of great interest, asserting as it does within the field of colonial government that right of the crown to govern all its subjects which in England had during the middle ages gradu-

[1] Declaration in *Maryland Archives*, viii. 100 *seq.*, 215 *seq.*
[2] *North Carolina Records*, i. 359.   [3] Chalmers, *Opinions*, 65.
[4] *New Jersey Documents*, ii. 100.   [5] Chalmers, *Opinions*, 66.

ally been secured against the hostile forces of local privilege and feudal anarchy. It is the recognition of this principle which chiefly distinguishes the modern State, whether it be an absolute monarchy or a representative republic, from the feudal organization of the middle ages.

It has been very commonly thought that this policy of securing direct control by the crown was inspired by the natural hostility of a tyrannical government to the local liberties of the colonies; but it must not be forgotten that, taking the colonies as a whole, the change was distinctly in the interest of better government. Royal tyranny may have been bad enough; but in the long run it was far better than the control of private and, to a large extent, irresponsible proprietors. May it not be said, too, that this union in dependence upon the crown worked in some measure toward that sense of common political interests which, imperfect as it was, was yet the indispensable condition for success in the struggle for independence, and paved the way for the "more perfect union" of the federal constitution?

The doctrine laid down by Chief Justice Holt was soon put into general operation. In Pennsylvania, Governor Fletcher of New York assumed control on the authority of a royal commission;[1] and although Penn succeeded with some difficulty in recovering his rights of government, yet a precedent had been set which might be cited on future occasions. The proceedings in Maryland were more serious. In 1691 the crown issued a commission to Sir Lionel Copley as governor of Maryland, thus establishing a royal government, without however depriving Lord Baltimore of his property rights in the soil.[2] The charter still stood; and finally, twenty-four years later, a Protestant Lord Baltimore was allowed to resume the government of the province.[3] In the Jerseys, the proprietary government had been restored after the revolution of 1688, but its position was by no means secure. There was a general feeling of discontent with the proprietary régime, and frequent peti-

---

[1] *Pennsylvania Records*, i. 352.   [2] *Maryland Archives*, viii. 263.
[3] *Ibid.*, vi. 25.

tions for the appointment of a royal governor were made.[1]
The situation was further complicated by the existence of
factions among the proprietors.[2]   As early as 1687 the proprietors had made propositions looking toward the surrender
of the government, but with a reservation of their property
rights.[3]   Finally terms of surrender were arranged, and in
1702 New Jersey became a royal province.[4]

Similar causes brought about similar results in the Carolinas.
In South Carolina, the oppressive treatment of the dissenters
by a party which received the support of the proprietors, and
the proprietors' veto of popular measures, combined to develop
the spirit of opposition.   Furthermore, the invasions by the
Spaniards and Indians seemed to show the inability of the
proprietors to maintain an effective defence of the province.
At length the growing discontent culminated in the rebellion
of 1719, when the popular party assumed control in the name
of the king, and a provisional government was chosen to serve
until the crown should take final action.[5]   The crown, on the
other hand, as early as 1706, had taken steps toward the overthrow of the proprietary government.   In 1705 the House of
Lords, after declaring null and void certain acts against dissenters, had urged the crown "to use the most effectual
Methods to deliver the said Province from the arbitrary Oppressions under which it now lies."   The Lords of Trade had then
recommended the institution of legal proceedings against the
charter in the Court of Queen's Bench, and the queen had
issued instructions to the law officers of the crown, although
nothing came of them at the time.[6]   Finally the uprising of
1719 gave the crown its opportunity.   The regency in council
declared that the proprietors had forfeited their charter, and
ordered the attorney-general to take out a writ of *scire facias*

[1] See, for example, the "Address of the Inhabitants of West Jersey,"
New Jersey Documents, ii. 380.

[2] *Ibid.*, 418.   [3] *Ibid.*, i. 535–539; propositions of 1688, *Ibid.*, ii. 26.

[4] *Ibid.*, ii. 452.

[5] "Narrative of the Proceedings of the People of South Carolina," in
Carroll, *Historical Collections*, ii. 141.

[6] Address of the House of Lords, in Oldmixon, *British Empire in
America*, i. 488; *Journals of the House of Lords*, xviii. 150–151.

against them.[1] The crown, without waiting for final action
by the courts, then proceeded to exercise its authority in
South Carolina by the appointment of Francis Nicholson as
governor.[2]

Of all the proprietary governments, that of North Carolina
had been the most notoriously inefficient. In this colony the
authority of the proprietors almost lapsed at times; and in
1711 there was practically a state of war between conflicting
claimants to the government.[3] The proprietary system, however, dragged out a wretched existence until 1729, when the
long negotiations between the crown and the proprietors came
to a close, in the final surrender of both provinces to the
crown.[4]

The surrender of North Carolina marked the last stage in
the course begun by Charles II. At one time or another the
crown had set up its own governors in every one of the proprietary and charter colonies; and at the end of this period
of transition all but four colonies had been brought into the
class of royal governments. Of these, two, Pennsylvania and
Maryland, represent the proprietary government, and two,
Rhode Island and Connecticut, the charter government.
Even these four were not altogether secure from attack. In
1702 an act of Parliament was proposed for bringing the proprietary governments into closer dependence upon the crown;
but although the proposition was supported by the Board of
Trade, it came to nothing.[5] Again, complaints made by Governors Dudley of Massachusetts and Cornbury of New York

[1] South Carolina Historical Society, *Collections*, i. 172, 256.

[2] *Ibid.*

[3] Chalmers, in Carroll, *Historical Collections*, ii. 301 *seq.*; Chalmers,
Revolt of the American Colonies, i. 398; *North Carolina Records*, i. 779
seq., 797, 801; Hawks, *History of North Carolina*, ii. 418.

[4] Act of Parliament completing the agreement with seven out of eight
proprietors. See *North Carolina Records*, iii. 32. Lord Carteret retained
his proprietary interest of one-eighth until 1744. For details on the surrender of the Carolina charter, see McCrady, *South Carolina under the Proprietary Government*, chaps. xxix., xxx.

[5] South Carolina Historical Society, *Collections*, i. 220; Chalmers, *Revolt*, i. 306, 342; *North Carolina Records*, i. 535 *seq.*, 552.

against the governments of Connecticut and Rhode Island, brought out the report of the crown law officers already referred to, declaring the right of the crown to "govern" all its subjects.[1] In 1711 the adoption of a uniform plan of colonial government was spoken of as desirable but impracticable, "the purchasing proprietyes and takeing away of usurpations being a work of time and trouble."[2] As late as 1721 the Massachusetts agent in London, Jeremiah Dummer, published his "Defence of the New-England Charters," designed to meet an impending attack on the charter governments; and even long afterward there was an unsuccessful attempt in Pennsylvania to overthrow the proprietary government of that colony.[3]

Those proprietary governments which were permitted to continue were nevertheless subjected to a considerable degree of royal control.   By the navigation laws the colonial governors were made, to a considerable extent, the administrators of these trade regulations; and by the statute 7 & 8 William III. it was provided that all governors of plantations should be approved by the crown.[4] Thus the proprietary governor himself became in a measure a royal officer responsible to the crown.   It is interesting to note that, in spite of the policy of direct royal control so generally adopted, in 1732, three years after the surrender of the Carolina charter, the crown by its charter to the Georgia trustees recurred temporarily to the old proprietary system.   The charter of Georgia had, however, a saving clause, in the provision that after twenty-one years the government of the colony was to revert to the crown.   Consequently in 1754, without a contest and as a matter of course, Georgia became a royal province.[5]

[1] See above. p. 18.

[2] Letter of Governor Hunter, *New Jersey Documents*, iv. 138.

[3] Franklin, *Works* (ed. Bigelow), iii. 286. Cf. Stillé, *Life and Times of John Dickinson*, ch. iii.

[4] c. 22, § xvi.: *Statutes at Large*, iii. 613. These provisions apparently applied also to the charter colonies, but they could hardly have been enforced upon an annually elected governor.

[5] Charter in Poore, *Charters and Constitutions*, i. 369; Chalmers, *Opinions*, 69 *seq.*

CHAPTER II.

THE EVOLUTION OF THE PROVINCIAL EXECUTIVE.

As the colonial executive only gradually came under royal control, so its ultimate form, that of a single head checked by a nominated council, was also at first undetermined. In the first century of colonization there were numerous experiments.

For the study of the executive, Virginia, as the oldest of the royal governments, again furnishes a convenient starting point. Under the first charter the resident government was vested in a council appointed by the superior council in England.[1] This council was to choose its own president, to whom certain minor functions were to be intrusted exclusively; and yet the right of the council to appoint and remove him at pleasure made that body the real executive, and justifies the classification of this early Virginia executive as of the collegiate type. This government proved unwieldy and ineffective; in 1609, therefore, the company received its new charter, which left it free to choose its own methods in the government of the colony.[2] As it was evident that a strong hand was needed, the principle of having a single head was adopted, and Lord Delaware was made governor, with absolute discretion in the choice of such councillors as he saw fit to employ.[3] This policy, demanded perhaps by the exigencies of the time, worked ill as a permanent system, inasmuch as the governors were nearly always arbitrary in their methods, and often mercenary and unscrupulous. Moreover, the fact that as yet the colony had no popular assembly was a source of especial

---

[1] .Royal orders in Brown, *Genesis of the United States*, i. 65.

[2] Poore, *Charters and Constitutions*, ii. 1893.

[3] Delaware's commission in Brown, *Genesis of the United States*, i. 375 *seq.*, especially 380.

danger; and there was therefore general rejoicing when the governor was at last "restrained to a Counseil ioyned with him."[1] The Ordinance of 1621, which was probably hardly more than a formal statement of the constitution actually introduced two years before, established two councils, the one legislative, the other executive. The governor, however, seems to have been little more than the first member of the council.[2]

It is hard to say what changes took place in the constitution of the executive on the introduction of the royal government, if indeed there were any real changes. The royal commissions of 1624 and 1625 were commissions to the governor and council, without any definite statement as to their mutual relations.[3] It is clear, however, that there was a period of conflict between two ideas. The governor contended for the theory of a single head, advised and to a certain extent checked by the council, yet possessing in himself the real executive authority; whereas the council claimed for itself a larger share of the executive power.[4] In 1631 the governor and council came into direct conflict. Governor Harvey complained that he could do nothing but what the council advised, and that his power extended no farther than to a casting vote;[5] while from the council, on the other hand, there were complaints of the overbearing conduct and usurpation of Harvey.[6]

Constitutional development in Virginia was interrupted by

[1] "A Declaration of the State of the Colonie," June, 1620, in Force, *Tracts*, iii. No. 5, p. 6.

[2] Ordinance in Hening, *Statutes*, i. 110; instructions to Governor Wyatt, *Ibid.*, 114 *seq.*

[3] Commission to Wyatt, 1624, in Rymer, *Fœdera*, xvii. 618; to Yeardley, "De Commissione directa Georgio Yardeley militi & aliis," *Ibid.*, xviii. 311.

[4] Compare, however, the letter to Sir Francis Wyatt, 1626, conceding that important actions should be determined by a majority of the council, in Sainsbury, *Calendar of State Papers, Colonial Series, America and West Indies*, 1574–1660, p. 79.

[5] Letter of Governor Harvey, 1631, *Ibid.*, 129. The instructions to Berkeley in 1641 direct that he shall have only a casting vote in the council. See § 5 of instructions, Appendix A below.

[6] Mathews to Wolstenholme, 1635, in Sainsbury, *Calendar of State Papers, Colonial Series, America and West Indies*, 1574–1660, p. 208.

the civil war; but by 1689 the governor was clearly separated from the council and possessed considerable power over it. Not only had he the right to make provisional appointments to fill vacancies in the council, but he might suspend members for causes which, by a later provision, were to be communicated to the home government. Moreover, when councillors were regularly appointed by the royal order, it was usually on the nomination of the governor.[1] The exact relation between the governor and the council continued to be matter of controversy; but there was now a rough definition of their relative positions, showing a single head, the governor, invested with the central executive power, but checked in its exercise by a nominated council more or less under his influence.[2] The system thus worked out in Virginia seems to have been the model for other royal provinces, and even to have influenced the proprietary governments to some extent.

The proprietary government in Maryland, established soon after the introduction of royal government in Virginia, adopted as the form of executive in the colony a governor with an advisory council, both appointed by the proprietor. The council in Maryland was at first very small: only three members were named in Calvert's commission of 1637.[3] It is not clear whether the taking of advice was at first compulsory upon the governor;[4] but the commissions of 1644 and 1666 expressly stated that the advice of the council should be taken, at least in important matters.[5] Though the councillors were regularly appointed by the proprietor, the governor was sometimes authorized to make additional appointments.[6]

---

[1] On this subject, see Beverly, *History of Virginia*, 202; Hartwell, Blair, and Chilton, *Present State of Virginia*, 22–24; Culpeper's instructions, *Calendar of Virginia State Papers*, i. 14; Howard's instructions, cited in Doyle, *English in America*, i. 352–353.

[2] For a fuller statement of the relation between the governor and the council, see below, ch. v.

[3] Bozman, *History of Maryland*, ii. 572.

[4] Note the clause "as he shall see cause," in the commission of 1637.

[5] Commission of 1644 in Bozman, *History of Maryland*, ii. 631; that of 1666, *Maryland Archives*, iii. 542.

[6] In 1648, the governor was authorized to appoint two or three coun-

In 1665 the Carolina proprietors issued a document called the "Concessions," by the provisions of which the executive consisted of a governor and a council of from six to twelve persons named by the governor.[1] The executive power was vested in the governor and council, but the governor, through his right of naming the councillors, held a position of practical independence. This system was soon superseded by the elaborate instrument known as the "Fundamental Constitutions," which provided for an organization of the proprietors themselves, called the "Palatine's Court," the president of which was the palatine chosen by the proprietors from their own number.[2] This was to be the chief executive body of the colony, though certain larger questions were to be settled by the Grand Council, consisting of the proprietors themselves and forty-two councillors chosen by a complicated process of election in which there was a strong aristocratic element.[3] It is clear that the collegiate idea of the executive was thus carried to an extreme point. The palatine who stood at the apex of the system was only a *primus inter pares*, and even the Palatine's Court did not possess full executive powers, since many of these were reserved to the Grand Council. Inasmuch as this system never became the actual constitution of the colony, it is idle to conjecture how it would have worked, though it may be noted that some of the formal provisions of the "Fundamental Constitutions" were observed for a considerable time.

In the absence of the palatine and his associate proprietors, the executive power in the province was vested in the governor, who was the proxy or deputy of the palatine, and the councillors, each of whom was the representative of some one of

cillors in addition to those named by the proprietor. See the commission to Governor Stone, in Bozman, *History of Maryland*, ii. 642 *seq.*, especially 647.

[1] *North Carolina Records*, i. 79.

[2] Later succession was on the basis of seniority. See § 1 of the instructions to Governor Ludwell, 1691, in Rivers, *Chapter in the Early History of South Carolina*, Appendix.

[3] "Fundamental Constitutions" in Poore, *Charters and Constitutions*, ii. 1397.

the proprietors.[1] For a time, it is true, the assembly was permitted to elect a certain number of commoners to the council;
but the proprietors found this practice unsatisfactory, and by
1691 it was abandoned.[2] The governor and the deputies, like
the Palatine's Court which they represented, constituted in
theory a collective executive;[3] though the independent position of the councillors was modified somewhat by the practice
of giving the governor blank deputations, which he might fill
out at his discretion. Appointment by the individual proprietors continued, however, to be the rule.[4]

Finally a change of some importance was made in the form
of the council, a change in form which implied also a change
in theory. Instead of instituting a body consisting of the
personal representatives of eight proprietors, the North Carolina instructions of 1718 organized a council of ten members
besides the governor, "as the custom is in his Majesty's other
colonies."[5] In South Carolina, similar action was taken in
1719. In the latter colony the people were inclined to emphasize the principle involved in the change, and refused to recognize the new constitution as valid. The discussion was closed
by the rebellion of the same year, and the consequent establishment of royal government in South Carolina.[6]

In North Carolina there was a controversy, similar to that
in Virginia in Harvey's time, arising from the desire of the
governor to acquire greater independence of the council.
Governor Everard in 1729 claimed an independent right of
nominating and removing public officers. Here, as in South

---

[1] " Temporary Laws " of 1671, in Rivers, *Sketch of the History of South
Carolina,* 351.

[2] Address to Governor Sothel, *Ibid.,* 426 ; also instructions to Ludwell,
1691, § 10.

[3] Letter of the Earl of Shaftesbury, *North Carolina Records,* i. 214. Cf.
Ludwell's instructions, 1691.

[4] For examples, see *North Carolina Records,* i. 346, ii. 175; South Carolina Historical Society, *Collections,* i. 111, 136 ; Rivers, *Sketch of the History of South Carolina,* 341.

[5] *North Carolina Records,* ii. 307. For later variations, see *Ibid.,* 454, 516.

[6] South Carolina Historical Society, *Collections,* i. 170 ; Carroll, *Historical Collections,* ii. 158, 169.

Carolina, however, the controversy was closed by the establishment of a royal government in the colony.[1]

Of the Carolina proprietors, two, Berkeley and Carteret, were also proprietors of New Jersey. The "Concessions" of New Jersey, like those of Carolina, vested executive powers in the governor and council jointly, but, on the other hand, authorized the governor to appoint the councillors, though the proprietors maintained a reserved right to appoint directly if they saw fit.[2] By later instructions it was provided that vacancies in the office of either governor or councillor should be filled by vote of the governor and council.[3] In 1683 the new proprietors of East Jersey proposed a system styled the "Fundamental Constitutions," which is of some interest as showing the political theories of the time.[4] By this instrument a large executive council was provided for, consisting of twenty-four proprietors and twelve freemen, and this large body was again subdivided into a number of committees. It is not surprising, however, that such a cumbersome system was never organized except on paper. In the meantime, the old form, by which the power was vested in the governor and council, was maintained, although the governor's power was very considerably checked by the council. Appointments were determined apparently by the governor and council jointly; commissions were issued by order of the council.[5]

The first government of New York was extremely simple. Complete political authority was vested in one man, Governor Nicolls, to whom the Duke of York granted all the powers conferred upon the proprietor by the charter of 1664. This despotic system was soon modified by the addition of a council, which was, however, to be appointed by the governor.[6]

[1] *North Carolina Records*, ii. 535, iii. 15.

[2] "Concessions" in *New Jersey Documents*, i. 28 *seq*. Cf. commission and instructions to Philip Carteret, *Ibid.*, 20, 21.

[3] Commission to Philip Carteret, 1674, in Leaming and Spicer, *Grants, Concessions*, etc., 58.

[4] *New Jersey Documents*, i. 395 *seq*.

[5] See minutes of the council, *New Jersey Documents*, xiii. 39–42, 46, 115, 174.

[6] Commission to Nicolls, *Pennsylvania Archives*, v. 509; Nicolls's

Governor Dongan's instructions of 1683 named some of the members of his council, but empowered him to suspend councillors and to fill the vacancies.[1] Finally, in 1688, the royal commission to Andros established the usual rule of the royal governments.[2]

The first royal commission for the government of New Hampshire provided for a collegiate executive, vesting executive powers in the president and council jointly.[3] Three years later, however, a commission was issued providing for a royal government in the usual form.[4]

In Pennsylvania the charter given to William Penn in 1681 was followed by a series of constitutional experiments. Passing over Penn's first commission to his deputy, Markham, which was purely provisional,[5] the "Frame of Government of 1682" was the first constitution of Pennsylvania. By this document the executive power was vested in a large body called the "Provincial Council," in which the governor was to preside and to have a "treble voice." He was also to have a limited power of appointment on the nomination of the council, but was to perform no public act of importance without the advice and consent of the council. This Provincial Council was composed of seventy-two members, of whom one third were annually elected by the freemen for terms of three years. The business of the council was divided among committees. Later, the number of councillors, having been found too large, was reduced successively to eighteen and twelve.[6] On Penn's departure from the colony in 1684, the government was left in the hands of this Provincial Council, which was to act in the name of the proprietor.[7] In 1687 Penn issued a commission to five

account, *Documentary History of New York* (1849), i. 87; instructions to Andros, 1674, *New York Documents*, iii. 216.

[1] *New York Documents*, iii. 331.

[2] Andros's commission and instructions, *Ibid.*, 537.

[3] Commission to Cutts, 1679, in *New Hampshire Provincial Papers*, i. 373.

[4] Commission to Cranfield, *Ibid.*, 433.

[5] *Charter and Laws of Pennsylvania*, 470.

[6] See Frames of Government of 1682, 1683, and 1696, *Pennsylvania Records*, i. Introd.

[7] *Ibid.*, 119.

councillors, authorizing them collectively to exercise the functions of a deputy-governor.[1] In the next year the governor's office was placed in the hands of one man;[2] but two years later there was a recurrence to the collegiate form, in a commission conferring the powers of the deputy-governor upon the council.[3] After the brief period of royal control, Penn adopted a form similar to that in the royal governments, by which a governor was appointed by the proprietor to act in conjunction with councillors, whose assent was required in all cases.[4] In 1701 the constitution of the colony was put into its permanent form, under which the governor was to be the chief executive, although checked by councillors who were to "assist" him "with the best of their advice." These councillors were appointed by the proprietor in the first instance, but they were afterward to be named by the governor.[5]

After this rapid survey of the different colonies, the results of the first century of constitutional experience may be briefly summed up. To represent the colonial executive as having assumed its final form at this time would be to give a false impression of the actual situation, inasmuch as questions were still open which gave rise to frequent controversies between governor and council. The general result, however, is clear. There was in each of the colonies, excluding the elective governments, a single head, the governor, appointed either by the crown or by the proprietor. This governor was checked by a council appointed generally by the superior authority in England, though usually on the recommendation of the governor, — a fact of considerable importance in determining the mutual relations of governor and council. To this general rule in regard to the appointment of councillors there were, however, two leading exceptions. In Pennsylvania they seem to have

[1] *Charter and Laws of Pennsylvania*, 514.

[2] Blackwell's commission in *Pennsylvania Records*, i. 228.

[3] An alternative commission sent out by Penn authorized the council to name three persons, *Ibid.*, 315.

[4] Commission to Markham, *Ibid.*, 475. In 1700 Penn again visited the colony to govern it in person for a time, appointing a council to assist him, *Ibid.*, 580.

[5] Proud, *History of Pennsylvania*, i. 451.

been nominated by the governor and presented by him to the council for acceptance.[1] In Massachusetts they were elected by the General Court, consisting of the council and the House of Representatives, and the choice was then subject to the veto of the governor.[2] The chief question still left open in all the colonies was, then, as to the exact extent to which the council should be allowed to control the action of the governor.

Still more important than these questions of organization was the gradual growth from loose and vague provisions toward a more accurate definition of the powers and duties of the executive. The nature of the early colonial governments was necessarily determined to a large extent by the conditions under which they were organized. The early governor was not the executive of a settled political community. In addition to his political functions, he was often the manager or the superintendent of an essentially commercial enterprise. Indeed, in the first stages of colonization, the most important of the governor's duties was the superintendence of the general work of settlement, such as the granting of lands, the development of natural resources, and the maintenance of friendly relations with the savages. It is hardly strange, then, that the political aspects of his office should have been overshadowed, or at least strongly modified, by the peculiar situation in which he was placed. It was inevitable that his political functions should be loosely defined.

This business aspect of the governor's office, his position as the manager of a large commercial establishment, so to speak, is clearly brought out in the instructions and correspondence of the earliest colonial governors. The Virginia president and council of 1607, and the first governors who succeeded them, were clearly the overseers of an industrial establishment intended to furnish revenue for the government

---

[1] Cf. commission to the council, 1701, in Proud, *History of Pennsylvania*, i. 451. For illustrations of practice, see *Pennsylvania Records*, ii. 68, 117, iii. 232, v. 1.

[2] Massachusetts Charter, 1691, in Poore, *Charters and Constitutions*, i. 942.

at home. The governor of Maryland received instructions not
only for the government of the colony, but for the management of the proprietor's private stock-farm.[1] Furthermore,
the turbulent elements in these early colonies made necessary
the enforcement of almost military discipline;[2] and this aspect
of the governor's office was also emphasized by the necessity
for constant watchfulness in order to guard the colony against
its savage neighbors. It was only natural, then, that in this
era more emphasis should be laid upon executive efficiency
than upon constitutional limitations.

The charters issued to the proprietors and to colonizing
companies were usually couched in very general terms. The
grantees were empowered to "punish, pardon, govern, and rule"
the inhabitants of the colony, though frequently the provision
was made that legislation and taxation should be with the
consent of the freemen. This limitation was imposed in the
charters of Maryland, Carolina, and Pennsylvania. The New
York charter reserved the right to hear appeals carried from
the provincial courts to the king in council, but contained no
restriction as to legislation and taxation.[3] The proprietors had
thus left to them a wide discretion in the constitution of their
colonial governments.

The first governor's commissions were correspondingly indefinite. The Virginia president and council of 1607 were
invested with powers legislative and judicial as well as executive.[4] The very brief commission to Lord Delaware in 1610

[1] *Calvert Papers* (Maryland Historical Society, *Fund-Publication*, No.
28), 194, 214. To the governors of the Carolinas were given full instructions
as to the manner of laying out town sites, and in regard to the development
of the natural resources of the colony. See instructions of 1669, in Rivers,
Sketch of the History of South Carolina, 347.

[2] An extreme illustration is to be found in the "Articles, Lawes, and
Orders, Diuine, Politique and Martiall" issued in Virginia in 1610 and
1611, which were really military regulations of the most extreme type,
adapted to the use of a disorderly soldiery in a hostile country. See Force,
Tracts, iii. No. 2.

[3] All these charters are given in Poore, *Charters and Constitutions*.
The Maryland charter is translated in Bozman, *History of Maryland*, ii. 9.

[4] "Articles," etc., in Brown, *Genesis of the United States*, i. 65 *seq*. Cf.
orders of the Virginia council, *Ibid.*, 75.

is worth citing. Delaware was commissioned governor and captain-general, with power to enforce martial law, "and upon all other cases as well Capitall as Criminall and upon all other accidents and occasions there happening, to rule, punish, pardone and governe," according to instructions given by the council in England, or in default of such instructions by his own discretion, or by such laws as he should see fit to enact either independently or with the advice of such a council as he should think proper to summon; in short, he received powers as absolute as the company by its patent could give, with the understanding, moreover, that if these powers were not sufficient, it would endeavor to meet his wants.[1] Here, then, in sweeping terms is a grant of legislative, executive, and judicial functions. The commission to Nicolls as governor of New York was couched in similar terms, showing that the Duke of York invested his deputy with the right of exercising all authority granted to himself as proprietor.[2]

These two commissions to Delaware and Nicolls respectively furnish the most striking instances of the brevity which was characteristic of all the early commissions.[3] Those issued by the crown immediately after the overthrow of the Virginia Company usually contained a formal grant of authority, a statement of the governor's military powers as commander-in-chief, a few lines regarding the constitution of the council, and some instructions of a special and temporary character. Finally, the governor was authorized to govern the colony as fully as any governor of the preceding five years had done. This vague reference to past usage as the measure of the governor's powers occurs as late as 1641.[4] Even in the Carolinas and the Jerseys, with their elaborate written constitutions, the commissions

---

[1] Delaware's commission, *Ibid.*, 376 *seq.*

[2] Nicolls's commission, *Pennsylvania Archives*, v. 509.

[3] With the founding of the Carolina and the Jersey colonies a change begins, inaugurating a period of elaborate constitutional definitions.

[4] See James I.'s special commission, 1624, in Rymer, *Fœdera*, xvii. 618–621 ; commissions of 1625 and 1626 in Chalmers, *Political Annals*, 111, 112, and Rymer, *Fœdera*, xviii. 311 ; commissions to Harvey, 1628, 1636, *Ibid.*, xviii. 980, xx. 3–5 ; Berkeley's commission, 1641, *Ibid.*, xx. 484.

were brief enough;[1] and the prematurely minute definitions of their fundamental documents had little or no practical constitutional value.[2] It was only very gradually that the commissions and instructions were so enlarged that a more accurate definition of powers was made possible.

The institution of royal governments, expressing as it did the nascent conception of the colonies as parts of a large political or, to anticipate contemporary phraseology, imperial system, contributed toward a more purely political conception of the governor's office. In the establishment of these governments, the king was but asserting his right and duty to govern his subjects; and since the governor was the king's representative, this vice-regal position gradually came to determine in large measure the powers of the colonial executive. The governor's prerogative was, in theory, the royal prerogative on a smaller scale and of course with important limitations. Nor was the influence of these new conceptions limited to the royal provinces; it was felt to a marked extent in the proprietary colonies as well.

The most noticeable feature of the earlier colonial constitutions is the absence of anything like the modern political principle of the separation of powers. In the Virginia government of 1607, and in Lord Delaware's commission of 1610, there was, as we have seen, a union of executive, judicial, and legislative functions.[3] In Maryland the right of legislation was vested in the proprietor and the freemen; but, in the intervals between the sessions of the assembly, the proprietor was specially empowered to issue ordinances having the force of

---

[1] See list of commissions and instructions below, Appendix B.

[2] It is interesting to note, in the youngest of the thirteen colonies, a return to the old practice, a repetition of the old vagueness in definition. Here, for example, is a contemporary description of Oglethorpe's authority in Georgia, quoted from a South Carolina paper: " The general Title they give him is *Father*. . . . If any difference arises, he is the Person that decides it. . . . He keeps a strict Discipline. . . . He does not allow them Rum, but in lieu gives them *English* Beer " (Jones, *History of Georgia*, i. 127–128). This statement seems to be quite outside the domain of exact or even approximately exact constitutional definitions.

[3] Above, p. 32.

law, provided that such ordinances should not prejudice the rights of persons in life, members, or property. This prerogative was granted to the governor by the early commissions, with the proviso that his enactments were not to be in conflict with laws already in force. Moreover, judicial jurisdiction in all cases civil and criminal was given him, to be exercised either alone or with his council.[1]

The precedents set in the older colonies were followed elsewhere. In New York, Governor Nicolls was invested with all the powers of the proprietor, including the right of legislation, which was actually exercised by him either alone or with the assent of the council and of the assize of justices, a body of his own nominees whose power could have been hardly more than advisory.[2] The Carolina charter, like that of Maryland, though it provided for legislation regularly by the proprietors with the consent of the freemen, also reserved to the proprietors or their representatives the right to issue ordinances having the force of law;[3] and the minutes of the governor and council show that such ordinances were actually passed.[4] Here also the governor and council were given judicial functions.[5] In New Hampshire the governor and council were authorized to continue the old taxes until suitable provision should be made by the assembly;[6] whereupon Governor Cranfield, on the failure of the assembly to raise the necessary revenue, took advantage of this power and continued the taxes, meeting with serious resistance, however, in the attempt to collect them.[7]

[1] See Calvert's commissions of 1637 and 1642, in Bozman, *History of Maryland*, ii. 572, 621. Cf. with the language of the charter, *Ibid.*, ii. 9.

[2] See commission to Nicolls, *Pennsylvania Archives*, v. 509. Cf. charter of 1664, in Poore, *Charters and Constitutions*, i. 783; Nicolls's account, *Documentary History of New York* (1849), i. 87; *Charter and Laws of Pennsylvania*, 3, 44, 53, 66.

[3] Charter of 1663, §§ 5, 6, in Poore, *Charters and Constitutions*, ii. 1382. Cf. the charter of Maryland

[4] Cf., for example, *North Carolina Records*, ii. 130.

[5] Instructions to Ludwell, 1691, §§ 15-17.

[6] Commissions to Cutts and Cranfield, *New Hampshire Provincial Papers*, i. 373, 433.

[7] *Ibid.*, 475, 496, 543-544.

The ordaining power was evidently pushed very far in these early years of New Hampshire's separate provincial government, for there are complaints that the governor and council made laws without the coöperation of the assembly.[1] Here also the president and council were endowed by the first provincial commission with judicial jurisdiction in all cases civil and criminal.[2] Everywhere, then, the governor is found exercising functions which are usually considered to be beyond the sphere of the executive department of the State.

The possession of legislative authority by the executive was hardly in accord with the old English tradition that legislation and taxation should be guarded by a representative body. It was not likely, therefore, that this branch of the governor's extra-executive power would survive the primitive conditions of the first colonial establishments. In Virginia the triumph of the liberal element in the company gave to the colony the famous assembly of 1619, the first representative body in America.[3] This grant was confirmed by the ordinance of 1621, and the governor's authority was thus brought within more moderate limits.[4] In spite of the existence of an assembly, however, the governors seem not to have given up their legislative powers at once; consequently in 1624 the assembly found it necessary to pass a formal act declaring expressly that the governor was not to make laws without the consent of the assembly.[5]

After the institution of the royal government in Virginia, the policy of the crown was for a time uncertain. The early commissions said nothing of an assembly; and the only recorded legislation of the next five years which has come down to us is in the form of proclamations by the governor.[6] On the other hand, it is certain that the assembly did not lapse altogether; for there is evidence that in 1627 the king recognized its

---

[1] See ordinances of governor and council, *Ibid.*, 463, 468, 473, 481; cf. p. 518.

[2] Commission to Cutts, *Ibid.*, 373.

[3] *Colonial Records of Virginia*, 81.

[4] Hening, *Statutes*, i. 110.

[5] *Ibid.*, 124, 129; Chalmers, *Political Annals*, 63-64.

[6] Hening, *Statutes*, i. 129-130.

existence and competency by submitting to it certain propositions relating to the tobacco trade, to which the assembly
replied by submitting counter-propositions.[1] The power of
the assembly was, however, still on a precarious footing. The
governor continued to assume for himself the rights of taxation and legislation, which were again expressly denied by the
assembly in acts of February and September, 1632.[2] This
abuse of power by the governor led to his expulsion by the
colonists; and though he was again forced upon them for a
time, yet a few years later the king, by his instructions to
Berkeley, gave to the assembly a formal recognition.[3] After
the Restoration the same Governor Berkeley was by his first
instructions directed to call the assembly within one month of
his arrival in the colony.[4]

The continued existence of some representative body was
now fairly assured; but there was still at times a disposition
to restrict its activity as far as possible. Lord Culpeper was
directed to summon an assembly only by special direction of
the crown,[5] and five years passed without any legislative
sessions.[6] On the other hand, the instruction to Lord
Howard of Effingham to "recommend" the assembly to allow
the governor and council, in case of emergency, to impose
duties, was a clear recognition of the assembly and of its
exclusive right to determine taxation.[7] The governor, nevertheless, seems still to have encroached upon the field of legis-

---

[1] Hening, *Statutes*, i. 129, 134; Neill, *Virginia Carolorum*, 55; Sainsbury,
Calendar of State Papers, Colonial Series, America and West Indies, 1574–
1660, pp. 86, 87, 89, 90.

[2] Chalmers, *Political Annals*, 118–119; letter of Richard Kemp, in
Sainsbury, *Calendar of State Papers, Colonial Series, America and West
Indies*, 1574–1660, p. 207; Hening, *Statutes*, i. 171, 196.

[3] Berkeley was to summon the assembly once a year, or oftener if urgent
occasion should require, having "as formerly" a *negative voice* upon its proceedings: Instructions, § 4, *Virginia Magazine*, ii. 281.

[4] Chalmers, *Political Annals*, 244; Instructions, 1662, § 2, *Virginia
Magazine*, iii. 15.

[5] Doyle, *English in America*, i. 344.

[6] There is, at least, no record of any acts of assembly between 1686 and
1691. See Hening, *Statutes*, iii.

[7] Doyle, *English in America*, i. 349–350.

lation by means of proclamations;[1] but, with a representative assembly controlling the purse, these abnormal features naturally passed away or became very exceptional.

In New York, James fought against the change as long as he could.   In reply to Andros's letter recommending an assembly, he wrote that assemblies were destructive to the peace of governments in which they were allowed.[2]   In 1680 occurred the Dyer case, in which the officers of the duke were resisted in the collection of duties imposed by the latter.[3]   The Court of Assizes, composed of the governor's own nominees, petitioned for a representative assembly; and James finally submitted, authorizing Governor Dongan in 1683 to call an assembly.[4]   This body at its first sessions enacted the so-called "Charter of Privileges," which asserted in strong terms the exclusive legislative authority of the assembly;[5] whereupon James took offence at the high tone assumed by it and disallowed the act.[6]   The royal commission of 1686 again vested full powers of legislation and taxation in the governor and council;[7] and in 1688 New York was annexed to the general government of New England, in which the same despotic system was already in force.[8]   The result of this latter experiment is too familiar to need repetition here.   In New York the Andros government went down before the Leisler rebellion; whereupon Leisler established a provisional government, assumed that the Charter of Privileges was in force, and called an assembly.[9]   This revolutionary organization was of course

---

[1] Beverly, *History of Virginia*, 80, 85.

[2] January, 1676: *New York Documents*, iii. 235.

[3] *Ibid.*, 246, 289 ; Chalmers, *Political Annals*, 582–583.

[4] Wood, *Sketch of Long Island*, 178; *New York Documents*, iii. 317–318; Dongan's instructions, *Ibid.*, 331.

[5] Brodhead, *History of New York*, ii. 659.

[6] Instructions to Dongan, *New York Documents*, iii. 370.

[7] Dongan's commission, 1686, *Ibid.*, 377.

[8] Commission and instructions to Andros, *Ibid.*, 537 *seq.*, especially 538.

[9] Leisler's writs, *Documentary History of New York* (1849), ii. 282–283; Brodhead, *History of New York*, ii. 615, 623; *New York Documents*, iii. 700, 717.

overthrown, but the new royal commission definitely recognized the assembly.[1]

The Andros commission for the government of New England was the last deliberate attempt to give the governor absolute powers in legislation, though in Georgia there was certainly for a time a very informal government under Oglethorpe.[2] Until 1751 there was no representative assembly within the latter colony, and the one then instituted was nothing more than an advisory body.[3] When Georgia became a royal government, however, an assembly was regularly organized.

Reference has been made to the power of issuing ordinances as exercised in Maryland, the Carolinas, and New Hampshire. This power, though certainly actually used in the beginning, seems, however, to have been allowed to lapse.[4] In New Hampshire, Governor Cranfield's effort to collect the old taxes continued by proclamation met, as has been seen, with vigorous resistance; hence in the commissions given after the revolution of 1688 the clause providing for this mode of continuing taxes was wisely omitted. Nevertheless, the power to issue ordinances continued to be exercised, but usually within reasonable limits. In two specified cases, namely, in the erection of courts and the regulation of fees, the governor was invested by his commission with quasi-legislative power; and although these rights were practically very much limited by the action of the assembly, yet they continued throughout the colonial era to be in theory a part of the governor's prerogative.[5]

Even after the governor had been forced to give up the power of legislating independently, he still claimed for himself, in many cases, a distinctly preponderating influence in

---

[1] Sloughter's commission, *New York Documents*, iii. 623.

[2] Wright, *Memoir of General James Oglethorpe*, 64.

[3] Jones, *History of Georgia*, i. 434–435.

[4] For Maryland, see *Maryland Archives*, iii. 103, 129, 194, v. 105; Calvert's commission, 1666, *Ibid.*, iii. 542. For Carolina, see "Grievances of the Assembly," in Rivers, *Sketch of the History of South Carolina*, 433.

[5] Commission to Bernard, 1758, § 15; instructions, § 44.

the process of legislation. In Virginia the royal instructions of 1682 directed that all bills should be drafted by the governor and council.[1] The Maryland proprietor claimed for himself or his governor the sole right of initiating legislation.[2] In Pennsylvania, Penn's first two constitutions provided that all laws should be prepared by the governor and Provincial Council; and measures thus prepared were then to be presented to the assembly for its simple approval or rejection.[3] A similar exclusive privilege was given to the Grand Council, the collegiate executive of the Carolina "Fundamental Constitutions."[4] These claims, however, were uniformly resisted. In Maryland, the proprietor, after an unsuccessful attempt to force legislation upon the assembly,[5] empowered the governor to approve bills presented by that body.[6] The Carolina governor and council had for a time, it is true, the initiative in legislation; but in 1682 this privilege was restricted by the provision that, if the council failed to propose a bill presented by a majority of the grand juries, the Parliament might assume the initiative.[7] Later the assembly denied altogether the right of the council to initiate legislation, and a prolonged deadlock ensued.[8] The instructions of 1691 did not distinctly

[1] Culpeper's instructions, cited by Doyle, *English in America*, i. 344.

[2] Lord Baltimore, by his commission to Leonard Calvert in 1637, declared his veto of all laws passed by the assembly, and submitted his own code to the freemen for their approval. The governor was thenceforth empowered to "propound" legislation to the assembly. See commission in Bozman, *History of Maryland*, ii. 572.

[3] Frames of Government of 1682 and 1683, in Poore, *Charters and Constitutions*, ii. 1520, 1527.

[4] Fundamental Constitutions, §§ 50–55, *Ibid.*, 1397.

[5] The assembly rejected the code of laws sent over by the proprietor, and passed another set. See *Maryland Archives*, i. 6, 9, 23.

[6] *Ibid.*, 31. In 1648 the proprietor sent over another set of laws to be accepted or rejected as a whole, but the assembly decided not to "meddle" with them at all; in the following year the proprietor again urged their passage, and some of them were passed, though the assembly still refused to enact them in a mass. See letters of the assembly and the proprietor, and laws passed, *Ibid.*, 238, 262 *seq.*, 299.

[7] Instructions to governor and council at Ashley River, in Rivers, *Sketch of the History of South Carolina*, 369, 395.

[8] Address to Governor Sothel, *Ibid.*, 422.

assert this right.[1] Royal instructions like those of the year
1682 in Virginia were quite exceptional, containing, as they
did, a grant of power such as was found in none of the royal
commissions of the eighteenth century.

In the earliest period of colonization, the governor was
sometimes a member of the assembly. In the Virginia
assembly of 1619, governor, council, and assembly all sat
together, and the governor seems to have made motions like
an ordinary member.[2] The ordinance of 1621 declared the
assembly to consist of the council of state (the governor
being a member) and two burgesses from each "town, hundred,
or other particular plantation." All decisions required a
majority vote, but the governor had, apparently in addition to
his vote as an individual member, the right of veto.[3] The
first Maryland assembly was similarly constituted. The governor presided, and his power was further increased by two
peculiar customs, one of which was the use of proxies. Thus,
on one division, the governor and one councillor are recorded
as having cast fourteen votes.[4] There is no indication that
these proxies were given for particular votes; they were apparently used at the discretion of the holder. A second peculiar
privilege enjoyed by the Maryland governor was that of issuing to persons not members of the council or regularly elected
as representatives special writs, giving them the right to sit
and vote in the assembly.[5] Such votes would under ordinary
conditions easily be controlled by the governor. The Carolina
"Fundamental Constitutions" provided that the governor,
the deputies, the nobility, and the elected representatives
should all sit together in parliament, except in certain cases
when they should separate into four houses. The first New
Hampshire constitution had given the executive power to a
president and council; but in view of the fact that by an early

[1] Ludwell's instructions, 1691, § 27. Cf. his private instructions, *North
Carolina Records*, i. 381.
[2] *Colonial Records of Virginia*, 9, 11, 12.
[3] Ordinance in Hening, *Statutes*, i. 110.
[4] *Maryland Archives*, i. 4, 9.
[5] *Ibid.*, 128–129; Bozman, *History of Maryland*, ii. 216.

statute a casting vote in the proceedings of the general assembly was given to the president, it seems evident that the president, council, and assembly sat as one body.[1]

The first important step toward legislative independence of the governor and council gained by the representative element in the assembly was the separation of the two houses. Just when the division took place in Virginia, it is not easy to determine. It has been said that it occurred in Culpeper's time;[2] but much earlier than this, in 1666, there is a distinct reference to the "house" of burgesses.[3] In Maryland the separation of the two houses came very early. In 1642 the burgesses requested a separation, which was at first refused; but in 1650 an act was passed providing for a division into two houses.[4] In New Hampshire and the Carolinas the single chamber system was soon discarded, and the governor and council were recognized as an upper house.[5] This division into two houses was the general rule in all the colonies except Pennsylvania, where the council lost all its formal legislative powers and became, at least in name, simply an executive body.[6]

After the division into two houses, the governor at first generally sat either as a member of the upper house or as its presiding officer.[7] Hutchinson, in his "History of Massachu-

---

[1] *New Hampshire Provincial Papers*, i. 407.

[2] Beverly, *History of Virginia*, 203.

[3] In that year, Governor Berkeley sent a message to the burgesses desiring that two or more of the council might join with them "in granting and confirming the sums of the levy." The burgesses replied that they conceived it "their privilege to lay the levy in the house." See Hening, *Statutes*, ii. 254.

[4] *Maryland Archives*, i. 130, 272. In 1660, Governor Fendall, who wished to win popularity at the expense of the proprietary interests, consented to a reunion of the two Houses, which was then desired by the lower House. The latter was then numerically superior to the upper house, and had thus something to gain from the change. The reunion, however, was only temporary (*Ibid.*, 390, 395 *seq.*).

[5] See, for example, *New Hampshire Provincial Papers*, ii. 155; *North Carolina Records*, i. 614; *Case of the Dissenters*, 31.

[6] Commission to the council, in Proud, *History of Pennsylvania*, i. 451; letter of Hannah Penn, 1724, *Ibid.*, ii. 179.

[7] *New Hampshire Provincial Papers*, ii. 155 (minutes of May, 1695);

setts," [1] says that Lord Bellomont, who was governor of Massachusetts in 1699, considered himself the head of the council in its legislative as well as in its executive capacity. Hutchinson thought, however, that this claim was the result of the unsettled condition of the constitution, and that the governor had strictly no right to vote on bills. Sewall's diary represents the governor as taking an active part in legislative business. An entry of the year 1715 refers to a certain tax-bill which had been read in the council and which Sewall desired to have postponed; but "the governor would have it voted then," and the vote was taken. [2]

In 1725 the question as to the governor's right to vote in the legislative sessions of the council was referred to the crown law-officers, who decided against the governor's claim; [3] but it is probable that this settlement of the questions at issue was not final, for in 1729 Governor Cosby of New York insisted on his right to sit and vote with the council. His action, however, called out a protest, in consequence of which the Board of Trade directed him not to act as a member of the legislative council; and thereafter Cosby's successors both in New York and in New Jersey allowed the council the privilege of sitting apart in its legislative capacity. [4] In North Carolina

Maryland Archives, i. 272, xiii. 329; *North Carolina Records*, iii. 310; Jones, *Present State of Virginia*, 63; Hartwell, Blair, and Chilton, *Present State of Virginia*, 39.

[1] II. 15, 107.

[2] *Sewall's Diary*, iii. 47. In Pennsylvania, the governor was himself a species of upper house, though the council was usually called upon for advice. The governor's right to amend bills was disputed only in financial legislation. See *Votes of Pennsylvania*, i. 129–133.

[3] Chalmers, *Opinions*, 238.

[4] *New York Documents*, v. 887, vi. 39. Cosby was succeeded in New Jersey by Lewis Morris, who before his appointment as governor had been a councillor, and as such had taken a strong stand against the claims of his predecessor. On his assumption of the government of New Jersey, he made an address to the councillors, promising them the privilege, for the first time, of holding their legislative sessions apart from the governor. See *New Jersey Documents*, xv. 4. Cf. Governor Belcher's apparently unsuccessful attempt to reverse this action, *Ibid.*, vii. 77–81. For New York, cf. Smith, *History of New York*, 310.

there was a similar conflict. Governor Burrington maintained that the council always sat in a double capacity, "the two capacities never being distinguished," and declared that the governor's right to be present at all debates was allowed everywhere. Here again the council finally gained its point, in that it sat apart in legislative sessions and had a separate presiding officer.[1]

In 1739 the South Carolina council declared its independence in the following vigorous terms: "The Governor or commander in chief being present during the debates of this House is of an unparliamentary nature, it is therefore resolved that we will enter into no debate during such his presence."[2] Governor Glen protested against this exclusion from the council, and was finally allowed to attend the sessions without taking any part in the debates.[3] In 1754, Georgia was organized as a royal province with a royal government of the strictest sort. The rule there was, — and this rule may be taken as an expression of the normal practice of the royal governments, — that when the council sat as an upper house, the lieutenant-governor, *if a member*, presided.[4] The council was thus, in form at least, an independent legislative house, having a distinct presiding officer.

This was the last step taken during the colonial era in the separation of legislative and executive functions. The governor retained a certain part in the process of legislation, first through his right of assent or veto, and secondly through his influence over the council, an influence which, though weakened by his withdrawal from the legislative sessions, was still strong over a body composed mainly of his own nominees.

Another branch of extra-executive powers possessed by the early governors has already been noted, namely, his judicial authority. This was necessarily much limited by the organization of a regular system of courts; but the governor and

[1] *North Carolina Records*, iii. 357, 478, iv. 446.
[2] Letter of Governor Glen, April 11, 1739, in South Carolina Historical Society, *Collections*, ii. 286.
[3] Letter of 1748, *Ibid.*, 303 *seq.*, especially 304.
[4] Stokes, *Constitution of the British Colonies*, 124.

council continued in most of the colonies to be the highest court of appeal within the province.[1]

The provincial governor, then, never became a purely executive officer, inasmuch as he continued to be invested with legislative and judicial functions of the highest importance. Nevertheless, much had been accomplished in the direction of a rational distribution of functions, in that the real control of legislation had passed irrevocably into the hands of the assembly, and the administration of justice was largely in the hands of a regularly organized judiciary. The result of this work of definition and separation, imperfect as it was, was the royal governor of the eighteenth century. With a few modifications, which have been already noted, the proprietary governors may properly be included in the same category with the royal. Thus, as a general term including both the proprietary and the royal governors, the name "provincial governor" will serve as a convenient if not precisely accurate title. The character of this office in its actual operation will form the subject of the succeeding chapter.

[1] See below, ch. vii.

CHAPTER III.

THE GOVERNOR'S APPOINTMENT, TENURE OF OFFICE, AND EMOLUMENTS.

THE provincial governor of the royal and proprietary colonies was appointed by the higher authority in England, though the appointment came in the one case from the crown, and in the other from a proprietor or a group of proprietors. As has been seen already, however, the crown had so far extended its control over the proprietary governments that the appointment of governors was subject to confirmation by the crown. The royal governors, on the other hand, were usually appointed on the recommendation of the Board of Trade, by order of the king in council.[1]

The methods by which these appointments were secured were similar to those employed in the other departments of the British public service in the days of the Whig ascendancy. In a report submitted to the Board of Trade in 1715 there is an interesting statement of the principles governing such appointments: "Governments have bin sometimes given as a reward for Services done to the Crown, and with design that such persons should thereby make their fortunes. But they are generally obtained by the favour of great Men to some of their dependants or relations, and they have bin sometimes given to persons who were oblidged to divide the profit of them

---

[1] See, for example, the record of the proceedings in the case of Josiah Hardy, appointed governor of New Jersey in 1761. After the reading of the representation of the Board of Trade proposing his appointment, it was ordered by the king in council that his appointment be made as proposed. The Board of Trade was then directed to prepare the draft of the governor's commission, which finally, after its approval by the Privy Council, went to the king for his signature. See *New Jersey Documents*, ix. 259, 262.

with those by whose means they were procured. The Qualifications of such persons for Government being seldom considered."[1] This is a severe indictment; but it is not difficult to
find specific cases sustaining these charges. Thus the Duke
of Newcastle, the great dispenser of public offices in the last
century, extended his activity to the colonies. In the North
Carolina records is a list of places said to be in his gift;[2] and
there is evidence that applications for the use of his influence
were made to him by anxious candidates for the colonial service.[3] The spirit of this office-jobbing is fairly well illustrated by a letter to the Secretary of State, Townshend, from
one John Lloyd. This gentleman explained that he had
resided nine years in South Carolina, "whither he came
because of ill-fortune in the stocks"; and he now asked for
the office either of lieutenant-governor without salary, or first
of the king's council, saying that "what he ' proposes by it
is a little power, and perhaps a little profit.'"[4] Chalmers
asserted that Eliseus Burgess sold his appointment as governor
of Massachusetts and New Hampshire for the sum of £1000.[5]
It is hardly strange, therefore, that under such conditions
characters like Culpeper and Cornbury were turned loose upon
the colonies.

During the latter part of the colonial era, appointments

---

[1] *North Carolina Records*, ii. 154 *seq.*, especially 158.

[2] *Ibid.*, iii. 80.

[3] Sir William Keith asked Newcastle to use his influence to secure the
former's appointment as governor of New Jersey (*New Jersey Documents*,
v. 446).

[4] South Carolina Historical Society, *Collections*, i. 245.

[5] Chalmers, *Revolt*, ii. 11. The securing of a commission was often a
very expensive process. Governor Wentworth's commission for New
Hampshire is said to have cost more than £300, part of which, at least, was
spent in getting the commission through the various formal stages after the
appointment had been made. Various fees had to be paid to different
functionaries. Jonathan Belcher, who was appointed governor of New
Jersey in 1747, found that there was great delay in the preparation of his
instructions, and on inquiry he was told that they were stopped for non-
payment of fees. He at once deposited £200, and "this unexpected Supply
set the Wheels into Motion." See *New Hampshire Provincial Papers*,
v. 929; *New Jersey Documents*, vi. 422.

were often made on more rational grounds, since, with in-
creasingly frequent communication between the colonies and
the mother country, the former naturally exerted increased
influence upon the choices made by the crown.   Thus, at the
beginning of the eighteenth century, Governor Spotswood
complained that the councillors had gained an undue sense of
their own powers from their success in securing the removal of
two of his predecessors.[1] Furthermore, the practice of sending agents to represent colonial interests naturally had its
influence, especially since these agents were often men of considerable importance.   There is one instance, indeed, in which
the agent sent to present the complaints of the colonists
against the governor was himself sent back with a governor's
commission.[2]

The appointment of colonists to the governor's chair was not
altogether uncommon in the eighteenth century.   Of the ten
royal governors of Massachusetts, four were Massachusetts
men. New Hampshire men also frequently received the
appointment of lieutenant-governor in that colony, and after
New Hampshire became a separate government both her governors were chosen from among the residents of the province.
On the appointment of the first of these, Benning Wentworth,
who had been a member of the provincial House of Representatives, the members of the House expressed their satisfaction with the choice of one "whose Interest is blended with
theirs."[3]   So in New Jersey, the first governor appointed, after
the "personal union" of that province with the government of
New York had been broken, was Lewis Morris, a representative colonist.   In Virginia and the other colonies, such appointments were occasionally made, but the practice was not
common.[4]   Though the conditions on which colonial appoint-

---

[1] *Letters of Governor Spotswood* (Virginia Historical Society, *Collections*,
ii.), 285.

[2] This was Governor Belcher of Massachusetts, who had represented the
assembly in their case against his predecessor Burnet. See Chalmers,
Revolt, ii. 132.

[3] *New Hampshire Provincial Papers*, iv. 646, v. 139.

[4] Governor Dinwiddie of Virginia was welcomed because he "formerly

ments were made were hardly calculated to secure the best results, the names of Spotswood of Virginia, Sharpe of Maryland, Morris of New Jersey, and Hutchinson of Massachusetts suffice to show that some provincial governors were neither unscrupulous nor inefficient. There were others, too, like Burnet of New York and Massachusetts, who showed an honorable willingness to make sacrifices for what they conceived to be the public interest.[1]

The governor's tenure of office may be considered under two aspects, — that defined by the terms of his commission and the practical aspect determined by actual conditions. His legal tenure, as stated by the commission, was during the king's pleasure,[2] though to this general rule of the royal governments there was one striking exception in the first century of the colonial era. In 1675 Thomas Culpeper received a commission for life as governor of Virginia; this commission, however, was forfeited for disobedience to orders, and no more royal commissions for life appear.[3] Upon the general prin-

liv'd amongst Us " and was " well acquainted with the Laws and Constitution of our Country ": *Dinwiddie Papers*, i. 27.

[1] For Burnet's efforts to secure the establishment of a post at Oswego by considerable personal advances which were never fully repaid, see *New York Documents*, v. 818, 846.

[2] See Bernard's commission for New Jersey, 1758, § 27 ; Smith, *History of New York*, 228.

[3] Patent to Culpeper, in Hening, *Statutes*, ·ii. 565. The commission given to Lord Delaware by the Virginia Company in 1610 was also a commission for life (Brown, *Genesis of the United States*, i. 375). In 1683 the proprietors of East Jersey issued a commission to Robert Barclay as governor for life; and at the same time a deputy-governor was named who was empowered to hold office for seven years. In later commissions of the New Jersey proprietors the term was stated as one year, or until some other appointment should be made (*New Jersey Documents*, i. 423, ii. 87, 301). The attempt to fix definite terms of office appears elsewhere. For example, the rules of the Virginia Company provided that all colonial commissions should be " onely for three yeares in certaine, and afterwards during the *Companies* pleasure "; and that no governor should in any case hold his office more than six years (" Orders and Constitutions of the Virginia Company," in Force, *Tracts*, iii. No. 6, p. 19). In the propositions issued by the proprietors of Carolina in 1663, it was provided that governors should hold office for terms of three years ; but the propositions were never carried

ciple that the governor's tenure depended on the king's pleasure there was a formal limitation, imposed by English custom, to the effect that all patents terminated on the death of the king. By acts of 7 & 8 William III. and 1 Anne, it was provided that commissions should continue for six months after the demise of the sovereign. At the expiration of that time the governor's authority lapsed, unless a new commission was issued.[1] In any case, the authority of the governor ceased on the arrival of his successor and the publication of the latter's commission.[2]

What, then, was the real duration of the governor's service as affected by the actual facts of the political situation in which he was placed? There were many circumstances that tended to make his position insecure. In the first place, the same sort of influence that gave him his office might be used with equal effect by other men: Douglass, a contemporary writer, speaks of the governor's position as "very slippery," of his liability to be called to account "upon frivolous and sometimes false complaints," and to be "superseded by some expectant at court."[3] Moreover, party changes in England were not without interest for governors in the colonies. A letter written by Lewis Morris, governor of New Jersey in 1742, shows his anxiety lest a probable change of ministry might affect his position.[4]

The removal of a governor for real misconduct was never an altogether easy task, though the colonial agencies made it

out ("Proposals of the Proprietors," in Rivers, *Sketch of the History of South Carolina*, 335).

[1] Chalmers, *Opinions*, 234 *seq.*

[2] *Ibid.*, 243.

[3] William Douglass, *Summary of the First Planting of the British Settlements in North America*, i. 474.

[4] He thought it "not unnaturall to suppose that those employ'd by the last [ministry] may not be look'd on in the most favourable light by their successors, and amongst the rest such a reptile as my selfe, (tho' now treading on the verge of life & far from being an advocate for arbitrary power), may be remov'd to make way for some new man that will think this government worth soliciting for": *Morris Papers* (New Jersey Historical Society, *Collections*, iv.), 145.

possible for the people of the provinces to make themselves
heard more effectively than would otherwise have been the
case. As has been seen, Governor Burnet of Massachusetts
was succeeded in office by the agent who had been sent to
represent the assembly in its controversy with the governor;[1]
and, though Governor Burnet died in office, the incident illustrates well the influence of some of these colonial agents.
Belcher himself, Burnet's successor, had occasion later to
realize the influence which an agent might bring to bear
against a distant governor, inasmuch as his own removal was
due very largely to the work of the New Hampshire agent.[2]
Chalmers deplored the extent to which this influence was used
against unpopular governors.[3] There can be no doubt that it
was often very effective. During the long periods in which
the royal and the colonial interests were in almost constant
conflict, when it was almost impossible, without a violation of
instructions, for a governor to get his salary or the necessary
grants for the conduct of government or even the military
supplies demanded by the crown, his position was trying in
the extreme.

Under these circumstances, one would naturally have expected a brief and uncertain tenure. There are instances,
however, which tell against this general view. Massachusetts,
during the eighty-two years from 1692 to 1774, the period of
the Province charter, had ten governors with an average term
of eight years.[4] North Carolina, during the thirty-four years
of the royal government up to the passage of the Stamp Act,
had only three governors with an average term of eleven years.
New Hampshire, after its separation from Massachusetts in
1741, had but two governors, the first serving until 1767.
These terms, however, are longer than the usual duration of

[1] See above, p. 48.

[2] *New Hampshire Provincial Papers*, v. 915 *seq.*

[3] "Having reduced to a miserable subservience the governors, they,
without difficulty, effected their recall, by those arts, which popular conven-
tions know how to use, either to gratify passion or to extend their privileges ": Chalmers, *Revolt*, i. 225.

[4] Two of these, Phips and Burnet, held their commissions at the time of
their deaths.

the governor's service. There is a striking reference to this instability in office in a passage in the history of Pennsylvania, once erroneously ascribed to Benjamin Franklin: "There is no Man, long or much conversant in this overgrown City [London], who hath not often found himself in Company with the Shades of departed Governors, doom'd to wander out the Residue of their Lives, full of the agonizing Remembrance of their passed Eminence, and the severe Sensation of present Neglect."[1]

A governor was usually assigned to a single province; but to this general rule there were several exceptions. The policy of James II. included not merely the reduction of charter and proprietary governments to the uniform royal type, but also the consolidation of provinces. Thus the commission to Andros in 1688 included not merely New England, but New York and New Jersey. This unwieldy province fell to pieces, however, with the overthrow of Andros; and, indeed, the attempt to consolidate the colonial governments was in the main given up, though for a long time it was a common practice to organize what may be called "personal unions," by which more governments than one were assigned to a single governor. The personal unions had certain advantages from a military point of view, a circumstance which was especially important in the last decade of the seventeenth century, at the opening of the great conflict with France for maritime and colonial supremacy as well as for the maintenance of the European political balance. Thus, in 1697 the Earl of Bellomont became governor of Massachusetts, New York, and New Hampshire;[2] and the appointments to Massachusetts and New Hampshire were combined under several of his successors. In 1702 the governments of New York and New Jersey were similarly combined. Pennsylvania and Delaware originally constituted but one government; but the lower counties on the Delaware were

---

[1] *Historical Review of the Constitution and Government of Pennsylvania* (1759), 77. Sometimes a governor after his removal remained in the province and joined the opposition (note the case of Keith, *Ibid.*). This essay, though not written by Franklin, seems to have been published with his sanction and coöperation. Cf. Franklin, *Works*, Bigelow ed., iii. 125–126, note.

[2] *New York Documents*, iv. 261.

restive under this arrangement, and finally secured from Penn permission to organize a separate legislature. This case is different from those just mentioned, in that the two provinces of Delaware and Pennsylvania, or rather perhaps the two divisions of the one province, had a common executive, with a joint council for both divisions.[1] In the other provinces above referred to, the union was merely personal: the same person who held the office of governor in one province held also the entirely distinct office of governor in the other.[2]

This combination of governments proved awkward in practice; for the governor maintained his regular residence in the larger province, and naturally his long periods of absence from the smaller colony led to grave difficulties.[3] The people of New Jersey, for example, felt strongly that their province was neglected by its absentee governors.[4] In New Hampshire also serious irregularities arose.[5] Indeed, in both colonies the situation gave rise to complications in the relations between governor and lieutenant-governor, especially in regard to the powers that might properly be exercised by the lieutenant-governor in the absence of the governor.[6] The chief difficulty of the system, however, lay in the fact that adjacent

[1] Charter of 1701, in Poore, *Charters and Constitutions*, ii. 1536; *Pennsylvania Records*, iii. 18, 143, 253, 254.

[2] This experiment was also tried for a time in the Carolinas (see commissions of 1691, 1693, 1694, and 1702). The governor, who resided in one province, might appoint a deputy in the other. In 1712 the two governments were separated. See South Carolina Historical Society, *Collections*, i. 128, 134, 136, 212; *North Carolina Records*, i. 554, 841.

[3] Governor Cornbury of New York is said to have been absent from New Jersey nine months of the year ("Address of the New Jersey assembly," *New Jersey Documents*, iii. 242). Governor Dudley of Massachusetts and New Hampshire resided in Boston, and visited New Hampshire for only comparatively short periods (Chalmers, *Revolt*, i. 325).

[4] *New Jersey Documents*, iii. 242–243, iv. 132–133.

[5] "Having determined to reside at Boston, the metropolis of the most powerful colony, he [Governor Dudley] adopted a mode of administration for New Hampshire, which promoted his profit without disturbing his ease. . . . In the principal Independents . . . he placed all power; as he allowed them to govern themselves, they procured for him, in return, a salary of one hundred and fifty pounds a year" (Chalmers, *Revolt*, i. 325–326).

[6] See below, pp. 56, 57.

provinces, like New York and New Jersey, or Massachusetts and New Hampshire, often had interests at variance with each other.   The New Jersey agent, in arguing for an independent New Jersey government, declared that a governor deriving his chief support from New York could not be induced to pass acts affecting unfavorably New York interests.[1]   The people of New Hampshire felt that Governor Belcher, in a controversy between the two provinces in regard to boundaries, had shown great partiality to the larger province, and had grossly abused his powers as governor of New Hampshire in order to secure a decision favorable to Massachusetts.[2]

The feeling in New Jersey and New Hampshire finally became too strong to be disregarded.   On the death of Governor Cosby in 1736, New Jersey presented several addresses praying for a separate government; and in 1738 Lewis Morris, formerly chief-justice of New York, was made governor.[3]   In 1741 Governor Belcher of Massachusetts was removed, and in the same year a separate governor was appointed for New Hampshire.[4]   From this time on the policy of personal unions was abandoned.

The newly-appointed governor, on his arrival in the province, published his commission, and then took the necessary oaths in the presence of the council.   The proceedings were sometimes attended with considerable ceremony.   Sir William Phips, the first governor of Massachusetts under the new charter, was conducted to the town-house by the military companies of Boston and Charlestown, and by the magistrates, ministers, and principal gentlemen of Boston and adjacent towns.[5]   The oaths prescribed for the governor were numerous and of various kinds.   The first was the simple oath of office. The following was the oath administered to the governor of New Hampshire in 1742: "You . . . Swear that you will

---

[1] *New Jersey Documents*, v. 453.

[2] See accounts in *New Hampshire Provincial Papers*, v. 915–921; Hutchinson, *History of Massachusetts*, ii. 349–350.

[3] *New Jersey Documents*, v. 435, 441, 450, vi. 1.

[4] *New Hampshire Provincial Papers*, v. 135, 915–921.

[5] Hutchinson, *History of Massachusetts*, ii. 20.

faithfully & Truely perform the Trust reposed in you by his Majesty's Comission and that you will administer Justice equally and impartially in all cases that shall come before you in judgment. So help you God." Other oaths had to do with the governor's duties to the central colonial administration, his allegiance to the crown, and his ecclesiastical obligations. He was required to take the oaths of allegiance and supremacy, to declare his fidelity to the Protestant succession, and to deny that there was any transubstantiation in the sacrament of the Lord's Supper. Finally he swore to enforce the various acts of Parliament relating to the colonies, especially the navigation laws.[1]

Ordinarily the governor was expected to reside within the province. Indeed, in 1680 an order in council was issued forbidding colonial governors to absent themselves from their provinces without leave;[2] and it afterward became customary to insert in the governor's instructions a clause forbidding him to come to Europe without special permission from the crown.[3]

Careful provision was made for the temporary succession in case of the governor's death or departure from the province. The earlier practice had been by no means uniform;[4] but gradually a rule was adopted for the royal governments, providing that, if the governor died or left the province, his place was to be taken by the lieutenant-governor, or in some cases

---

[1] *New Hampshire Provincial Papers*, v. 592. See also commission to Bernard of New Jersey, 1758, § 3; and instructions to Allen of New Hampshire, 1692, p. 63; to Cornbury of New Jersey, 1702, p. 490; to Dudley of Massachusetts, 1702, p. 102; to Dobbs of North Carolina, 1754, § 2; to Dunmore of Virginia, 1771, § 2.

[2] Doyle, *English in America*, i. 349. The proposed Virginia charter of 1676 insisted either on residence in the colony or on the appointment of a deputy (Hening, *Statutes*, ii. 532).

[3] Instructions to Bernard, § 89; to Dunmore, § 89; to Dobbs, § 130.

[4] According to the first royal commissions in Virginia, the councillors were to elect a substitute (see commissions of Yeardley and Harvey, in Rymer, *Fœdera*, xviii. 311, 980). This rule was at first followed in the Carolinas (Ludwell's instructions, 1691, § 34). The early Maryland governors were allowed to appoint their own deputies (Calvert's commission, 1637, in Bozman, *History of Maryland*, ii. 572; cf. *Ibid.*, 293-307).

by a commander-in-chief.   In the absence of any lieutenant-governor or commander-in-chief, the rule as at first laid down provided that the council as a whole should assume the government;[1] but this plan was found to have its disadvantages, and therefore in 1707 Queen Anne issued a new general instruction providing that thereafter the senior councillor should execute the commission in the governor's absence.[2] How far this instruction was carried out is not quite clear; Chalmers says that even in the royal governments it was not universally enforced until the reign of George III.[3] It is certain that in the proprietary province of Pennsylvania the council continued to act as a whole in the absence of the governor;[4] and that in at least one of the royal governments the royal order met with direct resistance.   The Massachusetts council held that the rights of government, in the absence of the governor and lieutenant-governor, were vested in the council as a whole; and it therefore disregarded the instruction which transferred its right to the senior councillor.[5]

The lieutenant-governor received a commission defining very briefly the powers and duties of his office.[6] He was authorized to exercise all the governor's powers in the latter's absence, subject to instructions and orders from the crown, and subject also to the orders and directions of the governor.   In ordinary cases these provisions furnished very little matter for dispute; but in the case of the so-called personal unions, which involved long absences on the part of the governor from one or the other of his two governments, they gave rise to very serious

[1] Commission to Cornbury of New Jersey, 1702, p. 499; Massachusetts Charter of 1691, in Poore, *Charters and Constitutions*, i. 942.

[2] Royal order of May, 1707, *Sewall's Diary*, iii. 33. Cf. Dudley's instructions of 1702, p. 115; commission to Bernard of New Jersey, 1758, § 26.   Members *ex officio* only were excluded.

[3] Chalmers, *Revolt*, i. 410.

[4] *Pennsylvania Records*, iv. 47; *Statutes at Large of Pennsylvania* (1896), ii. 190, 436.

[5] Hutchinson, *History of Massachusetts*, ii. 191; *Sewall's Diary*, iii. 35–38.

[6] See commission to Wentworth of New Hampshire, 1717, in Appendix A below.

difficulties, which may best be illustrated by specific examples. Lord Cornbury, governor of both New York and New Jersey, spent the larger part of the year in New York, and hence was absent from his province of New Jersey during that time. The question arose as to whether his absence was of the same nature as that for which the commission provided, by stating that the lieutenant-governor should exercise the authority of the governor during the latter's absence from the province. Cornbury held that while he was in New York, the lieutenant-governor had no power to act in New Jersey, basing his argument upon the fiction that while he was present in either of his provinces he was to be regarded as legally present in both.[1] As Cornbury was strong enough to enforce his views, the lieutenant-governor became a mere nonentity, and the province was reduced to the necessity of being without a resident executive head during the greater part of the year.[2] Precisely the same dispute arose in New Hampshire, where Governor Shute claimed that during his absence from New Hampshire he was still entitled to exercise his full powers. In this case the home government seems to have sided with the governor, for the refractory lieutenant-governor was removed and a successor appointed.[3] The same difficulty recurred when Jonathan Belcher was governor of New Hampshire and Massachusetts; and the home government again seems to have taken the governor's side.[4] The question ceased to have practical importance only when independent governors were assigned to New Jersey and New Hampshire.

In exceptional circumstances the lieutenant-governor remained in charge of the province for considerable periods of time. In Virginia, for example, titular governors were at different times appointed, who held the title and part of the emoluments of the office, while they left the actual conduct of

---

[1] *New Jersey Documents*, iii. 109–111.

[2] *Ibid.*, 242 *seq.*

[3] *New Hampshire Provincial Papers*, iii. 704 *seq.* Lieutenant-Governor Wentworth says that he was empowered by the governor to dissolve the assembly "if he saw meet" (*Ibid.*, iv. 44).

[4] *Ibid.*, 669.

government in the hands of a resident lieutenant-governor. The salary actually received by this resident governor was, sometimes at least, the result of a bargain between him and his nominal superior in office, though fortunately this trading was not common in the continental colonies.[1]

Except as a possible temporary successor of the governor, the lieutenant-governor had not regularly any independent powers; in some provinces indeed, especially in the smaller ones, there was often no lieutenant-governor at all.[2] Sometimes, but by no means always, the lieutenant-governor was a member of the council or its president;[3] but in general his office seems to have been one of comparatively little importance. It is therefore hardly strange that such an officer, without any definite political sphere, should at times have been a discordant element in the provincial constitution, as was in fact often the case.[4]

When, in the absence of both governor and lieutenant-governor, the government was assumed by the council or by the senior councillor, certain constitutional limitations were imposed. For example, the instructions forbade this provisional

[1] In 1704 the Earl of Orkney was appointed titular governor of Virginia, and held this office for more than thirty years. The lieutenant-governor for the time being made special agreements with the earl for a division of the salary and other emoluments of the office. Orkney was succeeded in this titular office by Lord Albemarle, and by Lord Loudoun, the unlucky British commander in the French and Indian War. In 1768, Lord Botetourt was appointed governor. He took up his residence in the province; whereupon the line of titular governors of Virginia came to an end (Campbell, *History of Virginia*, 375, 556; Oldmixon, *British Empire in America*, i. 400 ; *Dinwiddie Papers*, i. 383, ii. 2, 411 ; Bancroft, *History of the United States*, iii. 298). A similar case occurred in Maryland, where, though " Franks was appointed governor, Hart was continued in command " (Chalmers, *Revolt*, ii. 66–67).

[2] In the proprietary colony of Pennsylvania, the proprietor himself was the governor-in-chief. His representative in the colony usually bore the title of deputy-governor or lieutenant-governor, though he was commonly referred to as governor. See Proud, *History of Pennsylvania*, ii. 5.

[3] *New Hampshire Provincial Papers*, iii. 661, 674.

[4] Notice, for example, in New Jersey, Governor Belcher's feeling about Lieutenant-Governor Pownall: *New Jersey Documents*, viii. (2) 190. See also *New Hampshire Provincial Papers*, iv. 669.

government, without a special order, to pass any acts not immediately necessary, or to dissolve the assembly, or to remove any officers without the consent of at least seven councillors. In any of these cases, immediate notice was to be given to the home government.[1] The exclusion of the Pennsylvania council from any direct participation in legislation seems to have held good even in the absence of the governor.[2]

The governor's support was provided in a variety of ways; but the most important part of his income was his salary. At the close of the French and Indian War, this salary was dependent on temporary, and often annual, grants of the assembly, though to this general rule four important exceptions must be noted. In Virginia and Maryland the assemblies had been induced to make permanent grants to the crown and the proprietor for the support of the provincial government, and had thus lost their power to determine the governor's salary.[3] In North Carolina, both under the proprietors and under the crown, the salary was paid out of the somewhat uncertain and fluctuating quit-rent revenues of the province.[4] In Georgia, the youngest of the colonies, the provincial establishment was maintained by the government in England.[5] This is a summary statement of the results of a long and bitter controversy over the question as to whether salary grants should be temporary or permanent, a question of the utmost importance, involving the relations of the governor to the assembly on the one hand, and to the home government on the

[1] See instructions to Bernard of New Jersey, 1758, § 90; to Dobbs of North Carolina, 1754, § 131 ; to Dunmore of Virginia, 1771, § 90.

[2] *Pennsylvania Records,* iv. 47.

[3] For Virginia, see Hening, *Statutes,* ii. 466, iii. 344, 490. For Maryland, see Bacon, *Laws,* 1692, ch. 4, and 1704, ch. 42; McMahon, *History of Maryland,* i. 178–180. The governor seems also to have received special grants (Bacon, *Laws,* 1747, ch. 25).

[4] See instructions to the receiver-general, 1712, in Hawks, *History of North Carolina,* ii. 402; Chalmers, *Revolt,* ii. 165, 195–196; *North Carolina Records,* iii. 295, iv. 164, v. 20, 77, 114, 788.

[5] Stokes, *Constitution of the British Colonies,* 139. Cf. Jones, *History of Georgia,* i. 511, ii. 78; and schedules of appropriations for salaries (containing no provision for governor's salary), in Jones, *Colonial Acts of Georgia,* 230, 250 *seq.*

other.[1] The history of this issue may properly be considered later in connection with the systematic study of the mutual relations of governor and assembly.

The amount of the governor's salary varied; and it is often difficult to estimate with the slightest approach to accuracy the real value of amounts that are stated in currency in various stages of depreciation. The largest salary was perhaps that received by the governor of Virginia, who was allowed £2000 out of the duty of two shillings per hogshead levied on tobacco.[2] The governor of New York in 1766 received a grant of £2000.[3] In the other colonies the salaries, as a rule, were £1000 or less in sterling money, though they are often stated at much higher rates in the depreciated colonial currency.[4]

In addition to the salary, the governor had various other sources of income. The most important of these were perhaps

[1] For results in New York, Massachusetts, and New Hampshire, see below, ch. ix. For Pennsylvania, see Proud, *History of Pennsylvania*, ii. 32 ; *Pennsylvania Records*, ii. 492, iii. 174; *Votes of Pennsylvania*, v. 18, 35. For South Carolina, see Chalmers, *Revolt*, ii. 168–174; South Carolina Historical Society, *Collections*, ii. 135; Cooper, *Statutes*, iv. 63, 137. For New Jersey, see Allinson, *Acts of Assembly*, chs. 180, 183, 214, 228, 238, 249, 252, 262, 274 ; Belcher's answers to queries of the Board of Trade, *New Jersey Documents*, viii. (2) 86; cf. also *Ibid.*, vi. 443, 445, ix. 384.

[2] See instructions to Dunmore, 1771, § 88.

[3] *New York Journal of Assembly*, ii. 791, 810. For Maryland, see Sharpe's Correspondence, *Maryland Archives*, vi. 433, ix. 47. For North Carolina, see *Colonial Records*, iv. 164, 585, v. 20, 77. In North Carolina the governor's salary varied from £700 to £1000; but it was often collected with extreme difficulty, if collected at all. For Georgia, see Jones, *History of Georgia*, i. 511, ii. 78. The salary here was at first £600, and later £1000, with the advantage of being secure and not dependent on the favor of the assembly.

[4] In South Carolina the salary for 1744 was £500, with an allowance of £100 for house rent. The same salary was given in 1766. The amounts recorded in 1758 and 1760 — £3500, with £700 for house rent — are evidently stated in the depreciated currency (see South Carolina Historical Society, *Collections*, ii. 189, 287; Cooper, *Statutes*, iv. 63, 137). Governor Shirley of Massachusetts received £1300 per annum from 1754 to 1756. In 1748 he had refused £1900, on the ground that it was not the equivalent of the £1000 sterling required by his instructions ; and he finally succeeded in getting £2400 in the colonial currency (*Massachusetts Province Laws*, iii. 450–454, and 1754–5, ch. 6 ; 1755–6, ch. 5).

the fees, which were collected on a great variety of occasions. The character of these fees may best be illustrated by a specific instance. In 1748 the New Jersey assembly passed an act fixing the governor's fees, among which were fees for marriage licenses, for letters of administration, for certificates of vessels, for certificates to persons desiring to go beyond sea, for licenses to purchase land of the Indians, for bills of health when required, for putting the governor's seal to a township patent, for attorneys' licenses, and for certain judicial proceedings in error. The amounts varied from the three shillings required for a writ of error, to the twenty shillings collected for every attorney's license to practise; the marriage license fee was ten shillings.[1]

In the beginning, these fees seem not to have been fixed by law.[2] Many of them were apparently regulated simply by "English custom," a vague limitation clearly liable to great abuse. Thus the South Carolina assembly complained that public officers were taking much larger fees than were "allowed by act of Parliament in England for the same & like things, and before the same be settled by act of Assembly here."[3] Although the governor was authorized, with the advice of his council, to regulate all fees of provincial officers, yet in many cases, as will be seen, the assembly took the matter into its own hands and passed acts regulating official fees, including those of the governor.[4]

Among other perquisites commonly allowed to the governor was a share of the fines and forfeitures, — usually a third,

---

[1] Allinson, *Acts of Assembly*, ch. 210. In Virginia there were fees of twenty shillings for a marriage license, of thirty-five shillings for a licensed "ordinary," and of forty shillings for a patent of naturalization (Hening, *Statutes*, iii. 397, 434, 445).

[2] The New Hampshire law of 4 George II. expressly says that governors' fees have not previously been regulated: *Acts and Laws of New Hampshire* (1771), ch. 108.

[3] Rivers, *Sketch of the History of South Carolina*, 434.

[4] See below, pp. 118 *seq.* Particular fees were also provided for by particular acts. For example, the Maryland Naturalization Act of 1692 allowed the governor a fee of £3 for drawing a patent of naturalization (Bacon, *Laws*, 1692, ch. 6).

sometimes a half.   For example, one third of the seizures and
forfeitures of vessels for violation of the navigation acts went
to the governor;[1] and similar provisions were made by acts of
the various colonial assemblies.[2]   The most peculiar perquisite
received by a colonial governor was one which seems to have
been a curious survival of the old feudal right of escheat.
This was a provision of a Delaware law of the twenty-fourth
year of the reign of King George II., by which the property of
persons dying intestate was to go to the governor.[3]   The governor also frequently received from the assembly presents or
grants for special services.   Thus, in 1742, the New Hampshire assembly voted the governor a present of £500 for "the
charge he has been at in coming to the Government, &c."[4]   In
spite of royal objections,[5] the practice continued.   Governor
Shirley of Massachusetts was granted £250 for his special
services with the Indians on the Kennebec;[6] and on Governor
Pownall's departure for England, in 1760, the General Court
made him a present of £200.[7]

[1] *Statutes at Large,* iii. 268 (15 Car. II., c. 7, § vi.); vi. 117 (12 Geo. II.,
c. 30, § v.) ; vii. 465 (4 Geo. III., c. 15, § xlii.).

[2] The following list, taken from the Delaware laws, illustrates the general
character of these perquisites: the governor received forfeitures for neglect
of official duty; for violation of quarantine regulations; half the penalty for
speaking in derogation of courts; the fines of attorneys practising without
licenses; half the forfeitures for bribery; and half the penalty of £200 incurred by sheriffs who served more than three years (*Laws of Delaware,*
1797, i. 58, 98, 120, 133, 148, 165).   In Virginia, one third of the fines for
violation of the provincial duty acts commonly went to the governor (Hening, *Statutes,* iv. 147, 315).

[3] *Laws of Delaware* (1797), i. 295.

[4] *New Hampshire Provincial Papers,* v. 623.   In 1696 the governor of
Maryland was at his own request presented with a piece of land in Annapolis.   A few years earlier the governor had received from the assembly
20,000 pounds of tobacco, "as a Token of their love, Respect and Esteeme
for his honorᵣ" (Bacon, *Laws,* 1696, ch. 24, § 9; *Maryland Archives,*
vii. 47).

[5] General instruction of 1703, *New Hampshire Provincial Papers,* iii.
251.   Cf. instructions to Hunter of New York, § 28.

[6] *Massachusetts Province Laws,* iii. 836.

[7] *Ibid.,* iv. 336.   In regard to a gift to the governor of North Carolina,
see *Colonial Records,* iii. 49.   In some of the colonies a special house was

The amount of the governor's income in any given case cannot be exactly stated. The governor of Virginia was perhaps the most fortunate in his receipts, at least when he was not obliged to share the spoils with some titular governor across the sea. Lieutenant-Governor Dinwiddie was able to allow to his absentee superior, Lord Albemarle, the sum of £1665; and assuming, as on the whole seems reasonable, that his own return was equal to that of other governors, the total income attached to the office may have been over £2600, and could hardly have been less than £2500.[1] The only estimate at hand for Virginia simply gives the amount as between £2000 and £3000.[2] In a few cases, however, it is possible to get somewhat more definite estimates. Thus Burnaby, in his " Travels," [3] gives the governor of Massachusetts an annual income, including perquisites, of about £1300 sterling. An interesting view of this financial aspect of the governor's office is given in some correspondence between Governor Sharpe of Maryland and his brother, William Sharpe, in England. The governor, after thanking his brother for his efforts to procure for him the government of New York, then considers prudently the financial returns of that post. It seems that William Sharpe had been informed on good authority that the New York government was not worth more than £1600, though it was commonly rated much higher, a circumstance apparently due to the fact that the profits of the office had been lessened by the diminution in the amount of land remaining to be granted by the governor. Governor Sharpe therefore concluded that, on the whole, an exchange would not be desirable, especially as the New York governor was dependent on the assembly.[4]

reserved for the governor: for Virginia, see Hening, *Statutes*, iii. 285; for South Carolina, Cooper, *Statutes*, ii. 380; for North Carolina, Martin, *Iredell's Public Acts*, i. 55; for Maryland, Bacon, *Laws*, 1742, ch. 24; for New York, Rogers, *Concise Account of North America*, 65.

[1] *Dinwiddie Papers*, ii. 534.

[2] *History of the British Dominions in North America*, pt. ii. 132.

[3] Page 139.

[4] Sharpe's Correspondence, *Maryland Archives*, ix. 47-48, 85. The government of New Jersey seems to have been one of the least profitable. It

In addition to these sources of income, it is probable that unscrupulous governors found other ways of enriching themselves, sometimes perhaps without resorting to direct dishonesty.[1] In general, then, the provincial governors seem to have been quite liberally paid, especially if we compare their incomes with those of our present State governors.[2]

is said that, while New Jersey was combined with New York, the governor's expenses in passing from one province to the other equalled, if they did not exceed, the profits of the New Jersey office (letter of Lewis Morris, *New Jersey Documents*, v. 315). Governor Belcher declared this government to be one of the least profitable in the king's gift (*Ibid.*, viii. (2) 176); Burnaby estimates it as worth from £800 to £1000 (*Travels*, 102).

[1] See Belcher's letter, *New Jersey Documents*, viii. (2) 175.

[2] For example, the estimated income of the royal governor of Massachusetts was £1300, while the salary of the governor of that State was until very recently only $5000. In the absence of the governor, the lieutenant-governor or the president of the council was regularly to receive one half of the salary due to the governor. See instructions to Bernard of New Jersey, 1758, § 91; to Dobbs of North Carolina, 1754, § 132; to Dunmore of Virginia, 1771, § 91.

CHAPTER IV.

THE GOVERNOR AS THE AGENT OF THE HOME GOVERNMENT.

THE provincial governor may be considered from two distinct standpoints. On the one hand, he was the centre of the local administration, the chief executive of the province; on the other hand, he was the agent of a higher authority, the guardian of interests broader than those of his single province. As will be seen later, it was not always easy, or even possible, to keep in harmonious action the two forces of local feeling and imperial interest. Indeed, their inevitable conflict constituted the chief difficulty of the governor's position, and gives to this study henceforth its chief interest. Neither aspect of the office can be ignored; in fact, even for purposes of discussion, it is not easy to separate the one from the other, inasmuch as there was hardly an important function exercised by the governor in which he did not act in both of these characters. For the sake of convenient classification, however, the governor may first be considered primarily as the agent of the central authority in England.

In this character, his first duty was to serve as a means of communication between the province and the home government. The governor, for example, recommended to the colonial assembly the legislation desired by the crown;[1] furthermore, he was expected to keep the home government informed on a wide range of topics connected with the condition of the province and with its administration. The instructions to Governor Bernard of New Jersey, in 1758, will serve

---

[1] See below, p. 161.

as a convenient illustration. He was required, first, to give full information regarding the natural and economic conditions of his province, including a map of the country with an exact description of the territory and the settlements upon it. Statistics of population and some account of commerce and industry were also required of him; and, further, the wants of the province were to be pointed out and means of improvement suggested. Again, it was important that the home government should be informed as to the military strength of the colonies. The governor was, therefore, to send an inventory of the military stores in the province, and to report exactly on its state of defence, giving some account of its neighbors and its relations with them, whether these neighbors were Indians or colonists from foreign countries. The civil administration was another subject on which full information was desired; therefore the accounts of the public revenue and lists of all officers employed at the public charge were to be submitted to the government in England. Moreover, as it was especially important that the progress of legislation should be exactly reported, the governor was required to transmit, for the approval of the crown, not only the statutes actually passed, but also a complete record of legislative proceedings as embodied in the journals of the council and assembly.[1]

Here, then, was provision for a system of official returns which, if faithfully and intelligently made, must have been of great value. Several valuable reports, it is true, were made by various governors in regard to the condition of their respective provinces; but it is clear that on the whole this duty of informing the home government was very much neglected. In 1712 Attorney-General Edward Northey declared that the governors did not observe the instruction requiring them to send home all laws of the provincial assemblies, referring in particular to one case in which an act of 1706 had not been received till 1711.[2] In 1732 the Board of Trade made a similar complaint;[3] and in 1745 the same body declared that

---

[1] Instructions to Bernard of New Jersey, 1758, §§ 28–31, 51, 68, 81–87.
[2] Chalmers, *Opinions*, 348.
[3] Chalmers, *Revolt*, ii. 119.

it was then more than three years since they had received any letters from the governor of North Carolina, and that he had been equally negligent in sending other public documents required. These complaints were repeated three years later.[1] The system of reports by governors was certainly very far from being what the instructions promised.

The provincial governor also stood in certain important relations to the officers of the royal service in the colonies. Of these officers there was a large number. For example, the "Description of South Carolina," attributed to Governor James Glen, enumerates the surveyor-general of land, the receiver-general of quit-rents, various admiralty officers, and the officers of the royal customs.[2] The governor was of course expected to support these officers to the best of his ability; but he was also required to suspend them from office, if necessary, making temporary appointments to fill vacancies until the royal pleasure should be known.[3]

In general, then, the governor was the regularly-constituted guardian of royal and British interests. It was his duty, not only to recommend desired legislation, but also to prevent the passage of all acts injurious to the interests of the crown and of the mother country.[4] He was to coöperate in the great military operations of the British government, and as far as possible to enlist the assembly of his own province in support of them. Whenever the provincial interest and the imperial interest — if we may use these phrases — should come into conflict, his controlling obligation was to be his duty to the crown. The traditional view in regard to the office is well illustrated by the declaration of Governor Benning Wentworth to the New Hampshire assembly: "My firm attachment to his Maj^{tys} Person family & Government challenges my first atten-

---

[1] *North Carolina Records*, iv. 756, 870. In 1742 the Board reported that, during the years 1730–1738, the governor of New York had sent over only the minutes and the laws of 1730, six acts of 1733, and some minutes of the council for 1736 (*Morris Papers*, 150).

[2] Carroll, *Historical Collections*, ii. 221.

[3] See, for example, instructions to Bernard of New Jersey, 1758, § 45.

[4] See below, pp. 162 *seq.*

tion — my next Pursuit shall be the Peace & Prosperity of his Maj[tys] good subjects of this Province." [1]

In addition to these various ways in which the governor acted as the representative of the king, the extension of parliamentary control over the colonies imposed upon him a gradually increasing number of functions of another sort, connected with the enforcement of acts of Parliament. One of the first navigation acts, the well-known statute of 12 Charles II., required the governor to take an oath to enforce all the provisions of the act, under penalty of removal from his office. [2] Another act of 15 Charles II. gave a fuller statement of the governor's duties, providing that persons importing goods into the colonies were to give their names and inventories to the governor, or to some person authorized by him, and that no vessel was to be unloaded until the master had notified the governor of its arrival and its name, and given evidence that it was of English build. To other penalties attending violations of this act, was added one for disobedience on the part of the governor, by which he was to be permanently disqualified for service as a royal governor, and to forfeit £1000. [3] The act of 7 & 8 William III. continued these penal provisions as to removal from office and forfeiture for violation of the statute. As these duties were imposed on proprietary as well as on royal governors, the act of 7 & 8 William III. required that all proprietary governors should be approved by the crown; and it was furthermore customary to ask of them special security for the observance of the acts of trade. [4]

Duties of the same sort were imposed by various acts of Anne and the Georges. For example, the act of 23 George II. prohibited the building and working of factories of iron and steel within the colonies, and directed the governor to enforce this prohibition and to close all such establishments. For failing to do this, he was to forfeit £500 and to be per-

---

[1] *New Hampshire Provincial Papers*, v. 753.
[2] c. 18, § ii.: *Statutes at Large*, iii. 182.
[3] c. 7, § viii.: *Ibid.*, 269.
[4] c. 22, § iv.: *Ibid.*, 610; *North Carolina Records*, i. 509, 799.

manently disqualified for holding any office of trust.[1] The act
of 4 George III. provided for a new oath covering all duties
imposed by previous acts of Parliament.[2] These various directions were collected and systematized in a separate set of instructions relating to trade, enumerating a formidable list of
acts of Parliament, each of which assigned to the governor
certain specific duties.[3]

It was only with great difficulty that the governor could be
held to the faithful performance of these duties. Indeed,
charges of negligence in regard to them were made very early.
In 1696 Edward Randolph complained that the governors did
not enforce the navigation laws.[4] Dudley's instructions of
1702 referred to abuses in the plantation trade as largely due
to remissness on the part of governors;[5] and there is evidence
to the same effect in the severe penalties imposed by various
statutes for neglect of these duties. Clearly, then, the governor was far from efficient in his execution of parliamentary
enactments.

Before leaving this subject, it is necessary to consider very
briefly the British system of colonial administration, so far as
it touches the governor. During the eighteenth century the
management and supervision of colonial affairs were largely in
the hands of the so-called Board of Trade, the origin of which
may be traced to a commission issued by the crown in 1696,
after a varied experience with other councils and committees
charged with the care of the colonies.[6] By this commission

---

[1] c. 29: *Statutes at Large*, vi. 490.

[2] c. 15, § xxxix.: *Ibid.*, vii. 464.

[3] See, for example, those issued to Bernard of New Jersey, 1758, *New
Jersey Documents*, ix. 77.

[4] *Maryland Archives*, iii. 484, v. 46; *New Jersey Documents*, ii. 116,
131, 358.

[5] See instructions, p. 116. The same complaint was made in regard to
other acts of Parliament. One of the articles of Bernard's instructions
(§ 24) recited the failure of governors to enforce fully the provisions of the
act fixing the rates of foreign coins.

[6] See Neill, *Virginia Carolorum*, 102; Sainsbury, *Calendar of State
Papers, Colonial Series, America and West Indies*, 1574–1660, pp. 198, 335,
483, 492, and 1669–1674, p. 407.

a board of commissioners was organized "for promoting the Trade of this Kingdom and for inspecting and improving His [Majesties] Plantations in America and elsewhere." These commissioners were particularly directed to examine the usual instructions given to the governors, to consider and report desirable alterations, to take an annual account of the administration of governors, to hear complaints of maladministration, and, finally, to recommend persons for appointment as governors, councillors, or other colonial officers.[1]

Until 1752, governors were directed to correspond both with the Board of Trade and with one of the principal secretaries of state;[2] but in that year a new order was issued, by which the position of the Board of Trade was somewhat strengthened. Thenceforth governors and other provincial officers were to be appointed on the nomination of the Board of Trade, which was also to prepare draughts of commissions and instructions; and governors were directed in all ordinary matters to correspond with the Board of Trade alone, communicating with the secretaries only on matters requiring the more immediate attention of the crown.[3] In 1766, however, this order was reversed, and the governors were directed as before to correspond with the secretaries of state as well as with the Board of Trade. Thus,[4] during the main part of the period under consideration, the governor's communication with the central administration was carried on through these two agencies, and in ordinary times chiefly through the Board of Trade. It was on recommendation of this body that he received his appointment, his instructions were prepared by it, and he was subject in many ways to its direction.

It seems clear that this system of colonial administration was inefficient. The most important criticism upon it is that of Thomas Pownall, who was at one time governor of Massachusetts, succeeding Shirley and preceding Francis Bernard.

---

[1] *New York Documents*, iv. 145.

[2] See, for example, instructions to Cornbury of New Jersey, 1702, § 102; to Dudley of Massachusetts, 1702, p. 115.

[3] *New York Documents*, vi. 757.

[4] *Ibid.*, vii. 848.

Pownall declared that the weakness of the system was largely
due to unwise division of authority. For example, the Board
of Trade which had the general supervision of the colonial
governors had not the right of final appointment or dismissal.
He thought that the administration for all the colonies should
have been exclusively in the hands of a single department;[1]
and his opinion is supported by the evidence already given as
to the failure of governors to maintain regular correspondence
with the Board of Trade.

[1] Pownall, *Administration of the Colonies*, 13 *seq.* Cf. Egerton, *British
Colonial Policy*, 116 *seq.*

CHAPTER V.

THE GOVERNOR'S COUNCIL.

THE governor was the head of the colonial executive; but in the exercise of his powers he was assisted, and to a certain extent checked, by an executive council, usually of twelve members. Except in two provinces, these councillors were appointed by the crown, usually on the governor's recommendation. The original rule, as stated in the governor's instructions, was that the governor should always keep before the Board of Trade a list of persons best qualified for appointment as councillors.[1] The number was originally six; but later a list of twelve eligible candidates was sometimes required.[2] This rule evidently was not always observed; hence, on the recommendation of the Board of Trade, it was finally so modified that the governor was simply required, as each vacancy occurred, to send in the names of three persons, from which the crown might make its choice.[3] When the number of councillors fell below seven, the governor was allowed to make provisional appointments, which were valid until acted upon by the crown, or until by other nominations the council had again seven members.[4] It was claimed in Virginia that the

---

[1] Instructions to Dongan of New York, 1686, § 8.

[2] Instructions to Burrington of North Carolina, 1730, § 6.

[3] The instructions to Bernard of New Jersey, 1758 (§ 7), required three from each of the two divisions of the province; those to Dobbs of North Carolina, 1754 (§ 7), do not specify any number of names.

[4] In some of the instructions the number was nine instead of seven. See commission to Bernard of New Jersey, 1758, § 6, and his instructions, § 8. Cf. commissions to Allen of New Hampshire, 1692, p. 58, and Cornbury of New Jersey, 1702, p. 492; instructions to Allen, p. 64; to Cornbury, § 10; to Dobbs of North Carolina, 1754, § 8; to Dunmore of Virginia, 1771, § 8.

governor kept the number of councillors as low as possible, in order that he might enjoy this right of appointment.[1]

The governor, in his nominations for the council, was directed to see that certain qualifications were complied with. For example, the councillors must be men of good life and "well affected to Our Government," of good estates, and not necessitous persons or much in debt; they must also be "inhabitants" of the province.[2] Clearly the intention was to secure, so far as possible, the substantial men of the colony, though undoubtedly many other elements had to be taken into consideration. Thus, in at least two colonies, it was not safe to ignore the principle of local representation within the province. The New Jersey proprietors, on their surrender of the two provinces of East Jersey and West Jersey, had expressed their wish that in the united province six councillors might be chosen from each side of the old line of division;[3] and this principle was recognized in the first royal instructions.[4] Still, it is evident that the rule was not strictly enforced, for in Belcher's time only two of the councillors represented the western division, an inequality which was made a ground of complaint against the governor. In 1758 Governor Bernard was instructed, in case of vacancies, to send in the names of three persons in each of the two divisions.[5] In New Hampshire there was no definite provision in regard to the matter; but in 1717 complaint was made to Governor Shute that by his appointment of six councillors, all from Portsmouth, an undue representation had been given to the merchants and traders.[6] Similar considerations undoubtedly presented themselves in other provinces.

---

[1] Hartwell, Blair, and Chilton, *Present State of Virginia*, 23.

[2] Instructions to Bernard of New Jersey, 1758, §§ 7, 9. Cf. §§ 7, 9 of instructions to Dobbs of North Carolina, 1754, and to Dunmore of Virginia, 1771.

[3] "Memorial of the Proprietors," *New Jersey Documents*, ii. 407.

[4] To Cornbury, 1702, § 9.

[5] *New Jersey Documents*, viii. (1) 18 *seq.* Cf. instructions to Bernard, 1758, § 7.

[6] *New Hampshire Provincial Papers*, iii. 675; Belknap, *History of New Hampshire*, ii. 18 *seq.*

It has generally been assumed, and with some degree of truth, that the governor had essentially his own way in the appointment of councillors; but such a statement would require some limitation.   Undoubtedly he was not at first under any effective restraint; but later he seems not to have been always successful in getting his nominations accepted, — a circumstance indicating the presence of counter-influences not always of a desirable kind.   In 1756 Governor Sharpe of Maryland complained that his recommendations for the council had been very generally disregarded.[1]

The councillors thus appointed might be removed only by the crown, though the governor had the right to suspend them for certain causes.[2]   A councillor absent for twelve months without the governor's consent, or for two years without leave from the crown, was to lose his position.[3]   The governor was directed to send immediately to the Board of Trade the names of all councillors suspended by him, with a statement of the grounds of suspension; but this arrangement left him so nearly unrestrained that it was afterward found necessary to require that all suspensions should have the consent of a majority of the council, to which the governor was to communicate the reasons for his action.   If, however, the reasons were of such a nature that they might not properly be communicated to the council, the governor was to transmit at once to the home government a full statement of his charges against the suspended councillors.[4]

Under these provisions the governor had considerable lati-

---

[1] He writes with some bitterness that he has been ordered to put into the council a person whose merits "are to me all invisible," unless "an easy Disposition & his having lately contracted Marriage with a Niece of His Ldp's " may be considered merits (*Maryland Archives*, vi. 400–401). Governor Belcher of New Jersey was often forced to see his own recommendations ignored and other appointments made (see *New Jersey Documents*, vii. 177, 595, 608–609).

[2] Commission to Bernard of New Jersey, 1758, §§ 4, 5.

[3] Instructions to Bernard of New Jersey, 1758, § 11.

[4] See § 10 of instructions respectively to Bernard of New Jersey, 1758; to Dobbs of North Carolina, 1754; to Dunmore of Virginia, 1771. Cf. instructions to Allen of New Hampshire, 1692, p. 64.

tude in the exercise of his right of suspension; indeed, even
in the final removal of councillors his influence often prevailed.
There can therefore be little doubt that this power was liable
to very serious abuse by governors who were disposed to take
advantage of it to get rid of their opponents in the council,
and to put into their places persons who might be relied upon
to support the governor's interest. This danger led to a
tendency on the part of the home government to check more
closely the governor's power of suspension, with the result
that in several cases suspended councillors were reinstated by
special order of the crown. Thus in 1706 the Board of Trade
ordered Lord Cornbury to reinstate Lewis Morris, a councillor
whom the former had suspended;[1] and in 1719, on Governor
Spotswood's proposal to suspend William Byrd for prolonged
absence from the colony, an order in council was issued directing in somewhat peremptory terms the councillor's retention
or reinstatement.[2] It is true that this reversal of the governor's action was not common; but the fact that it was possible
and had actually taken place was of no little significance.

There were two colonies in which the constitution of the
council differed from the regular type just described. These
colonies were Pennsylvania and Massachusetts. When Penn
left his colony in 1701, he issued a commission to ten persons
to constitute a Council of State, empowering the governor for
the future to fill any vacancies that might arise and, if he saw
fit, to add to the number of councillors.[3] This provision
seemed to give the governor greater control of the constitution
of the council than was the case in other colonies; but it is
evident that his power was very much restricted either by
subsequent instructions or simply by usage, for in actual practice the council itself had an important part in the admission
of new members.[4] The exact method of the removal of coun-

[1] *New Jersey Documents*, iii. 95, 124, 154.

[2] *Calendar of Virginia State Papers*, i. 195. For a similar case in
North Carolina, see *Colonial Records*, vi. 558, 1015.

[3] Commission in Proud, *History of Pennsylvania*, i. 451.

[4] For example, in 1702 the governor proposed the name of John Finney
as councillor; whereupon the council ordered that he should forthwith be

cillors is not quite clear; but it would seem that the power of dismissal lay in the hands of the governor and council, possibly in those of the governor alone.[1] Thus in Pennsylvania, as in the royal governments, there was a nominated council, in the appointment of which the governor had a predominant influence.

In the Massachusetts council is found a radical departure from the principle of the royal government, in that the council was there not appointed, but elected. The explanation of this circumstance lies in the peculiar character of the second Massachusetts charter. In granting this instrument, the crown had determined not to restore the old independent system which had grown up under the first charter, but to put in its place the principle of direct control by the crown. The old republican traditions, however, were too deeply rooted in the affections of the people to be lightly put aside, and consequently concessions were necessary. Indeed, the charter of 1691 was distinctly a compromise, under which the governor was here, as elsewhere, to be appointed by the crown, though the old principle of popular control of the executive was to survive in the constitution of the council.

The charter declared that there should be a council of twenty-eight members, more than double the usual number in the other colonies. Of these twenty-eight members, eighteen at least were to be from the old Massachusetts Bay jurisdiction, four from Plymouth, three from Maine, and one from the territory between the Sagadahoc and Nova Scotia. As each of these divisions must have at least the representation here assigned, only two members were left without designation. This council was to be chosen annually by the General Court; but the charter provided that the General Court should consist of the council and the House of Representatives, and further, that the governor should have the right of veto upon all acts and orders of the General Court.[2]

admitted: *Pennsylvania Records*, ii. 68. For similar cases, see *Ibid.*, ii. 117 (1703), iii. 232 (1724), 529 (1733), v. 1 (1745).

[1] For example, in 1706 the governor was called upon to remove a member of the council (*Ibid.*, ii. 279).

[2] Charter of 1691, in Poore, *Charters and Constitutions*, i. 942.

The first councillors were named by the crown; consequently an election did not occur till 1692. On that occasion the House of Representatives claimed the right to elect councillors; but the council also claimed the right to participate in the election, and finally carried the day.[1] The members of the council were regularly elected by joint ballot of the two Houses;[2] and though in this ballot the lower house had of course a decided numerical advantage, yet as a rule the influence of the council was sufficient to prevent sweeping changes.

That the governor's right of veto was no mere formality is shown by the circumstance that in 1693 Governor Phips negatived a candidate who had opposed his appointment as governor.[3] Again, in 1703 Governor Dudley placed his veto upon five councillors, two of whom were the next year again elected by the General Court but again disallowed by the governor.[4] The most striking case is that of Governor Belcher, who in 1741, at the time of the famous land-bank craze, negatived thirteen councillors; whereupon the House retaliated by refusing to fill the vacancies, thereby establishing a precedent which was followed by succeeding Houses.[5] Nevertheless conflicts of this sort were less common than might have been expected, inasmuch as both the House and the governor seem usually to have avoided radical action. In 1729, in the heat of the struggle over the salary question, only four of the twenty-eight councillors were changed, notwithstanding the fact that the council had opposed the extreme demands of the House.[6]

The Massachusetts council, then, departed from the ordinary type in two important particulars. In the first place, it had a much larger number of members, — always an important consideration in determining the character of such a body; and, secondly, it was constituted on an entirely different principle, in that it received its members not by appointment but by

[1] Hutchinson, *History of Massachusetts*, ii. 16.
[2] See, for example, *Journal of the House*, 1723, pp. 2–3.
[3] Hutchinson, *History of Massachusetts*, ii. 70.
[4] *Ibid.*, 136–137; *Sewall's Diary*, ii. 78, 103.
[5] Hutchinson, *History of Massachusetts*, iii. 152.
[6] *Ibid.*, ii. 323.

election, an election checked, however, by the governor's veto.

Before this subject is left, it should be stated that besides the regular members of the council there were other so-called extraordinary members.   Thus, by order of the crown, surveyor-generals of customs were *ex officio* members of the councils in their respective districts;[1] and by a later provision the same privilege was given to the royal superintendent of Indian affairs.[2]   As might be expected, these extraordinary councillors seem to have been regarded with some jealousy by the regular members.[3]   Sometimes also the lieutenant-governor was a member of the council.[4]   In Massachusetts, Stoughton, the first lieutenant-governor, acted in the first place as a councillor *ex officio*, but in 1693 he was elected as one of the regular twenty-eight councillors.[5]   Thereafter, until 1732, the lieutenant-governors sat in council, but did not vote unless they had been regularly elected.   In that year Governor Belcher, influenced, it is said, by personal dislike of Lieutenant-Governor Phips, forbade the latter to sit unless elected.   In regard to this action, Hutchinson insists that in the intention of those who drew up the charter the lieutenant-governor was to have a seat in the council, and cites in support of his position a minute of the Board of Trade to that effect, made just before the charter passed the seals.[6]

The councillors were not, as a rule, salaried officers, though in Virginia they received an allowance out of the permanent fund for the support of the government.[7]   In general, how-

---

[1] *New Jersey Documents*, v. 348.

[2] Stokes, *Constitution of the British Colonies*, 237.   Cf. *Ibid.*, 123.

[3] In Virginia the councillors at first refused to allow Surveyor-General Dinwiddie to act with them, — whether because they disliked the interference of outsiders in their local affairs, or, as Chalmers says, on account of aristocratic prejudices, it is difficult to say.   See Chalmers, *Revolt*, ii. 199.

[4] *Maryland Archives*, viii. 365, 366; *New Hampshire Provincial Papers*, iii. 661, 674, 756.

[5] Hutchinson, *History of Massachusetts*, ii. 70.

[6] *Ibid.*, iii. 174.

[7] See instructions to Dunmore, 1771, § 88.   In Maryland they were for a time similarly paid out of the proprietary fund; but this fund was finally

ever, like the members of the lower house, they had to content themselves with *per diem* allowances during the sessions of the assembly.[1]

As an executive board, the council was of course subject to the governor's call,[2] though in some cases it met at stated periods. Thus in the New Jersey records are found references to regular quarterly meetings; and in Pennsylvania there was a rule providing for weekly meetings.[3] For the conduct of executive business the commission required a quorum of three;[4] but by the instructions the governor was directed not to act with less than five, except in emergencies in which so large a number could not be had.[5] In the larger Massachusetts council of twenty-eight members, the quorum was fixed at seven.[6] In executive meetings the governor presided and proposed matters for consideration; but he was directed to allow the council freedom of debate and vote.[7]

engrossed by the governors. They were then provided for by temporary grants of the assembly, until the lower house at length refused to continue the grants (Sharpe's Correspondence, *Maryland Archives*, vi. 46–48; *Votes and Proceedings of the Lower House*, Nov. 16, 1753, May 1 and 4, 1756). In Pennsylvania, where the council was only an executive board, councillors had no pecuniary compensation (speech of the governor, 1757, *Votes of Pennsylvania*, iv. 750–751). .

   1 In North Carolina in 1761 the allowance was 7s. 6d. In 1757 the Board of Trade recommended an allowance of £50 per annum, to be paid out of the quit-rents of the province. See *North Carolina Records*, v. 787–788, vi. 620. Cf. *Massachusetts Province Laws*, i. 100, ii. 410, 591, 1074; *Acts and Laws of New Hampshire* (1771), ch. 47; Allinson, *Acts of Assembly*, ch. 631, § v.

   2 Stokes, *Constitution of the British Colonies*, 124; Hartwell, Blair, and Chilton, *Present State of Virginia*, 34.

   3 *New Jersey Documents*, viii. (1) 103; *Pennsylvania Records*, ii. 597, iii. 56.

   4 See commission to Bernard of New Jersey, 1758, § 5; to Dobbs of North Carolina, 1760, p. 526.

   5 See § 6 of instructions respectively to Bernard, 1758; to Dobbs, 1754; to Dunmore of Virginia, 1771.

   6 Charter of 1691, in Poore, *Charters and Constitutions*, i. 942.

   7 Stokes, *Constitution of the British Colonies*, 124; Hartwell, Blair, and Chilton, *Present State of Virginia*, 21, 32. See also instructions to Bernard of New Jersey, 1758, § 5; to Allen of New Hampshire, 1692, p. 63; to

Having considered the organization of the council, let us now turn our attention to its functions. These were of three general classes. In the first place, the council with the governor had some judicial functions, and constituted a court for the trial of certain kinds of offences. In the second place, it was the upper house of the provincial legislature. Finally, it was an executive body to assist, to advise, and in a measure to control the governor in the exercise of his executive functions. The judicial functions of the council will be considered incidentally in connection with the judicial powers of the governor, and its legislative work in connection with the relation of the governor to the assembly. For the present, then, the council may be considered as an executive, advisory body.

An accurate definition of its powers and duties as an executive board is not easy. In the absence of definite statements, many matters were determined by mere usage; and even when definite statements did exist, they were often modified by the same unwritten law. The personal element must therefore be taken into account, in order to get an adequate conception of the relative powers of governor and council in any given province and at any given time.

One function of the council is however very clear: it was at least an advisory body.[1] This phase of the councillor's position was expressed in his oath of office, by which he was bound "at all times freely" to give his advice to the governor

Cornbury of New Jersey, 1702, § 7; to Dudley of Massachusetts, 1702, p. 102 ; to Dobbs of North Carolina, 1754, § 5; to Dunmore of Virginia, 1771, § 5.

[1] In 1666 Governor Calvert of Maryland was required to "advise as there shall bee occasion with those who are or shall be of our Councill there . . . upon all emergent occasions touching . . . the goode Governm^t of our said Province and the people there" (*Maryland Archives,* iii. 545). The Massachusetts charter of 1691 provided for a council to " be advising and assisting to the Governour " (Poore, *Charters and Constitutions,* i. 948). Penn commissioned the council of his colony "to consult and assist with the best of their advice and counsel, me, or my Lieutenant, or Deputy Governor, for the time being, in all public affairs and matters relating to the said government, and to the peace, safety and well-being of the people thereof " (Proud, *History of Pennsylvania,* i. 451).

"for the good management of the publick affairs of this government."[1] The councillors had also to restrain as well as to assist the governor in the exercise of his powers. In the commission and instructions to the governor was a long list of matters in which his power was limited by the proviso that he was to act only with the advice and consent of the council. Thus, the commission and instructions to Governor Bernard of New Jersey in 1758 contained a number of such restrictions as the following: the advice and consent of the council were required in calling assemblies;[2] in erecting courts and regulating their jurisdiction;[3] in issuing warrants for the expenditure of public money;[4] in declaring martial law;[5] and, finally, in taking any action not definitely provided for in the commission.[6]

In appointments made by the governor the advice and consent of the council were not at first distinctly required.[7] The respective rights of the governor and council within this field became in consequence the subject of frequent controversy. In 1709, however, in the instructions to Governor Hunter of New York, occurred the provision that commissions to judges and justices of the peace should be issued with the advice and consent of the council;[8] and this restriction was repeated in subsequent instructions. The rule was still more forcibly laid down afterwards, when the governor was directed not to appoint judges or justices without the consent of at least three of the council. The Board of Trade explained the necessity for this new statement on the ground that the old provision, though clearly requiring the advice and consent of the council, had not been strictly adhered to by the governors.[9] In Massa-

[1] *Massachusetts Province Laws*, i. 78.

[2] See instructions, § 12, and commission, § 7.

[3] Commission, § 15.

[4] Instructions, § 19. [5] *Ibid.*, § 72.

[6] *Ibid.*, § 88.

[7] See instructions to Allen of New Hampshire, 1692, and to Cornbury of New Jersey, 1702.

[8] § 43.

[9] Instructions to Bernard of New Jersey, 1758, § 41; to Dunmore of Virginia, 1771, § 45. Note especially the instructions to Dobbs of North

chusetts the consent of the council to appointments had been definitely required by the charter of 1691.[1]   Indeed, the council had even gone so far as to claim the right of nominating officers, a power which was only with some difficulty resumed by the governor.[2]

The advice of the council was of course asked and given on a great variety of other questions, though the extent to which the practice was carried naturally depended upon the personal characteristics of the governor on the one side, and of the councillors on the other.   Some governors excluded the council from the conduct of public affairs as far as possible, while others were inclined to throw responsibility upon it.[3] The temptation to shift responsibility was particularly strong in questions of legislation.   Indeed, governors often asked advice as to whether they might properly give their consent to particular bills, even though before coming to the governor at all a bill must have been previously passed by the council sitting as an upper house.   Governor Shute of Massachusetts, for example, asked the opinion of his council whether he might, consistently with his instructions, pass an act laying duties on English goods.   The council gave its opinion that he might not.[4]   Again, Governor Sharpe of Maryland asked advice on the question of approving a supply bill, which among other provisions imposed a tax on the proprietary estates.[5]

There is at least one instance, however, in which the council gave advice with some reluctance.   The Massachusetts councillors, having passed a bill, were then called upon by the governor to decide whether he might sign it consistently with his instructions.   They insisted, however, that having already declared their concurrence as an upper house they could

Carolina, 1754, § 62, and the explanatory note by the Board of Trade, *North Carolina Records*, v. 1104.

[1] Poore, *Charters and Constitutions*, i. 942.

[2] Chalmers, *Revolt*, i. 284.

[3] See remarks on Stoughton and Dummer in Hutchinson, *History of Massachusetts*, ii. 79.

[4] *Ibid.*, 205.

[5] He writes: "I presume their Advice will be in some Sort my Iustification" (*Maryland Archives*, vi. 428).

not give any further advice. Nevertheless, they continued to assert that the bill was for the public welfare; and the governor seems to have accepted this declaration as a convenient excuse, for he signed the bill, urging in defence of his action the advice of his council.[1]

In Pennsylvania the question of asking advice in legislation became an issue of great importance. It will be remembered that in this colony the council was a purely executive body, without any direct participation in legislation, although by the terms of their commission the councillors were to advise the governor in all public matters relating to the government and to the peace and welfare of the people.[2] This provision would seem to include the giving of advice on legislation; but the assembly was inclined to resent any interference whatever in this field. In 1709, Governor Gookin complained that the assembly would not allow him to communicate the supply bill to the council for its advice; and he therefore thought it necessary to enter into an argument in defence of his position.[3]

During the governorship of his successor the issue was quite clearly defined. Governor Keith had been instructed that, in order to impose a necessary check upon the otherwise uncontrolled action of the governor and assembly, he was to take no action in legislative matters without the advice and consent of the council.[4] The council, it must be remembered, was looked upon as the bulwark of proprietary interests, a view which only increased the hostility of the assembly. Keith now adopted a distinctly popular policy, by allying himself with the assembly as against the proprietary interest and its representative, the council. The result was that the proprietary instructions were so often ignored that the widow Penn at length found it necessary to intervene. Keith was censured for departing from his instructions, and new instructions were issued that completely tied his hands in matters of

---

[1] Hutchinson, *History of Massachusetts*, ii. 297 ; *Massachusetts Province Laws*, ii. 486.

[2] Commission in Proud, *History of Pennsylvania*, i. 451.

[3] *Pennsylvania Records*, ii. 492.

[4] Instruction of 1724, in Proud, *History of Pennsylvania*, ii. 178 *seq.*

legislation.   He was directed for the future to advise with the council upon every meeting or adjournment of the assembly; to make no speech and send no message not approved by the council, if practicable; to return no bills without advice, and to approve none without the consent of a majority of the council.[1]   Keith argued that by the existing charter the council was no part of the legislature and had no right to restrain the governor's action in that department.   He even went so far as to maintain that the council was not legally anything more than a council of state, "to advise, and to be present, as solemn witnesses to the Governor's actions."[2]   He soon paid the penalty of his insubordination, however, with the loss of his office.[3]

It is clear that the instructions of the widow Penn were not always strictly observed.   Nevertheless, the council was so frequently asked to give advice that it seems often to have assumed almost the character of an upper house.   For example, it discussed and amended bills for various purposes,[4] although sometimes the governor passed a bill in the face of opposition from the council.   Thus, in 1759, the assembly passed a bill for the issue of paper money, whereupon the council made a formal protest against the governor's action as inconsistent with his instructions.   The protest, however, was ignored and the bill passed.[5]

The questions referred to the council were not confined to matters of legislation.   There is an interesting case in Massachusetts in which the councillors were called upon to give their opinion as to the interpretation of the clauses in the charter which defined the governor's military power.   They were reluctant to give advice under such circumstances, and one of them declared that such questions of interpretation belonged to the judges, not to the council.   They finally returned a noncommittal answer.[6]

[1] Proud, *History of Pennsylvania*, ii. 179, note.
[2] *Votes of Assembly*, quoted *Ibid.*, 180–181 *seq.*, notes.
[3] *Ibid.*, 183.
[4] See, for example, *Pennsylvania Records*, vii. 444.
[5] *Ibid.*, viii. 357 *seq.*   [6] *Sewall's Diary*, iii. 313.

It has been seen that the reference to the council of such a question as the propriety of signing particular bills seemed often to offer a convenient means of shifting responsibility. The home government saw this danger, and laid down emphatically the principle of the governor's personal responsibility. In the year 1758, for example, Governor Fauquier of Virginia approved the law reducing the salaries of ministers; but the act was disallowed on the ground that it had been passed contrary to the governor's instructions, and Fauquier was reprimanded. In defence of his action, he presented the excuse that he had passed the law by the advice of his council and contrary to his own better judgment; but the Board of Trade declined to admit this defence, insisting that the advice of the council could not free the governor from personal accountability.[1]

More important than any formal statement of rights and duties, is the question as to the real influence of the council in the government of the province, — as to the extent to which it actually controlled the governor's action. This is clearly a difficult question, depending as it does largely upon those personal elements that refuse to submit to convenient generalization or exact definition. It has been very generally assumed, and not unnaturally, that a body constituted like the provincial council was necessarily subservient to the governor, exercising practically little or no check upon his action; and it would not be difficult to find contemporary opinions tending to confirm this view. Governor Hutchinson, in his "History of Massachusetts,"[2] comparing the elective council of his province with the nominated council of the other royal governments, speaks of the latter as so closely dependent upon the governor that it could hardly be considered as a distinct branch. The same ground is taken by Dummer, in his "Defence of the New-England Charters."[3] Moreover, governors were sometimes charged with keeping the council subservient by means of a judicious system of patronage.[4]

---

[1] Chalmers, *Revolt*, ii. 356–357.
[2] II. 16.   [3] Pp. 40–41.
[4] "A Short Discourse on the Present State of the Colonies in America"

To present only this side of the case, however, would be to give a false impression. The governor's control of the constitution of the council was by no means absolute, a fact which must be borne in mind in any fair consideration of the sweeping charges of subserviency brought against the provincial councils. If there are many instances of subservient councils, there are also cases of direct conflict between governor and council. Take, for example, the case of the Virginia council, which by one author was represented as completely under the governor's thumb.[1] By other writers the situation was viewed in a very different light. Chalmers says of this council during the reign of Queen Anne: "From the constitution of this province, twelve counsellors enjoyed almost every power," even attempting to control governors and frequently succeeding in securing their recall. According to the same authority, a combination of six councillors secured the recall of Governor Nicholson.[2] Governor Spotswood, who succeeded to the government a few years later, made frequent complaints in his letters of the factious and unreasonable claims of the council, saying that it was under the control of a family who had succeeded so well as to remove two governors while they themselves had kept their seats, and whom he now suspected of intriguing against himself.[3] Here, then, clearly enough was a strong aristocratic body very different from the subservient creatures of the governor whom we might have expected to find. In 1711 Governor Hunter of New Jersey complained of the council's obstinate resistance to public measures upon which governor and representatives were agreed.[4] In 1749 the governor and assembly of New Jersey had one agent in London,

---

(1726), by M. Bladen, in *North Carolina Records*, ii. 626 *seq.*, especially 631; Hartwell, Blair, and Chilton, *Present State of Virginia*, 24, 32–33.

[1] Hartwell, Blair, and Chilton, *Present State of Virginia*, 32.

[2] Chalmers, *Revolt*, i. 317–318.

[3] *Letters of Governor Spotswood* (Virginia Historical Society, *Collections*, ii.), *passim*, especially 285, 311 *seq.*

[4] *New Jersey Documents*, iv. 51–62. Governor Hunter was accused at this time of having a sort of kitchen cabinet (*Ibid.*, 119. Cf. the case of Governor Belcher, *Ibid.*, vii. 183, 251).

and the council another.[1] The case of Governor Keith and the Pennsylvania council has already been referred to. These instances are enough to show that the councillors must not be regarded necessarily as mere figureheads, since they are seen to have been often men who could and did act even in opposition to the governor's favorite measures. Indeed, with the increasing number of restrictions upon the governor's power of suspension and appointment, it became more and more difficult to get rid of opposition within the council, or even to prevent opponents from becoming councillors.

With these limitations always in mind, it must be said, however, that as a rule the council could be relied upon to support the governor in his defence of his own prerogative and of the interests of the crown. This fact was clearly shown by the action of the council in legislation, in which it generally supported the governor against the lower house. For example, bills that were likely to be opposed by the governor were usually stopped in the council, a practice of which a good illustration is to be found in Maryland politics during the years 1753–1759. This was a stormy period of conflict between the governor and the assembly over supply bills, and yet during the six years there is no record of any veto by the governor: all bills presented to him were approved, and this fact clearly indicates that obnoxious legislation was blocked by the upper house.[2] Indeed, the council was sometimes even more conservative than the governor. Thus in South Carolina, on one occasion, the councillors, at the expense of their popularity, opposed the bills for the issue of paper money, although these measures had the support of the governor as well as of the assembly.[3] In Pennsylvania Governor Keith adopted the policy of winning popular support by an alliance with the assembly; and it was the resistance of the council to this design that brought on the discussion as to the powers of the council.[4] A later governor approved a bill for the issue of

[1] *New Jersey Documents*, vii. 302.
[2] *Votes and Proceedings of the Lower House*, Nov. 17, 1753–April 17, 1759.
[3] South Carolina Historical Society, *Collections*, i. 302.
[4] Proud, *History of Pennsylvania*, ch. xxv.

paper money, in the face of a protest by the council against the bill on the ground that it was dangerous in its tendencies and inconsistent with the governor's instructions.[1]

The efforts made in Pennsylvania to get rid altogether of the intervention of the council have been already noticed. In Maryland, too, which was very probably under the influence of Pennsylvania ideas, the doctrine prevailed that "the Upper House is no Part of our Constitution."[2] A more practical expression of this jealousy of the council is seen in the assembly's policy of denying the council any right to initiate or to amend money bills.[3] Furthermore, the value of the council as a barrier against radical legislation was also much impaired by its very constitution: appointed as it was by the crown, it had little of that popular local support which alone could give it any great weight or influence. The royalist writer, Anthony Stokes, thought that if this difficulty had been met, if the council had been made a local, hereditary aristocracy with interests bound up with those of the crown, the Revolution might have been prevented.[4]

It is interesting to note that the Massachusetts elective council showed very nearly the same constitutional tendencies as the nominated councils of the other colonies. Though chosen by a vote in which the lower house predominated, it was distinctly conservative, partly perhaps from the fear of incurring a veto from the governor on its next election, partly owing to the personal influence of the governor exercised in other ways, and partly, without doubt, because of the conservative influence of executive responsibility. A certain phase of popular feeling on this point is illustrated by an interesting anonymous pamphlet of the year 1708, which charged the councillors, in language more forcible than refined, with subser-

[1] *Pennsylvania Records,* viii. 358.

[2] *Maryland Archives,* ix. 120. Note also a message of the House: "What are the Rights and Privileges of those Gentlemen, that are said to constitute another Branch, we know nothing about; as it is a Branch undevised in our Charter, and unknown in it's Original" (*Votes and Proceedings of the Lower House,* Dec. 1, 1757).

[3] See below, pp. 122 *seq.*

[4] *Constitution of the British Colonies,* 137-138.

iency to the governor, censuring their timidity in strong terms; and furthermore contrasted unfavorably the elective council of Massachusetts with the nominated councils of the other colonies.[1] There is an entry in the diary of Samuel Sewall which gives a similar impression.[2] That this view was not always the correct one, however, is shown by Dudley's statement that there were "commonwealthsmen" even in the council, and by the fact that Lord Bellomont had serious differences with his council.[3] Nevertheless, the governor's veto seems on the whole to have been effective in keeping the opposition out of the council; for in the heat of the controversy over the salary question, the council took the governor's side, and in 1719, in a long struggle between the council and the House over the impost bill, laying a tax on British goods, the council urged as its ground of objection that the bill was contrary to the governor's instructions.[4] Hutchinson said of the council that it was too dependent on both governor and people, being at different times under the influence of the one or the other, adding that "the most likely way to secure a seat for many years" was "to be of no importance."[5]

In addition to other causes which have already been suggested, the conservatism of the council was due very largely to the presence of several men of official position. For example, in 1765 there were in the council the lieutenant-governor, the secretary of the province, judges of the Superior Court, and the attorney-general; and Hutchinson says that, with very few exceptions, the judges of the Superior Court had been elected to the council. Now these were all appointees either of the crown or of the governor, and hence as a rule — to use a contemporary phrase — "government men." Hutchinson himself was for some years both councillor and lieutenant-governor, and seems to have been a sort of leader in the business of the

---

[1] "Deplorable State of New England," in Massachusetts Historical Society, *Collections*, 5th Series, vi. 113.

[2] For example, iii. 47.

[3] Chalmers, *Revolt*, i. 315.

[4] Council records, *Massachusetts Province Laws*, ii. 158–161.

[5] *History of Massachusetts*, ii. 15–17.

council. In 1766, however, a radical change was made. The House then assumed an aggressive attitude, striking off from the list of councillors the lieutenant-governor and the most prominent of the official members, with the result that the relation of the council to the House and the governor respectively was entirely changed. The leadership of the council now passed from the hands of Hutchinson into those of Bowdoin, a popular leader, under whose management the council was brought into sympathy with the lower house.[1] It was this altered disposition of the council, no doubt, which caused a provision to be inserted in the Massachusetts Government Act, to the effect that the councillors should hereafter be appointed, as in the other colonies, by the crown upon the governor's recommendation.

To sum up what has been noted as to the position of the council in the provincial constitution, it may be said that, although it is a mistake to suppose that the council was always or necessarily under the control of the governor, yet, as might have been expected from its constitution, it was usually on the governor's side in his contests with the assembly, exercising upon the whole a conservative influence. Furthermore, it is evident that this conservative tendency was found in the elective council of Massachusetts as well as in the nominated councils of the other colonies. In the words of Hutchinson, "neither in Massachusetts, nor in the royal governments, do we meet with that glorious independence, which makes the House of Lords the bulwark of the British constitution, and which has sometimes saved the liberties of the people from threatened incroachment, and at other times put a stop to advances making upon the royal prerogative."[2]

---

[1] *History of Massachusetts*, iii. 148–150, 156.
[2] *Ibid.*, ii. 17.

CHAPTER VI.

THE GOVERNOR'S EXECUTIVE POWERS.

In the study of the powers and duties of the provincial governor, the first inquiry must be as to the documents in which these powers and duties are stated, the instruments through which the governor's authority was conferred and defined. There are two classes of instruments which have more nearly than the others that quality of permanence which is associated with a rigid constitution or a fundamental law. The first class may be represented by a single instance. When New Netherland passed from the Dutch to the English in 1664, the two parties agreed upon so-called "Articles of Capitulation," an instrument containing some important constitutional provisions. For example, it declared "That the town of Manhatans shall choose Deputies, and those Deputies shall have free voices in all public affairs, as much as any other Deputies"; another clause provided for the election of certain inferior civil officers and magistrates; and there were also provisions regarding the rights of individuals. On the whole, however, there seems to have been little here to determine the framework of the provincial constitution.[1]

The second class of instruments, the charters, are much more important; yet even these, with the exception of the Massachusetts Province Charter of 1691, are of comparatively little value for the present purpose. In the first place, the royal governments, as a rule, had no charters; the only one of any political significance was the so-called Province Charter of Massachusetts in 1691. In the two proprietary governments which survived the general wreck, Maryland and Penn-

[1] *New York Documents*, ii. 250–253.

sylvania, there were, it is true, the charters to the origina
proprietors; but the Massachusetts charter is the only one
among either royal or proprietary governments which assumes
to mark out in any systematic way the form of the provincial
constitution, and to define with any degree of accuracy the
relative powers of governor and assembly.   Nevertheless, the
charters did contain certain broad limitations, imposed in
the one case by the crown upon the proprietors, and in the
other by the crown upon itself.   It must be said, moreover, in
general terms, that in the proprietary governments the proprietors delegated to their governors the powers granted to
themselves by their charters.   All these cases, however, may
fairly be regarded as exceptional, as variations from the strict
type of the provincial government.

The main clue to a correct understanding of the powers of
the provincial governor is to be found in the vice-regal character of his office.   He was the agent, the representative of
the crown.   He succeeded, with certain necessary limitations
imposed by his subordinate position, to the traditions of the
royal prerogative as defined by long-standing usage and modified by the development of parliamentary control.[1]   Not only
did this vice-regal conception determine the provisions of the
commission; it also fixed the interpretation of these provisions,
or supplied a rule of action in matters concerning which the
commission itself was silent.   Naturally the question was
constantly arising as to whether a particular power was or was
not an essential part of the royal prerogative.   Governors
claimed, for example, that the interference of the assembly in
military affairs and in appointments was an invasion of the
prerogative; while the assembly, on its part, repeatedly based
its privileges on the usages of the House of Commons.   An
interesting case in point arose from the practice of presenting
the speaker to the governor for the latter's approval.   Since
assent was always given as a matter of course, in England this
custom had become a mere formality; and such was usually
the case in the colonies.   In a few cases, however, the gover-

[1] Pownall, *Administration of the Colonies*, 55; Chalmers, *Political Annals*, 683.

nor undertook to make his prerogative a reality by rejecting the choice of the House.[1]

The terms of the commission echoed the old phrases of the royal prerogative; and often old powers of the crown which had ceased to have practical meaning at home were revived in it. Thus, in accordance with the old constitutional tradition which gave the king as the fountain of justice the right to erect courts of justice, the royal commission gave the governor as the king's representative this independent right of establishing courts.

With this fundamental principle in mind, the main features of the commission may be easily summed up. The king was the fountain of honor and privilege, and had thus the right to create offices and to fill them: therefore the provincial governor had the right to appoint all officers. The king was commander-in-chief of the army and navy: the governor was captain-general of the provincial military forces, as well as vice-admiral. The king, by virtue of his prerogative, might prorogue and dissolve Parliaments, although this power was limited by the triennial and septennial acts: the governor's commission, however, conferred it without limitation. The king had the right of legislation in conjunction with the two houses of Parliament: the governor was empowered to make laws with the consent of the council and assembly. The similarity is even more striking in minor points. The governor, like the king, had in theory the right to grant charters of incorporation to cities and towns, and to establish ports, markets, and fairs; he had the right of pardon, except for treason and felony; and in ecclesiastical matters he had certain rights of appointment to benefices. The character of the governor's office as drawn in the commission is thus clearly vice-regal.

Besides the commission, a set of instructions was given to each governor on his appointment, and these were supplemented from time to time by so-called "additional instructions." The two documents taken together formed what may be roughly called the constitution of the province; they were drafted by

---

[1] See below, pp. 149 *seq.*

the Board of Trade, receiving their final sanction through orders in council.[1] As to the distinctive characters of these two documents respectively, it may be said, in the first place, that the commission was an essentially public document, while the instructions were not. The commission was published at the accession of the governor, and was generally inscribed on the council books.[2] The instructions, on the other hand, were not regularly published, though it would appear that in Virginia it was at first customary to publish them, and that the discontinuance of the old usage was considered a grievance.[3] The governor was, however, directed to communicate to the council those clauses which had to do with matters in which its consent was necessary, together with such other articles as he might think fit for the information of the council and assembly.[4] The instructions thus given out were usually articles bearing on controverted points or limiting the governor's assent to certain kinds of legislation.

The commission contained the grant of power, while the instructions told how that power should be used and often limited its scope. For example, the commission empowered the governor to act with a quorum of three councillors: the instructions required a quorum of five, except in emergencies. The commission authorized him to appoint judicial officers: the instructions made necessary the advice and consent of the council for the making of such appointments. The commission authorized him to erect courts: the instructions usually forbade the erection of new courts without special warrant from the crown. Finally, the commission empowered him to make laws in conjunction with the council and assembly: the instructions forbade him to assent to certain classes of laws.

An interesting question arises here as to the exact legal effect of action taken by the governor within the lines of his commission but in violation of his instructions. A case in point occurred in 1762. Governor Hardy of New Jersey was

---

[1] See e. g. *New York Documents*, vi. 791, 793.

[2] Stokes, *Constitution of the British Colonies*, 177.

[3] Hartwell, Blair, and Chilton, *Present State of Virginia*, 21.

[4] See instructions to Bernard, § 4.

authorized by his commission in general terms to appoint judges and other officers for the administration of justice. His instructions, however, expressly directed that the duration of such appointments should not be during good behavior but subject to recall at pleasure. In spite of these directions, Hardy, on his arrival in the province, appointed three judges of the Supreme Court, with commissions authorizing them to serve during good behavior; whereupon the validity of these commissions was questioned and the matter was referred to Attorney-General Yorke for his opinion. That officer held that the judges' commissions were illegal and invalid, on the ground that, although the power conferred by the governor's commission was general, yet since the instructions, which restricted his authority, were referred to in the commission, they must be regarded as incorporated into the latter document and hence as limiting the power conferred by it.[1]

It has been said that the commission and instructions may together be regarded as the constitution of the province. Thomas Pownall, one of the ablest students of colonial administration, and himself at one time governor of Massachusetts, claimed for the royal commission something of that fixity and permanence which mark the so-called rigid constitutions of our own time. "This the King's commission," he writes, "is barely a commission during pleasure, to the person therein named as governor, yet it provides for a succession without vacancy, or interregnum, and is not revoked but by a like commission, with like powers: It becomes the known, established constitution of that province which hath been established on it, and whose laws, courts, and whole frame of legislature and judicature, are founded on it: It is the charter of that province: It is the indefeasible and unalterable right of those people . . . and therefore not to be altered; but by such means as any reform or new establishment may take place in Great Britain: It cannot, in its essential parts, be altered or destroyed

---

[1] *New Jersey Documents*, ix. 349 *seq.*, 380. The Attorney-General held, however, that although such appointments were "illegal, yet that the Judgments given and acts done by such Judges will be good," as in the case of officers *de facto*.

by any royal instructions or proclamation; or by letters from secretaries of state: It cannot be superceded, or in part annulled, by the issuing out of any other commissions not known to this constitution." [1]

It is probable that this was a prevalent view among the colonists themselves, though its strict legal accuracy may perhaps be open to question. It must be said, also, that the commissions and instructions were remarkably free from arbitrary alterations. There was, it is true, a development from simplicity to complexity, from the extremely vague and general terms of the early commissions to the elaborate and fairly accurate definition of powers found in the commissions and instructions of the royal governors toward the close of the colonial period. This progress is palpably marked by the striking increase in the length of these documents, as seen by contrasting the first brief royal commissions in Virginia after the overthrow of the London Company with the formidable commissions of the next century, accompanied as they were by instructions like those to Governor Dobbs in 1754, which contained more than a hundred articles. During the last century of provincial government, however, this expansion was mainly in the direction of a more accurate definition of powers previously given, together with a few further limitations imposed upon the governor's freedom of action. The commission of a new governor in Massachusetts or New York differed very slightly, if at all, from that of his immediate predecessor; and such changes as were made usually came about gradually, and did not seriously affect the stability of the provincial constitution.

In addition to the set of instructions given to the governor on his assignment to a province, he received from time to time other instructions, some of which had a permanent character and were thus likely to be included in the regular set of instructions to the next governor, while others were merely orders and directions intended to serve temporary ends. These additional instructions might take the form either of orders in council, or of instructions from the Board of Trade or the

---

[1] Pownall, *Administration of the Colonies*, 54.

secretaries of state. The instructions relating to trade formed a distinct body of articles governing the conduct of the governor as the agent of the home government in the enforcement of the navigation laws.

But these were not the only instruments that defined the governor's powers or imposed duties upon him. He had further to govern "according to such reasonable Laws and Statutes" as might be enacted by the provincial legislature.[1] These laws might, and frequently did, conflict with the directions of the royal commission or instructions, and many of them were disallowed for that reason; but a still larger number — such as those providing for appointments by the assembly, or interfering with the management of military operations, or containing provisions inconsistent with those instructions which limited the governor's assent to bills — were passed and went into operation. This result came about partly because in many cases the acts were merely temporary, partly because they were not noticed, and partly also because the assembly was strong enough to have its own way. Such acts, though often disallowed, do not seem to have been ordinarily regarded as *ipso facto* null and void because they were in conflict with a fundamental law.[2]

The governor's authority was also modified to an important extent by local usages of various sorts. Irregularities once weakly or inadvertently acquiesced in gradually became too deeply rooted to be disturbed, and often resulted in a serious diminution of the governor's powers. Finally, with the development of parliamentary control over the colonies, another element arose which must be taken into account, namely, acts of Parliament conferring privileges and imposing duties upon the provincial governors. Such provisions appear in the navigation acts of the reign of Charles II., and they were extended

---

[1] See commission to Bernard, § 10.

[2] Note, however, the opinion of the attorney-general of Barbadoes on the act of the assembly of that colony providing for the creation of paper money. He held that the assembly could not enact a law taking from the governor powers conferred on him by his commission. See Chalmers, *Opinions*, 373 *seq.*

by statutes of William III. and later sovereigns.   In general, these acts imposed upon the governor the duty of coöperation in the enforcement of the navigation laws.[1]

Of these various instruments by which the governor's powers were either conferred or defined, the most important were the commission and the instructions, interpreted by the analogy of the royal prerogative and modified by usages springing up in each province.   Before leaving this subject and proceeding to a discussion of the particular powers granted and defined in these ways, it may not be out of place to quote the quaint phraseology of a contemporary writer, probably James Glen, once a royal governor of South Carolina.   He writes: "The Governor is appointed by Patent, by the title of Governor in Chief, and Captain-General in and over the province; He receives also a Vice Admiral's Commission: But alas! these high sounding titles convey very little Power, and I have often wished that Governors had more; I cannot, however, help making this disinterested Remark, that though a Virtuous Person might be trusted with a little more power, perhaps there may be as much already given, as can safely be delegated to a weak or a wicked Person; and considering, that such may in ill times happen to be employed, a wise and good Prince will therefore guard against it."[2]

Historically one of the first departments of executive power to assume prominence was the military power, the command of the armed forces of the State.   By the English constitution the king was regarded as the commander-in-chief of the army and navy; he had the sole right to raise armies and fleets and to regulate them; it was his prerogative to establish and garrison forts and other places of strength.[3]   In this, as in other matters, the governor was the king's representative.   His commission authorized him, either directly or through officers of his appointment, to arm, muster, and command all persons

[1] See above, p. 68.

[2] Glen, *Description of South Carolina*, in Carroll, *Historical Collections*, ii. 220.

[3] Blackstone, *Commentaries*, i. 262.

residing within his province; to transfer them from place to place; to resist all enemies, pirates, or rebels; if necessary, to transport troops to other provinces in order to defend such places against invasion; to pursue enemies out of the province; in short, to do anything properly belonging to-the office of commander-in-chief. These powers were to be exercised by the governor independently. Furthermore, he might, with the advice and consent of the council, establish fortifications and furnish them with supplies;[1] and in time of actual war he might also with the council's consent execute martial law.[2]

Similar powers were given to the proprietors of Maryland and Pennsylvania. The proprietor of Maryland, for example, was authorized to execute all powers properly belonging to the office of captain-general; to summon to his standards all the inhabitants of the province; to wage war; and to execute martial law.[3] The Massachusetts charter of 1691 conferred like powers upon the new royal governor, but with two important restrictions, namely, that the governor was forbidden to take men out of the colony without the consent of the General Court or without their own free consent, or to execute martial law without the approval of the council.[4]

The governor was thus the head of the provincial military system, with the right of appointing subordinate military officers, and also of calling upon all inhabitants for military service in the defence of the province or in the suppression of rebellion. He was not, however, permitted by his instructions to declare martial law except in time of war, and then only with the advice and consent of the council.

In practical operation, however, the scope of the military powers of the governor was far from being as large as the terms

[1] Commission to Bernard of New Jersey, 1758, §§ 19, 20; to Allen of New Hampshire, 1692, p. 60; to Cornbury of New Jersey, 1702, p. 496; to Dobbs of North Carolina, 1761, p. 529.

[2] Instructions to Bernard, § 72; to Dudley of Massachusetts, 1702, p. 110; to Dobbs, 1754, § 113; to Dunmore of Virginia, 1771, § 78.

[3] Charter of Maryland, 1632, § 12, in Bozman, *History of Maryland,* ii. 9; charter to William Penn, 1681, in Poore, *Charters and Constitutions,* ii. 1509.

[4] Massachusetts charter of 1691, in Poore, i. 942.

of the commission would indicate. Even if the governor's powers as thus defined received the fullest recognition, they must have been quite useless without financial support from the assembly, a support which was often grudgingly and uncertainly given.[1] Moreover, some positive limitations were imposed either by law or by custom, as, for example, in the instance already noticed regarding the clause of the Massachusetts charter which required the consent of the General Court for the transportation of troops out of the province. The same principle, though not similarly embodied in the fundamental laws of the various provinces, seems to have been insisted on by other provincial assemblies.[2]

Furthermore, the right of the provincial governor to command the military service of the citizens and to maintain proper discipline depended largely, even for its legal sanction, upon acts of the assembly, which were known as the militia laws. The general character of this legislation may be sufficiently indicated by citing as an example the Georgia statute of 1755. This law provided, in the first place, for the enlistment of all males between the ages of sixteen and sixty, and authorized the governor to issue orders regulating the number of men in each company. It fixed penalties for neglect of

---

[1] Governor Dinwiddie of Virginia writes on one occasion that it is impracticable to conduct any expedition with dependence upon assemblies. See *Dinwiddie Papers*, i. 325.

[2] For assertions of the operation of this principle in Virginia, see *Ibid.*, i. 135, 377; Hening, *Statutes*, vi. 548, vii. 17. A Maryland act of 1650 denied the governor's right to compel freemen to serve out of the province; but in 1661 this authority was granted for a brief period. In 1757, however, Governor Sharpe of Maryland had to meet the same objections from the assembly to the call for service beyond the frontier (*Maryland Archives*, i. 302, 407, ix. 121 *seq.*). In the same year the Pennsylvania assembly refused to allow the militia of that province to be transported to the Carolinas (*Ibid.*, ix. 7). In 1759 the North Carolina militia refused to march out of the province against the Cherokees, on the ground that they were not obliged by law to do so (*North Carolina Records*, vi. 119, 141–142). The Georgia militia law of 1755 expressly confined the use of the militia to the province (Jones, *Colonial Acts of Georgia*, p. 9, § 14). Cf. the letter of Governor Morris, *New Jersey Documents*, vi. 186; Allinson, *Acts of Assembly*, 1746, ch. 200, and 1757, ch. 294.

military obligations by officers or men. It authorized the governor, in case of invasion or insurrection, to raise, with the advice and consent of his council, as many regiments as he might consider necessary and march them to such places within the province as he might think fit. It gave him authority also to draft men and to impress boats and arms.[1]

The assemblies realized the importance of this method of holding the governor in check, and often pushed it to an extreme point, requiring the governor, as a rule, to depend upon temporary acts for the enforcement of the simplest military obligations. Terms of one, two, and three years were commonly set for the duration of these militia acts.[2] Some of the colonies remained for long periods of time without any militia law, or at least without any which was effective. In North Carolina it was only after several years of unsuccessful effort on the part of the governor that the assembly was finally persuaded to pass satisfactory measures.[3] When the acts were of short duration, it was often difficult to secure regular renewals. In 1752, for example, Governor Clinton of New York complained that for four years the assembly had neglected to pass the regular annual militia law.[4] In New Jersey, as well as in Pennsylvania, the Quaker influence was a source of embarrassment.[5]

These were not the only ways in which the assemblies showed their jealousy of the governor's military powers. An interesting illustration of the kind of opposition which a governor had to meet in the conduct of military operations is to be found in

---

[1] Jones, *Colonial Acts of Georgia*, 9 *seq.* Cf. *Acts and Laws of New Hampshire* (1771), ch. 67 (act of 1718).

[2] The New York and New Jersey acts usually ran for one year only (*New York Acts of Assembly*, 1691–1718, pp. 53, 137, 146, 149, 216, 232; *Laws of New York*, 1691–1773, chs. 563, 573, 598, 617; Allinson, *New Jersey Acts of Assembly*, 1746, ch. 200). In Virginia, Maryland, and Pennsylvania the periods varied from one to seven years (Hening, *Statutes of Virginia*, v. 99, vi. 118, 350, 544, 564, vii. 92, 106, 115, 364; Bacon, *Laws of Maryland*, 1692, ch. 83, 1714, ch. 3, and *passim;* Cooper, *Statutes of South Carolina*, ix. *passim*, especially p. 645).

[3] *North Carolina Records*, iv. 816, 834, 917.

[4] *New York Documents*, vi 765.

[5] *New Jersey Documents*, vi. 104–105. Cf. *Ibid.*, iii. 167, 338.

POINT PARK COLLEGE LIBRARY

the conflict between Governor Sharpe and the Maryland assembly during the French and Indian War. The governor wished to collect troops for an expedition to the westward, claiming that he was empowered to do so both by his commission and by an act of 1715, which, as he held, was still in force. The assembly denied both of these propositions, and moreover insisted that the act in question applied only to cases of actual invasion. The governor, on the other hand, maintained that there was a state of invasion; whereupon the assembly argued that, although there had been incursions, there had been no invasion, a distinction which the governor characterized as nothing but a quibble. The assembly held that the mere apprehension of an invasion was not a sufficient ground for marching the militia; while the governor very naturally insisted that such an interpretation would prevent him from taking action until the enemy might be in the heart of the province.[1] To illustrate popular opinion within the province, Governor Sharpe cites the proposal of Hammond, a leading member of the assembly. This gentleman proposed merely to "recommend" the people of the province to supply themselves with arms and to learn how to use them, saying that, in his opinion, anything more than such a recommendation would "abridge the Liberty, to which as Englishmen they have an inviolable Right."[2]

The Pennsylvania militia law passed in 1755 was characterized by Governor Dinwiddie of Virginia as a "Joke on all military Affars,"[3] and was finally disallowed by the home government because it provided for the election of officers by ballot and failed to fix proper penalties for neglect of military obligations.[4] Occasionally in times of pressing danger the assembly

[1] For this controversy, see *Votes and Proceedings of the Lower House*, 1758, Feb. 23, March 6, April 1, May 5, 8; Sharpe to Pitt, August, 1758, *Maryland Archives*, ix. 249.

[2] Sharpe to Calvert, *Ibid.*, vi. 491.

[3] *Dinwiddie Papers*, ii. 313.

[4] *Votes of Pennsylvania*, iv. 629. In June, 1757, the assembly voted that there was no propriety in subjecting the people of a whole community to the rules and regulations imposed upon the mercenary soldiers of the crown. In response to the governor's suggestion that the Delaware assem-

saw the necessity of giving the governor a looser rein;[1] but
the tendency was rather to tie up the appropriations so closely
as to limit his freedom of action as far as possible. It will be
seen later that this process was carried so far as to deprive the
governor of his legitimate executive functions.

In a consideration of the militia, as in other departments of
the colonial government, the double character of the governor
must be kept in mind. He was the head of the provincial
administration, but he was more than that: he was the agent
of the crown, charged with the maintenance of its interests in
America; and consequently, in the discharge of his duties he
was often led beyond the limits of his own province. In some
instances royal governors were invested with a certain control
of the militia of the neighboring charter colonies: for example,
Governor Phips of Massachusetts was put in command of the
militia of Rhode Island and New Hampshire, and Governor
Fletcher of New York in command of the Connecticut militia.
Both of these cases, however, may fairly be regarded as exceptional; and ultimately the charter colonies asserted successfully their independence in this as in other departments of
government.[2]

bly had set a good example, particularly by conferring upon the governor
the right to make regulations for the government of the militia, the assembly declared that the governor would find it difficult to persuade a free
people to agree with him (*Ibid.*, iv. 716).

[1] In Virginia, for example, the governor was at times allowed a moderate discretion in the use of funds for military purposes (see e. g. Hening,
Statutes, v. 93). For similar acts in South Carolina, see Cooper, *Statutes*,
ii. 320, 333. The governor had authority over regular troops only when no
general officer of the crown was in the province; at such times he might
give orders to the military for the service of the province (see Stokes, *Constitution of the British Colonies*, 187-188).

[2] The commission to Phips first named him captain-general in Rhode
Island, Connecticut and New Hampshire. Phips visited Rhode Island, but
was unsuccessful in his attempt to secure recognition (Hutchinson, *History
of Massachusetts*, ii. 20; *New York Documents*, iv. 30). Governor Fletcher
of New York found the same difficulty in enforcing his authority in Connecticut under his commission of 1693. He visited the latter colony and
offered Governor Treat a commission for the command of the Connecticut militia. Treat, however, refused this recognition of Fletcher's superior authority, and his example was followed by other officers of the

Nevertheless, the governor did have an important part in the general military operations carried on by the crown in America. As early as 1687, Governor Dongan received a royal letter directing him to defend the Indian allies, to demand satisfaction from the governor of Canada, and to call on the other provincial governments for assistance.[1] In 1692, Governor Fletcher, then of Pennsylvania, was directed to assist the governor of New York with troops, and to agree with the governors of New England, Maryland, and Virginia about the quotas required from their respective colonies.[2] A circular letter of the year 1754, sent to the governors of the different colonies, shows fairly well the sort of coöperation expected. The circular begins with an account of the military preparations then making, and proceeds with instructions to the governors to take proper measures for collecting troops. They were to provide stores, to aid the royal officers in their movements, to enforce the orders of the latter, to secure adequate appropriations from their assemblies, and finally to confer with the royal officers and with the other governors in regard to the general plan of operations.[3] In response to these directions, the governors of North Carolina, Maryland, and Virginia ar-

---

colonial militia. Fletcher then issued a commission declaring all former commissions invalid; but he was finally obliged to leave the colony without any tangible results to show for his visit. The Board of Trade decided that the crown might appoint a commander-in-chief for the colonies in time of war, but that in time of peace the militia of each colony should be commanded solely by its governor according to its charter. In the commissions and instructions to Dudley and Shute of Massachusetts there were similar provisions with reference to the Rhode Island militia. See Fletcher's commission, *New York Documents*, iv. 29; Trumbull, *History of Connecticut*, i. 392–395, and Appendix, xxv.; Dudley's instructions, pp. 101–102. Cf. Chalmers, *Revolt*, ii. 11; *New Jersey Documents*, ii 411.

[1] *New York Documents*, iii. 503.

[2] *Maryland Archives*, viii. 540. In 1709 three governors, Ingoldsby of New York, Saltonstall of Connecticut, and Gookin of Pennsylvania, sat together as a military council at Fort Ann, issuing commissions to military commanders and signing military orders of various sorts. It is noticeable that the list includes a proprietary and an elective as well as a royal governor. See *New Jersey Documents*, xiii. 343, 346.

[3] *North Carolina Records*, v. 144 d.

ranged a plan for the Ohio expedition, with Governor Sharpe of Maryland as commander of the combined forces.[1] The governor most prominent in this line of activity was Shirley of Massachusetts, who held at one time the chief command of all the forces in America.[2] Governor Sharpe of Maryland was conspicuously active in the same way, as was also Governor Dinwiddie of Virginia.[3]

The same difficulties which the governor had to meet in conducting the military administration of his own province of course made themselves felt with additional force in this broader sphere of activity. Popular jealousy of the governor was reinforced by the strongly-marked spirit of local selfishness then prevalent among the colonists; and furthermore, as has been already shown, there was in the provincial assemblies a strong opposition to any extended plan of military operations beyond the lines of their respective provinces.

In this study of the governor's military functions, it has been found, first, that he was the commander-in-chief of the military forces of the province, charged with its defence and authorized by his commission to demand the military service of its inhabitants; secondly, that he was intrusted with important responsibilities in connection with the general military operations of the crown in America; and, finally, that in both of these directions he was closely dependent upon the assembly, not only for supplies, but also for the legal machinery necessary for the enforcement of his military authority.

Besides being commander-in-chief of the provincial forces, the governor had also the title of vice-admiral, though this name carried with it very little real power, inasmuch as the colonies had of course no naval establishments worth mentioning. The governor's admiralty powers, as defined in his vice-admiral's commission, gave him authority to collect the

---

[1] *North Carolina Records*, v. 144 f.

[2] There is a record of a council of war, held by Governor Shirley in his capacity of commander-in-chief, at which were present the royal governor of New York, the proprietary governors of Maryland and Pennsylvania, and the elective governor of Connecticut. See *Maryland Archives*, vi. 315.

[3] *Ibid.*, vols. vi., ix., *passim;* especially vi. 3, 73, 107, 350, ix. 323.

royal admiralty dues and to punish all offenders against maritime law; and for these purposes he was to maintain and
supervise admiralty courts and to appoint all necessary sub-
ordinates. He might issue commissions to ships' officers
authorizing them to execute martial law on board their vessels,
and he might also grant letters of marque and reprisal, though
this latter right was closely limited and could not be independently used except against powers at war with Great
Britain. When war had actually broken out, such commissions to privateers were usually issued on the governor's
warrant by the judge of the Admiralty Court, who was an
appointee of the crown. The governor was also brought into
direct relations with the royal naval officers, to whom he was
directed to give due assistance.[1]

One of the usual functions of the executive in any constitution is that of representing the State in its relations with
other States, that is to say, in the department of foreign relations. This function was one of the prerogatives of the
English crown. Blackstone says: "With regard to foreign
concerns, the king is the delegate or representative of his
people. . . . What is done by the royal authority, with regard
to foreign powers, is the act of the whole nation." As a consequence of this principle, the king had the prerogative of war
and peace, the sole right of sending and receiving ambassadors
and of making treaties with foreign States and princes.[2] It
is, of course, at once clear that this principle, if applicable to
the governor at all, could be so only in an extremely limited
sense, inasmuch as the provincial governor was not the head of
a state. The province, if it might be regarded as a state in
any sense, was clearly a dependent one, having no relations
with other states except through the medium of the home gov-

---

[1] See the vice-admiral's commission to the governor of New Jersey, 1759,
New Jersey Documents, ix. 195; instructions to Cornbury of New Jersey,
1702, §§ 60–62; to Dunmore of Virginia, 1771, §§ 61, 63; to Dudley of
Massachusetts, 1702, pp. 110, 114; to Bernard of New Jersey, 1758, §§ 76–
77; Stokes, *Constitution of the British Colonies*, 185; commission to
Bernard, §§ 21, 22.

[2] Blackstone, *Commentaries*, i. 252–261.

ernment. Nevertheless, each colony had two important kinds
of external relations, to which may be applied in a rough way
the principle already stated. These were its relations with
the Indian tribes on its frontiers and with other colonies.

The statements of the two proprietary charters in regard to
external affairs may first be considered. The Maryland charter
referred to the proximity of barbarous tribes, and simply gave
the proprietor power to make war against such enemies of the
province.[1] The charter to William Penn contained a similar
article, preceded, however, by another which expressly denied
the right of the proprietor to maintain any correspondence with
states at enmity with the crown or to declare war against
friendly states.[2] This article, considered in connection with
the absence of any clause in the Maryland charter conferring
the right of making war and peace, appears to give evidence
that the proprietors had no independent authority other than
the mere right of protecting themselves from attack.

The case is still clearer when the position of the royal governor is considered. Obviously, the subordinate officer of the
crown could not have the power to involve the state in war or
to conclude any authoritative peace, — a plain inference, which
is supported by the terms of the royal instructions. By one of
his instructions the governor was authorized to take temporary
action, with the advice and consent of the council, in matters
not covered by his commission; but there was a proviso that
he was not under any circumstances to declare war, except
against the Indians in case of emergency; and even in such
cases immediate notice was to be given to the home government.[3] To show that this exceptional power of declaring war
was not only granted, but was actually used in a number of
instances, two or three examples will suffice. Thus in 1722

---

[1] Bozman, *History of Maryland,* ii. 9.

[2] Poore, *Charters and Constitutions,* ii. 1509.

[3] Instructions to Bernard of New Jersey, 1758, § 88; to Allen of New
Hampshire, 1692, p. 68; to Dudley of Massachusetts, 1702, p. 115; to
Dobbs of North Carolina, 1754, § 129; to Dunmore of Virginia, 1771, § 87.
Note also the clause in regard to maintaining friendly correspondence with
the Indians: instructions to Bernard, § 74 (instruction to encourage the
Indians); to Dudley, p. 113; to Dobbs, § 125; to Dunmore, § 59.

Governor Shute of Massachusetts, with the advice of his council, issued a declaration of war against the Indians, and in 1755 Governor Shirley was formally requested to do the same.[1] In 1745 the governor and council of New Hampshire also agreed upon a similar declaration of war.[2]

The commission and instructions contained no distinct grant of power to make treaties; the governor was simply told in somewhat vague terms to maintain a good correspondence with the Indians.[3] That treaties were frequently made by the governors, however, is proved by abundant examples, one of which is seen in the case of Governor Glen of South Carolina, who in a letter of the year 1746 describes his circuit among the Indian tribes for the purpose of negotiating with them.[4] In 1749 and 1754 Indian treaties were also negotiated by the governors of the provinces of New Hampshire and Massachusetts.[5] When these cases and others that might be cited are borne in mind, together with that clause of the governor's instructions which authorized him, in matters not covered by his instructions, to take action with the advice and consent of his council, it is clear that the governor with the council had in this lower plane the treaty-making power.[6] Nevertheless, it should be said that toward the close of the colonial period the governor's sphere of activity was limited by the appointment of special

[1] Hutchinson, *History of Massachusetts*, ii. 251 ; *Massachusetts Province Laws*, iii. 948 (extract from council records).

[2] *New Hampshire Provincial Papers*, v. 105, 374.

[3] See above, p. 107, note 3.

[4] South Carolina Historical Society, *Collections*, ii. 294.

[5] *New Hampshire Provincial Papers*, v. 131 ; Hutchinson, *History of Massachusetts*, iii. 26. Cf. *Provincial Papers*, i. 588, iii. 545–546, 693 *seq.*, 705 ; Hutchinson, ii. 124.

[6] Cf. *North Carolina Records*, ii. 56 ; *Dinwiddie Papers*, ii. 298. The governor seems also to have had more or less right of supervision over the ordinary intercourse between Indians and whites. In Pennsylvania and Georgia there were laws requiring the governor's license for trade with the Indians. In Virginia and North Carolina, at least, the governor's consent was required for the purchase of land from the Indians. See instructions to Dunmore of Virginia, 1771, § 59 ; *Pennsylvania Records*, v. 194–196 ; *New Hampshire Provincial Papers*, ii. 17 ; Jones, *Colonial Acts of Georgia*, 190 ; Hening, *Statutes*, iv. 461 ; Martin, *Iredell's Public Acts*, i. 23.

royal agents for Indian affairs, and later by that of a general superintendent of Indian affairs.

The governor was also the natural representative of the province in its relations with other colonies. It has been seen that, in the general system of military operations in the country, the governors were necessarily brought into close correspondence with each other; and also that in the closely related department of Indian affairs the colonies were led into similar communication and correspondence, conducted usually by the governor, though often on consultation with the assembly.[1] Among the most common subjects of negotiation among the different colonies were various questions relating to boundaries. At first such negotiations seem to have been left to the governor;[2] but gradually there grew up a custom of referring them to commissioners chosen by the assemblies, a method which was distinctly recommended by royal instructions of the year 1730.[3]

In conclusion, then, it may be said that, although the governor had little or nothing to do with what may properly be called foreign affairs, yet he was the natural representative of the colony in its external relations. He had a limited power of declaring war against the Indians, and he might make treaties with them, though in both these cases the consent of the council was required. He was also the natural representative of his own province in its dealings with other provinces, though even here his activity was limited to a certain extent

---

[1] Hutchinson, *History of Massachusetts*, ii. 287; *Maryland Archives*, vi. 10, vii. 265, 319.

[2] *North Carolina Records*, i. 505, ii. 204; *Maryland Archives*, iii. 496.

[3] *New Hampshire Provincial Papers*, iv. 568. There is one other interesting phase of intercolonial relations which is worth noting, namely, that relating to the extradition of escaped criminals. Instances of this sort were rare; but when they did occur the governor seems to have been the medium of communication. Thus in 1698 Governor Basse of New Jersey refused to obey the order of the New York Admiralty Court for the surrender of a pirate (*New Jersey Documents*, ii. 229); and in 1759 Governor Sharpe of Maryland sent to the governor of Pennsylvania an order for the extradition of offenders who had escaped to that province (*Maryland Archives*, ix. 335–336).

by the participation of the assembly through its election of commissioners.

Another essential part of the royal prerogative was the appointing power. The king was the fountain of honor and privilege, with the right to establish offices and to dispose of them;[1] and this essentially executive power was naturally intrusted to the provincial governor. Both the Maryland and the Pennsylvania charter conferred it in express terms upon the proprietor, who may be regarded as the governor-in-chief of the proprietary province. The Maryland proprietor was empowered to appoint judges, magistrates, and other officers "of what kind, for what cause, and with what power soever," whether on land or sea;[2] and similar authority was given to William Penn and his heirs.[3] The Massachusetts charter of 1691 gave the governor somewhat more limited powers, allowing him to appoint judicial and military officers, but requiring that important administrative positions be filled by the General Court.[4] The royal commissions conferred the right of appointment under two separate heads, providing first that the governor have the right of naming military officers, a natural part of his prerogative as commander-in-chief; and secondly that, in consequence of his general obligation to maintain courts and enforce the law, he should have the right to appoint civil officers of various sorts.

The authority to name military officers was so plainly a matter of course that it was generally admitted. Moreover, in this class of appointments the governor was independent, being required by neither commission nor instructions to ask consent of the council. This independence was, however, a natural consequence of the peculiar character of military command, with its necessity for a concentration of authority.[5] Nevertheless, in Pennsylvania an effort was made to limit

[1] Blackstone, *Commentaries*, i. 271.

[2] Charter of 1632, § vii., in Bozman, *History of Maryland*, ii. 9.
[3] Charter of 1681, in Poore, *Charters and Constitutions*, ii. 1509.
[4] *Ibid.*, i. 942.
[5] See commission to Bernard of New Jersey, 1758, § 19; to Allen of New Hampshire, 1692, p. 60; to Dobbs of North Carolina, 1761, p. 529.

somewhat this power of independent appointment by a provision of the militia act, which required the election of officers by ballot. This obnoxious provision, however, led to the disallowance of the act of 1755.[1]

The appointment of civil officers is a subject of much more importance. The governor's commission empowered him to appoint judges, justices of the peace, sheriffs, "and other necessary Officers and Ministers . . . for the better Administration of Justice and putting the Laws in Execution."[2] This power of appointment appears to have been at first unlimited; the only restriction imposed was the direction "to take care" in the nomination of the principal officers to select "men of good life," of "good estates and abilities," "well affected to Our Government," and not "necessitous people, or much in debt."[3] The power of removal was given in terms almost as liberal; the governor was merely forbidden to make removals without good cause, a statement of which was to be duly submitted to the home government.[4] Soon, however, it was felt that additional safeguards were necessary, particularly in order to secure proper judicial appointments; whereupon the rule was made that commissions to judges and justices of the peace should be issued only with the advice and consent of the council.[5] In 1754 the Board of Trade declared that the rule of concurrent action by the council, though plainly implied in previous instructions, had not been strictly adhered to; consequently the governor was then bound, in more specific and

[1] *Votes of Pennsylvania*, iv. 629. On this whole paragraph, cf. above, pp. 99 *seq.*

[2] Commission to Bernard of New Jersey, 1758, § 16; to Allen of New Hampshire, 1692, p. 59; to Dobbs of North Carolina, 1761, p. 528.

[3] Instructions to Allen, p. 64; to Dudley of Massachusetts, 1702, p. 102; to Dobbs, 1754, § 9; to Bernard, § 9.

[4] See instructions to Allen of New Hampshire, 1692, p. 66; to Cornbury of New Jersey, 1702, § 41. It should be said, however, that the Massachusetts charter of 1691 distinctly required the consent of the council to all civil appointments made by the governor. See Poore, *Charters and Constitutions*, i. 942.

[5] Instructions to Hunter of New York, 1709, § 43; to Burrington of North Carolina, 1730, § 44; to Morris of New Jersey, 1738, § 36.

unmistakable terms, not to appoint judicial officers without the advice and consent of at least three councillors signified in council.[1]

After this glance at the formal provisions of the commission and instructions, the actual practice of the different colonies may well be examined. In the first place, the concurrent action of the council in appointments was so fruitful a source of controversy that it is difficult to lay down any general rule applicable to the practice of all the colonies. On the one hand, the council sometimes undertook to assume undue control. Thus in Massachusetts the actual nomination of officers was at first left in the hands of the council, from which it was finally wrested with considerable difficulty.[2] In North Carolina also the records show that, during the period of the royal government, justices and sheriffs were regularly appointed and removed by orders in council.[3] On the other hand, the governor was restive under restrictions of any kind. For example, in 1711, Governor Spotswood of Virginia complained of an "unreasonable" proposal of the assembly to make the consent of the council necessary in appointments.[4] Again, in 1730, Governor Belcher of New Hampshire informed his council that the nomination and appointment of officers belonged to him, but that he was willing to listen to the objections of the council and to give them due consideration;[5] and afterwards, when governor of New Jersey, he took similar ground.[6] It is clear that the more specific directions of 1754 were needed.

[1] Instructions to Dobbs of North Carolina, 1754, § 62; to Bernard of New Jersey, 1758, § 41; to Dunmore of Virginia, 1771, § 45. The provision in regard to removal was unchanged. Cf. Bernard's instructions, § 42; cf. *North Carolina Records*, v. 1104.

[2] Hutchinson, *History of Massachusetts*, ii. 20; Chalmers, *Revolt*, i. 284.

[3] *North Carolina Records*, vi. 218, 762, 771.

[4] *Letters of Governor Spotswood* (Virginia Historical Society, *Collections*, i.), 53–54.

[5] *New Hampshire Provincial Papers*, iv. 773.

[6] See a letter from John Cox to James Alexander, May, 1748: "We had A long dispute About the Power of the Councill he was in Efect for Making

The amount of patronage thus placed in the governor's hands varied in the different colonies. In Massachusetts many of the important officers were appointed by the General Court, subject in this as in all other matters to the governor's approval; and, as will be seen later, this practice had its influence on the other colonies.[1] In Virginia the governor's patronage, according to an account published in 1727, was very extensive, including the appointment not only of all military officers by commission during the governor's pleasure, but of nearly all civil officers of importance.[2] In New Hampshire, in 1730, appointments were with very few exceptions in the hands of the governor.[3] Anthony Stokes, the writer of a valuable work on the colonial constitution, but a man of distinctly royalist tendencies, laid down the general rule that the governor had the disposal of all offices not specifically retained within the direct control of the crown, and even that vacancies arising in such royal appointments were temporarily filled by him.[4] There is, however, another side to the question. In South Carolina the patronage of the governor was insignificant, being limited chiefly to the appointment of military officers and justices of the peace, "offices of no profit, and some trouble."[5] Such limitations were due partly to encroachments by the assembly and partly to the tendency of the home government to keep in its own hands some of the more important appointments. In addition to the offices connected with the customs and the Indian department, the crown reserved for its own appointment the offices of secretary of the province,

of us Solemn Witnesses to his Appointments by Consenting to Persons he Should Name & propose And I insisted On what I concieved to be our rights — Which at last Ended in a declaration that tho his Sentiments were So Yet he would Not appoint officers Without Advice of Councill" (*New Jersey Documents*, vii. 129.)

[1] See below, ch. x.
[2] Hartwell, Blair, and Chilton, *Present State of Virginia*, 20 seq.
[3] *New Hampshire Provincial Papers*, iv. 533.
[4] *Constitution of the British Colonies*, 184.
[5] Glen, *Description of South Carolina*, in Carroll, *Historical Collections*, ii. 221.

chief-justice, attorney-general, auditor-general, receiver-general, and sometimes that of clerk of the assembly.[1]

In reply to the question which now arises as to the way in which this power vested in the governor was exercised, it must be said that much of it was corruptly used.   Maryland furnishes a glaring example of a regular traffic in offices, though for this practice the proprietor and not the governor was chiefly to blame.[2]   In South Carolina a similar corrupt use of patronage was charged against one of the acting governors, of whom it was said that with him four hundred pounds would make a provost marshall.[3]   Some governors, apparently, were inclined to provide for their families out of this colonial patronage, while others used it to extend their influence and to promote the passage of measures in which they were interested.[4]   An

[1] Glen, *Description of South Carolina*, in Carroll, *Historical Collections*, ii. 221 ; *Documentary History of New York* (1849), i. 770–772 (Tryon's report of 1774); *North Carolina Records*, vi. 620 ; *New Jersey Documents*, vii. 246, viii. (2), 86, ix. 257, 620.   In Maryland, proprietary influence in colonial appointments was very marked; in one instance the proprietor even went so far as to commission a justice of the peace.   Furthermore, even when the appointment was not made by the proprietor directly, the governor was tied up by orders to appoint particular persons.   Governor Sharpe complained that he was not allowed to dispose of the most honorable and lucrative offices, and that persons who desired offices would apply to the proprietor's secretary (*Maryland Archives*, v. 117, vi. 184, 238, 400, ix. 34–35).   Stokes condemned severely the common practice of granting commissions in England to persons who exercised colonial offices by deputy, saying that in his opinion the governor thus lost weight (*Constitution of the British Colonies*, 138).

[2] This traffic was largely carried on by Cecilius Calvert, secretary to the proprietor.   With other friends of the proprietor, he was accustomed to levy certain charges upon persons appointed to office in the colony, requiring the judges of the colonial land office, for example, to remit to him a part of their profits.   Sharpe writes an interesting letter to the secretary about the case of a certain Mr. and Mrs. Graham, who had always received fifty pounds per annum from the present sheriff.   Another relative asked to be allowed to appoint the next incumbent, in order that he might continue to receive the fifty pounds a year assigned by the proprietor; whereupon the governor is charged with the ungracious duty of making the most advantageous bargains.   See Sharpe's Correspondence, *Maryland Archives*, vi. 238, ix. 64.

[3] South Carolina Historical Society, *Collections*, i. 237.

[4] Governor Dobbs of North Carolina successfully recommended his son

illustration of this latter use of the power is suggested by the complaint of an eminent contemporary authority, to the effect that the governor, by the diminution of his patronage, was left without means of stopping the mouths of demagogues.[1] Again, Governor Dobbs of North Carolina revenged himself on the leader of the opposition in the assembly by depriving the gentleman of all his offices;[2] and Governor Morris of New Jersey appointed to a judgeship the late speaker of the assembly, "who had been as serviceable as he could."[3] This question of the use of patronage will occur again when the relation of the governor to the assembly is considered.

It was inevitable that such abuse of power should lead to efforts on the part of the assembly to restrict its exercise. The first step taken was the imposition of certain qualifications for appointment, a provision which was aimed particularly at the practice of appointing non-residents to colonial offices. An early statute of New Jersey directed that none but resident freeholders should be appointed to offices, civil or military, within the province.[4] A similar residential qualification for offices in the colony was fixed by the Maryland assembly in 1704.[5] In 1705 Virginia passed more thoroughgoing acts governing the appointment of sheriffs, declaring that a candidate for that office must be a justice of the peace, and that he must have resided in the province at least three years.[6] Another illustration of popular distrust of the appointing power is to be found in the fact that numerous efforts were made to

for appointment to the council. Governor Cosby of New Jersey urged the appointment of "my son Billy" as secretary of the province, a post to which he had already given his son a provisional appointment until the royal pleasure should be known. See *North Carolina Records,* v. 440, 649; *New Jersey Documents,* v. 321.

[1] Stokes, *Constitution of the British Colonies,* 138.

[2] *North Carolina Records,* vi. 218.

[3] *Morris Papers,* 48.

[4] A special exception was made of the office of secretary. See Leaming and Spicer, *Grants, Concessions,* etc., 368 *seq.,* especially 370; Allinson, *Acts of Assembly,* 1748, ch. 208.

[5] Bacon, *Laws,* 1704, ch. 93.

[6] Hening, *Statutes,* iii. 246, 250.

regulate the tenure of certain offices in the gift of the governor. A Maryland act of 1662, for example, provided for the annual appointment of sheriffs, with the limitation that no person should fill the office for two successive terms; and later acts of the same province fixed a tenure first of two and then of three years.[1] Similar acts were passed in North Carolina, New Jersey, and Delaware.[2]

Occasionally still more serious limitations were laid upon the governor's right of nomination. A Maryland law of 1662, for example, enacted that the commissioners of the county courts should annually present to the proprietor or the governor the names of three persons who had not been sheriffs during the previous year, from which the governor was to choose one. The act was temporary, however, and the restriction was abandoned.[3] Elsewhere the attempt met with better success. A Virginia act of 1705 provided that the county courts should annually present to the governor the names of three persons as candidates for the office of sheriff, one of whom the governor was required to appoint.[4] In Pennsylvania the people had from the beginning a similar share in the nomination of sheriffs and coroners.[5]

The assembly had, furthermore, an indirect and somewhat questionable method of controlling appointments through its power over the purse. Indeed, it was a common practice of the colonial assemblies to withhold altogether the salaries of judges whose appointment they disapproved. In New York, salaries were granted annually and specifically by name to the person then holding the office; the governors claimed, and

---

[1] *Maryland Archives*, i. 450; Bacon, *Laws*, 1692, ch. 25; 1715, ch. 46, § 10.

[2] Martin, *Iredell's Public Acts*, i. 42; *Laws of Delaware* (1797), i. 63. Cf. also Leaming and Spicer, *Grants, Concessions*, etc., 368 *seq.;* Allinson, *Acts of Assembly*, 1748, ch. 208.

[3] *Maryland Archives*, i. 451, v. 138, 469.

[4] Hening, *Statutes*, iii. 246.

[5] See Frames of Government of 1682 and 1683, in Poore, *Charters and Constitutions*, ii. 1522, 1529; Charter of Privileges, 1701, *Ibid.*, 1538; *Statutes at Large of Pennsylvania* (1896), ii. 272. Cf. *Laws of Delaware* (1797), i. 63.

apparently with reason, that this was done for the purpose of controlling appointments.[1]

Thus in almost all the colonies the appointing power was subject to important limitations imposed by colonial statutes. Not content with these checks, however, the assemblies entered upon a more radical course of action: from measures restricting the exercise of the appointing power, they went on to wrest from the governor and to take into their own hands the actual power of appointment itself. This policy of the assemblies, and the long and bitter conflicts to which it gave rise, may best be studied after a consideration of the governor's relations with the assembly.[2]

In the early part of the colonial era the financial powers of the governor had, as has been seen, been very extensive. The introduction of representative assemblies, however, gradually deprived him of these abnormal powers, rendering him dependent upon the assembly for supplies. Naturally, the legislatures of those days were not inclined to grant any larger supplies than they considered strictly necessary for the support of the government; and, furthermore, the body which granted money began to claim the right of determining how that money should be spent. Hence the financial powers of the governor became very much reduced. There were, however, two important functions of this class which continued to hold their place in the royal commission and instructions, namely, the regulation of salaries and fees, and the issue of warrants for the expenditure of money.

The royal instructions directed the governor, with the advice and consent of the council, to regulate all salaries and fees of provincial officers.[3]

Of these two functions the regulation of salaries may first be considered. It is clear that when, as was usually the case, official salaries were paid by special grants of the assembly,

---

[1] *New York Documents,* v. 844, vi. 432–437, 764.

[2] Cf. ch. x. below.

[3] Instructions to Bernard of New Jersey, 1758, § 44; to Allen of New Hampshire, 1692, p. 66; to Dudley of Massachusetts, 1702, p. 108; to Dobbs of North Carolina, 1754, § 65; to Dunmore of Virginia, 1771, § 48.

their amounts must of necessity have been determined by the same authority.   In Virginia, however, where a considerable portion of the provincial establishment was provided for by a permanent fund settled by the assembly upon the crown, not only was the governor directed to regulate the salaries of officers, but he had the power to do so.[1]   In New York there was a spirited contest over the question.   In that colony, in the early part of the last century, it was customary, in granting supplies, to pass at the same time resolutions fixing the salaries of the various officials.   Governor William Burnet, who held office in 1720, at first issued his warrants in accordance with these resolutions, though six years later he refused to obey the resolves of the assembly.   His successor, Montgomerie, however, seems practically to have yielded the point to the assembly, which by 1729 had completely gained its end.[2]   Salaries were thenceforth regularly fixed by annual acts of appropriation, and the regulation of official salaries thus passed entirely out of the governor's hands.[3]

The question as to the regulation of fees is more difficult. It is clear that the governor's prerogative in this matter was not exclusive, inasmuch as acts of assembly for the regulation of officers' fees begin early and are numerous.   In Maryland a law was passed, in 1676, providing that no officer mentioned in the act should take other fees than those specified;[4] and from 1699 to 1763 a large number of similar laws are recorded.[5]   Virginia enacted a law regulating fees as early as 1699.[6]   Several such acts were passed in North Carolina; indeed, in 1736, Governor Johnston himself recommended the regulation of fees by the legislature, and some

[1] Act of assembly, in Hening, *Statutes*, iii. 490, especially § 10; instructions to Dunmore of Virginia, 1771, § 88.

[2] *New York Journal of Assembly*, i. 448, 580, 585, 646, 700; *New York Documents*, v. 878–879, 885.

[3] Opinion of Attorney-General Bradley, *New York Documents*, v. 901-903.

[4] *Maryland Archives*, ii. 532.   For earlier acts, see *Ibid.*, i. 21, 229.

[5] Bacon, *Laws*, 1699, ch. 49 ; 1700, ch. 7 ; 1704, chs. 4, 86 ; 1708, ch. 19 ; 1709, ch. 15 ; 1711, ch. 19 ; 1714, ch. 5 (for four years); 1763, ch. 18, § 87 *seq.*

[6] Hening, *Statutes*, iii. 195.

years later a law was finally agreed upon.[1] Johnston's successor objected to this measure on the ground that it was inconsistent with that article of the instructions which authorized the governor to regulate fees; but the Board of Trade decided that such legislation was not inconsistent with the instructions.[2] Without adding to this list of acts passed by the assemblies for the regulation of official fees, it may be said that the practice was general.[3]

It is equally clear, however, that fees were frequently settled by the governor and council without the intervention of the assembly. In some of the colonies there were no acts regulating fees until a very late date, and consequently there was room for action by the governor, who seems not to have been slow to exercise his power. New Jersey, for example, furnishes a considerable list of ordinances issued by governors for the regulation of fees, beginning with one issued by the first royal governor and continuing to the time of Governor Belcher, who assumed the office in 1747.[4] Other cases may be found in the records of New Hampshire, New York, Maryland, and Virginia.[5] Popular feeling, however, was so strongly against the practice that the assembly of New Jersey, in its remonstrance against Lord Cornbury, declared that it considered the

---

[1] *North Carolina Records*, iv. 229, 916.

[2] *Ibid.*, v. 643, 750.

[3] For New Jersey, see Allinson, *Acts of Assembly*, 1743, ch. 195, and 1748, ch. 210; for Georgia, Jones, *Colonial Acts of Georgia*, 321 *seq.*; for New Hampshire, *Provincial Laws*, chs. 64, 108; for South Carolina, Cooper, *Statutes*, iii. 326, 414, and Chalmers, *Revolt*, ii. 175; for Massachusetts, *Province Laws*, iii. 1743-4 ch. 10, 1744-5 ch. 13, 1746-7 ch. 24, 1750-51 ch. 8, 1752-3 ch. 28, 1756-7 ch. 30. Cf. Proud, *History of Pennsylvania*, ii. 51.

[4] *New Jersey Documents*, iii. 176, v. 338, xiv. 260, 388; Allinson, *Acts of Assembly*, Appendix.

[5] In 1642 the governor and council of Maryland published a table of officers' fees. In 1669 the council expressly declared the right of the proprietor to settle fees; and in 1682 a similar declaration was made by the proprietor himself on the failure of the House to take action. See *Maryland Archives*, i. 162, ii. 176, vii. 401; also *New York Acts of Assembly*, 1691-1718, pp. 115-123; *New Hampshire Provincial Papers*, i. 454; *Dinwiddie Papers* (Virginia), i. 44-46; *North Carolina Records*, vi. 288.

settling of fees otherwise than by a legislative act to be a great grievance and repugnant to Magna Charta; [1] and a similar position was taken by the assemblies of several other colonies. [2]

The attitude of the home government in regard to the question seems not to have been consistent throughout. In 1708, after the remonstrance of the New Jersey assembly against the conduct of Lord Cornbury, the Board of Trade declared its opinion "that no fee is lawful, unless it be Warranted by Prescription, or Erected by the Legislature "; [3] but it is doubtful just how much is meant by the phrase "warranted by prescription." In the next year the act of assembly regulating fees was disallowed, and the new governor, Hunter, was ordered, with the advice of the council, to establish fees "upon a reasonable footing." This he did by ordinance. [4] In New Hampshire, where by 1730 officers' fees were fixed by law, the governor was directed by the home government to see that no fees were taken in the province, "but what are according to law." [5] A South Carolina law regulating fees was condemned by the home government, but apparently on the ground that fees were unduly reduced. [6] In 1757, the Board of Trade instructed Governor Dobbs of North Carolina that acts of assembly regulating fees were not inconsistent with the royal instructions, but recognized also a concurrent right of the governor and council. [7]

Apart from the question of strict right, it may then be said that, although the royal instructions placed in the governor's hands the regulation of official fees, the function came to be exercised mainly by the assemblies. Some governors, it is

[1] *New Jersey Documents*, iii. 176.

[2] *New York Documents*, v. 296; McMahon, *History of Maryland*, i. 284; Proud, *History of Pennsylvania*, ii. 51; *North Carolina Records*, iii. 151, vi. 288; *Dinwiddie Papers*, i. 44–46.

[3] *New Jersey Documents*, iii. 327.   [4] *Ibid.*, v. 338.

[5] *New Hampshire Provincial Papers*, iv. 573.

[6] South Carolina Historical Society, *Collections*, iii. 332; Chalmers, *Revolt*, ii. 175.

[7] *North Carolina Records*, v. 750. In 1754, the protest of the Virginia burgesses against fees not sanctioned by law was rejected. *Dinwiddie Papers*, i. 44–47, 362.

true, still used their right to a limited extent; but fees were for the most part regulated by statutes that provided penalties for the exaction of other or larger amounts than those specified.

The other important financial function expressly vested in the governor by his instructions was the general oversight of public expenditures. To this end, it was ordered that all money raised should be expended only by warrant of the governor, with the advice and consent of the council. The exercise of this power was checked on two sides: the instructions provided, in the first place, that all accounts should be sent to the home government; and, in the second place, that the assembly should be allowed to inspect the accounts of money appropriated by law. The latter provision was probably the more effective safeguard.[1]

The real extent and importance of this power conferred on the governor can be determined only by an examination of the financial methods prevalent in the different colonies. The important question is, of course, whether the requirement of the governor's warrant was merely formal, perhaps designed to check expenditures by other officers, or whether it was meant that the governor should have a real voice. At first, before the practice of making minutely exact appropriations became general, the governor and council seem actually to have possessed considerable discretion in the disposition of money.[2] The assembly at that time appears hardly to have realized its power, — a conclusion suggested by the fact that the New Jersey militia act of 1704 was criticised by the Board of Trade as giving the governor too much discretion in the expenditure of certain funds created by the act.[3] This earlier confidence

[1] See instructions to Bernard of New Jersey, 1758, §§ 19, 20; to Allen of New Hampshire, 1692, p. 65; to Dudley of Massachusetts, 1702, p. 105; to Dobbs of North Carolina, 1754, §§ 29, 30; to Dunmore of Virginia, 1771, §§ 21, 22.

[2] See e. g. *Maryland Archives*, viii. 404; *Charter and Laws of Pennsylvania*, 281; *New Hampshire Provincial Papers*, ii. 84, iii. 165 *seq.* Note the general absence of detailed appropriations in the early statute books and legislative proceedings.

[3] *New Jersey Documents*, iii. 126.

in the judgment and integrity of governors soon passed away, however, as it became evident that many of them were undoubtedly corrupt.   In evidence of the lack of principle among them, reference has already been made to an official report on the condition of the plantations.   Governor Cornbury of New York was a particularly notorious offender; and it is practically certain that such cases as his had much to do with the distinctly different policy followed by the assemblies of the eighteenth century.   Indeed, this doubt as to the integrity of the executive was expressly stated in the official proceedings of the legislature of New York as a reason why means should be taken to prevent corrupt expenditure.[1]   The natural tendency of all legislative bodies to define appropriations closely probably worked to the same end.   At any rate, the result is perfectly clear: a glance at the statute books of almost any colony will show that, by the close of the colonial era, the general rule consisted in making detailed appropriations for short periods of time.[2]

In the making of these appropriations the governor had a gradually decreasing influence.   He had himself only a right of veto upon appropriation bills as a whole; but the council, as the upper house of the assembly, afforded to a certain extent a representation of the policy of the executive.   The lower house, however, soon came to resent the interference of the council in financial matters, and a jealousy sprang up, of which an early illustration is to be found in the Virginia House of Burgesses.   This body, in 1666, in reply to the governor's request that certain members of the council should coöperate with the burgesses in making up the public levy, asserted its right to "lay the levy in the house," promising that bills should then be presented to the governor for his assent or dissent.[3]   In 1704 and 1705 the New York council

---

[1] *New York Journal of Assembly,* i. 170–171.

[2] See e. g. *New Hampshire Provincial Papers,* v. 393; *New York Journal of Assembly,* i. 700, 784, 790–791, ii. 9, 14; *New York Documents,* v. 901–903; Cooper, *Statutes,* iv. 6, 14, 18, 45, 53, 103. 128; *Massachusetts Province Laws, passim,* e. g. 1743–4 ch. 2, 1753–4 ch. 24.

[3] Hening, *Statutes,* ii. 254.

returned with amendments supply bills sent up by the House of Representatives; whereupon the House resolved that it was "inconvenient" to allow the council to amend money bills, and returned the bills, having paid no attention to the amendments.[1] The Board of Trade vigorously opposed this action of the assembly; but the House stood firm. In 1711 the controversy was renewed with the same result. Again in 1750 and 1754 the House refused to admit amendments by the council, and finally carried its point. Thereafter money bills seem to have been passed without interference from the council in the form of amendments.[2]

In spite of the opposition of the home government, which never looked favorably upon the pretensions of the assemblies, the same policy was followed with more or less consistency in the other colonies.[3] When the question was raised in New Jersey in 1740, the Board of Trade declared that the council had an undoubted right to amend money bills; but such opposition from a distant authority could hardly effect much against a local representative body which held the purse-strings in its hands, and consequently the New Jersey House of Representatives continued to deny to the council the right of amending money bills.[4] In this matter, as in many others, the colonial assemblies showed that they regarded themselves as inheritors of the rights and privileges of the House of Commons.

It may easily be seen that the financial functions of the

[1] *New York Journal of Assembly*, i. 189–190, 201 ; Chalmers, *Revolt*, i. 358.

[2] *New York Journal of Assembly*, i. 306 *seq.*, ii. 289, 381 *seq.*, and *passim*, to the close of the volume.

[3] *Votes and Proceedings of the Lower House of the Assembly of Maryland*, April 28, 1756, May 9, 1758 ; *North Carolina Records*, vi. 909; *Pennsylvania Records*, iii. 534, vi. 40 ; *Votes of Pennsylvania*, iv. 516–522; *Morris Papers*, 283 ; *New Jersey Documents*, v. 10. The Maryland lower house, on April 28, 1756, spoke of its "ancient and undoubted Rights, in Case of all Bills for Grant of Aids or Supplies, to direct, limit, and appoint, in such Bills, the Ends, Purposes, Considerations, . . . and Qualifications, of such Grants, which ought not to be changed by the Upper House": *Votes and Proceedings*, etc., as above.

[4] *Morris Papers*, 84 ; *New Jersey Documents*, vii. 407, viii. 28–31.

governor were widely different from those of an executive intrusted with the preparation of the budget. He might simply recommend in general terms such appropriations as he desired, without having any part in the actual work of legislation. Indeed, the conditions that have just been described generally left the governor and council in the position of a mere accounting board, to check expenditures made in accordance with appropriations of the legislature.[1] Moreover, not content with this restriction of the governor's powers, the assembly went on to more radical measures, finally placing the actual administration of the finances in the hands of its own officers. The consideration of these measures will be taken up in connection with the study of the gradual assumption of executive functions by the assembly, either for itself or for its appointees.[2]

Certain minor functions intrusted to the governor may now be briefly considered. First and perhaps most important of these was the pardoning power, a common prerogative of the executive. In the English system the right of pardon belonged to the king, on the theory that criminal offences were offences against the crown; "for," says Blackstone, "it is reasonable that he only who is injured should have the power of forgiving."[3] This power, within certain limits, passed naturally to

[1] Even this right was sometimes interfered with, or at least not clearly recognized (see *New Jersey Documents*, xiv. 197; Cooper, *Statutes*, iii. 206 *seq.*, 333; South Carolina Historical Society, *Collections*, ii. 195). Of course the mere failure to mention the governor's warrant in appropriation bills is hardly conclusive evidence that it was not required in practice. In fact, the statute books of the different colonies contain frequent references to the governor's warrant as necessary for the expenditure of public money (*North Carolina Records*, v. 190; *New Hampshire Provincial Papers*, iii. 526–529; Hening, *Statutes*, iv. 26, 279; Cooper, *Statutes*, iii. 529; Allinson, *Acts of Assembly*, chs. 397, 631). There were some cases in which the assembly, by assuming itself the right to pass upon claims in detail, deprived this function of the governor and council of nearly all of its importance (see e. g. South Carolina Historical Society, *Collections*, ii. 195; cf. Cooper, *Statutes*, iii. 206; for action of the New Hampshire and Massachusetts assemblies, cf. below, p. 181.

[2] See below, ch. x.

[3] *Commentaries*, i. 269.

the governors, who represented the crown in the colonies. The proprietary charters of Maryland and Pennsylvania each conferred the right of pardon upon the proprietor, — the Maryland charter for all offences against the laws of the province, the Pennsylvania charter for all except cases of treason and wilful murder.[1] The royal commissions and instructions conferred the power upon the governor, with the same restrictions as those imposed by the Pennsylvania charter, granting him in those excepted cases the right of reprieve until the royal pleasure should be made known. He was also authorized to remit fines and forfeitures not exceeding ten pounds. This right of pardon was granted to him to be exercised independently, without reference to the concurrent action of the council.[2]

The rule just stated applies to all of the colonies, with the possible exceptions of Pennsylvania and of Maryland. In Pennsylvania the governor seems to have asked the advice of the council with reference to pardons, though the exact question of right is not clear.[3] The first recorded Maryland commission, that to Leonard Calvert in 1637, gave the governor the right of pardon except for high treason;[4] the commission to Charles Calvert in 1666 gave him indefinitely the full powers of the proprietor under the charter;[5] during the period when Maryland was a royal province, the pardoning power was granted in the same terms as in the other provinces;[6] and it seems probable, on the whole, that in this as in other matters the practice of the royal government was continued after the return to the proprietary constitution.

The general, almost universal rule, then, was that the gov-

---

[1] Charter of Maryland in Bozman, *History of Maryland,* ii. 9; of Pennsylvania, in Poore, *Charters and Constitutions,* ii. 1509.

[2] Commission to Bernard of New Jersey, 1758, § 17; to Allen of New Hampshire, 1692, p. 60; to Dobbs of North Carolina, 1761, p. 528. Cf. instructions to Bernard, § 56; to Dobbs, 1754, § 95; to Dunmore of Virginia, 1771, § 43.

[3] *Pennsylvania Records,* iii. 40–42, 110, iv. 503.

[4] Bozman, *History of Maryland,* ii. Appendix.

[5] *Maryland Archives,* iii. 543.

[6] See commission to Lionel Copley, 1691, p. 267; instructions, p. 275.

ernor exercised the pardoning power except in cases of treason and wilful murder; that he had the power of reprieve in those cases; and, finally, that his action was independent, not requiring the concurrence of the governor and council.

Other minor functions of the governor may be dismissed very briefly. The governor was the keeper of the public seal of the province, required in the more important state processes.[1] In many of the royal provinces he was authorized, with the advice of the council, to grant lands, reserving such quit-rents as seemed to him reasonable.[2] An extended consideration of this latter subject would bring up all the questions of land administration in the colonies, and is hardly in place here. It may, however, be noted that this power was especially liable to abuse. The governors of New York, in particular, were charged with corrupt management of the royal lands, on the ground that they granted them away for low quit-rents in return for certain arrangements by which they were to receive a share in the profits of the transactions.[3]

The right to issue charters of incorporation, including charters to towns, furnishes another interesting illustration of the governor's position as the representative of the crown. The king had the right to issue charters of incorporation;[4] hence in the provincial governments the governor was naturally invested with the same authority, though towns and other organizations were also incorporated by act of assembly.[5]

[1] Hartwell, Blair, and Chilton, *Present State of Virginia*, 20; Stokes, *Constitution of the British Colonies*, 185; commission to Bernard of New Jersey, 1758, § 13.

[2] Commission to Hunter of New York, 1709, p. 97; to Dobbs of North Carolina, 1761, p. 531; blank commission in Stokes, *Constitution of the British Colonies*, 162. Cf. instructions to Dunmore of Virginia, 1771, § 54; to Dudley of Massachusetts, 1702, p. 106.

[3] Lewis Morris to the Board of Trade, 1733, *New Jersey Documents*, v. 353. Cf. *Ibid.*, 363.

[4] Blackstone, *Commentaries*, i. 273.

[5] See charters of Maryland and Pennsylvania, in Bozman, *History of Maryland*, ii. 16; Poore, *Charters and Constitutions*, ii. 1512. For examples of charters issued by the governor, see *North Carolina Records*, iv. 43; *New Hampshire Provincial Papers*, ii. 107, 722, v. 90. For acts of assembly, see *New Hampshire Provincial Papers*, iii. 620, iv. 262;

Another prerogative was that of establishing markets, fairs, ports, and havens. The right was given to the governor by his commission,[1] and there are some illustrations of its exercise by the governor and council;[2] but here again the assembly sometimes interposed its action.[3]

The earlier royal governors possessed another power, which, if not always effective, at least involved an important principle. The royal instructions for a number of years immediately before and immediately after the beginning of the eighteenth century contained clauses authorizing the governor to exercise a sort of censorship of the press, that is, providing that no press was to be set up and no book or other matter printed without the governor's license.[4] This censorship was for some time actually enforced in Massachusetts, but finally broke down during the administration of Governor Shute. In 1719–1720 Shute attempted first to prevent and then to punish the publication of an attack by the House of Representatives upon the surveyor of the woods. The attorney-general and the council, however, declined to take any responsibility in the matter, asserting that there was no ground on which to support a prosecution; whereupon the governor complained to the Board of Trade, which, as Chalmers says, "observed the most prudent silence."[5] In 1721, Shute recommended a measure to punish the authors of factious and seditious papers. The House refused to take such action, however, resolving that "to suffer no books to be printed without license from the governor will be attended with innumerable inconveniences and danger."[6] "The last instance of an attempt to enforce

Hening, *Statutes*, iii. 94; *North Carolina Records*, v. 63. Cf. commissions to Bernard of New Jersey, 1758, § 20; to Allen of New Hampshire, 1692, p. 60; to Dobbs of North Carolina, 1761, p. 529.

[1] Commission to Bernard, § 24; to Allen, p. 61; to Dobbs, p. 531.

[2] *Maryland Archives*, v. 31, 47, 92.

[3] Cooper, *Statutes*, iii. 214–217; Hening, *Statutes*, iii. 54, 404, 428; Bacon, *Laws*, 1684 ch. 2, 1688 ch. 6; Jones, *Colonial Acts of Georgia*, 57.

[4] See instructions to Dongan of New York, 1686, p. 375; to Copley of Maryland, 1691, p. 279; to Allen of New Hampshire, 1692, p. 68; to Cornbury of New Jersey, 1702, § 98.

[5] Chalmers, *Revolt*, ii. 12, 19, 20.

[6] Hutchinson, *History of Massachusetts*, ii. 223.

the licensing of the press in Massachusetts " occurred in 1723, and the prosecution then failed.   The home government seems finally to have given up the obnoxious provision, omitting it altogether in the later instructions.[1]

The provincial governor represented the crown also in certain ecclesiastical privileges and functions.   The English king was the head and governor of the English church, though, as Blackstone says with some *naïveté*, the reasons on which this prerogative was founded were reasons rather of divinity than of law.   By virtue of this position the king exercised a certain control over the ecclesiastical assemblies of the realm; his assent was necessary to the validity of church canons; and he had the right of nomination to bishoprics and some other preferments.   He was, in short, the ultimate resort in all ecclesiastical causes.[2]

The subject of ecclesiastical jurisdiction in the colonies is by no means free from difficulties.   According to the royal commission issued to the Bishop of London in 1728, the colonies had not been subject to any ecclesiastical jurisdiction other than that of the king himself, as the supreme governor of the church of England.[3]   On the other hand, the royal instructions to governors of New York in 1686 and 1690 expressly refer to the ecclesiastical jurisdiction first of the Archbishop of Canterbury and then of the Bishop of London. At any rate, three important privileges were reserved to the governor by the commission and instructions: these were the rights of collation to benefices, granting marriage licenses, and probate of wills.[4]   The royal commission to Bishop Gibson in 1728 gave him a general spiritual jurisdiction over the colonial churches, and authorized him to appoint commissaries

---

[1] See C. A. Duniway, *The History of Restrictions upon Freedom of the Press in Massachusetts*, ch. 3. (Unpublished thesis in the library of Harvard University).

[2] Blackstone, *Commentaries*, i. 278.

[3] *New York Documents*, v. 849.   Cf. the letter of Bishop Sherlock in 1759, *Ibid.*, vii. 360.

[4] See commission to Dongan of New York, 1686, p. 379, and instructions, §§ 31–39; instructions to Sloughter of New York, 1690, p. 688.

in the colonies to act in his name.[1] The right of collation to benefices, however, remained as before in the governor's hands, together with the granting of marriage licenses and the probate of wills.[2]

Besides attending to these specific duties, the governor was expected to exercise a general oversight of the church in the province. He was required to see that "God Almighty be devoutly and duly served" throughout his government, and that the liturgy and other forms of the church of England were regularly observed. He was in general to support the Bishop of London in the exercise of his spiritual jurisdiction, and in particular to induct no ministers who were not duly certified by the bishop. When ministers proved unfit for their duties, the governor was to use the best means for securing their removal.[3]

In practice, this division of functions between the governor on the one side and the Bishop of London and his commissaries on the other, did not always work as smoothly as might have been wished. A classic illustration is the case of Commissary Blair of Virginia, who was engaged in constant altercations with Governors Andros and Nicholson of that province, the latter of whom in particular was charged with having seriously encroached upon the prerogative of the Bishop of London.[4]

The whole theory of the ecclesiastical authority of the governor and the Bishop of London was greatly disturbed by the action of the colonists themselves through their assemblies. In the Puritan colonies of New England, in Pennsylvania, Delaware, and New Jersey, the church of England had no legal recognition as an established church.[5] In New York a

---

[1] *New York Documents*, v. 849.

[2] See e. g. instructions to Morris of New Jersey, 1738, § 60; to Bernard of New Jersey, 1758, § 64.

[3] See instructions to Bernard of New Jersey, 1758, §§ 59–67; to Dunmore of Virginia, 1771, §§ 66–75. Cf. those to Dongan of New York, 1686, §§ 31–39.

[4] See various documents in Perry, *Papers relating to the History of the Church in Virginia*, 32 *seq.*, 131 *seq.*

[5] For New Jersey especially, see Allinson, *Acts of Assembly; New Jersey Documents*, iv. 155, 161; Burnaby, *Travels*, 102.

general act was passed for the establishment of six Protestant
ministers; but, though it contained no distinct reference to
the church of England, yet under its provisions Episcopal
churches were actually supported by public taxation.[1]   In the
Carolinas the church of England was in theory the established
church, and from time to time legal provisions were made
for its support.   This support, however, was very uncertain,
especially in North Carolina, and there was often no security
that the ministers and vestrymen would be *bonâ fide* adherents
to the established order of the church of England.[2]

Where there was an establishment, the governor's prerogative suffered through various statutory provisions enacted in
the interest of the vestries.   Virginia acts of 1642 and 1662
gave the parishes themselves the right of presentation, and
called upon the governor to induct ministers so presented.[3]
The royal attorney-general ruled that this right of presentation
lapsed after six months, and that the governor then had the
right to collate.[4]   As a matter of fact, however, ministers
were commonly not inducted at all, but were engaged from
year to year by the vestries, upon which they became almost
wholly dependent.   Indeed, the neglect of Governor Nicholson
to secure proper presentation and induction of clergymen
formed one of the most serious charges made against him by
Commissary Blair.[5]   In 1748 the assembly went a step farther,
by passing an act which declared expressly that the vestries
had the right of presentation for twelve months after a vacancy had occurred, a provision which the Bishop of London

[1] Act of 1693 in Trott, *Ecclesiastical Laws*, 263.   Cf. titles of acts of
1703 and 1705, *Ibid.*, 276; also Perry, *History of the American Episcopal
Church*, i. ch. ix., and illustrative notes, p. 171.

[2] See South Carolina act of 1706, in Trott, *Ecclesiastical Laws*, 5; Glen,
Description of South Carolina, in Carroll, *Historical Collections*, ii. 222;
Cooper, *Statutes*, ii. 366, iii. 174, iv. 266; North Carolina act of 1715, in
Trott, *Ecclesiastical Laws*, 83; *North Carolina Records*, vi. Preface, xxix-
xxxiii, and 10, 714, 720; vii. 150.

[3] Hening, *Statutes*, ii. 46.

[4] Opinion of Attorney-General Northey, 1703, in Perry, *Papers relating
to the History of the Church in Virginia*, 127.

[5] *Ibid.*, 132.

interpreted as taking away from the crown the patronage of all livings and giving it to the vestries.[1]

The situation in the Carolinas was less satisfactory than that in Virginia. In South Carolina the church act of 1706 provided that ministers should be chosen by a majority of the inhabitants of the several parishes "that are of the Religion of the Church of England"; and the practice of election seems to have been continued down to the revolutionary era.[2] In North Carolina the act of 1715 empowered the churchwardens and vestry to procure ministers; and there were various subsequent acts, which were disallowed by the crown because of encroachments upon the authority of the governor. Finally in 1765 an act was passed which was silent as to the right of presentation, leaving it, according to the interpretation of the Bishop of London, "in the crown to be exercised by the Governor by virtue of his Patent from the King."[3]

Nevertheless, the governor's ecclesiastical functions were by no means purely nominal. In Maryland the church establishment act of 1702 expressly provided for the maintenance of ministers, who were to be "presented, inducted or appointed" by the governor;[4] and the right of presentation seems to have been actually exercised later by the proprietor or the governor.[5] Furthermore, in North Carolina the governor and council had by statute the right to suspend ministers for improper conduct; and, in Virginia and Maryland at least, they acted as a species of ecclesiastical court.[6] It may fairly be said that, although the authority of the governor almost nowhere in practice reached the standard set by the royal commission and instructions, it was yet possible for him in many

[1] Perry, *Papers relating to the History of the Church of Virginia*, 462; Hening, *Statutes*, vi. 90.

[2] Trott, *Ecclesiastical Laws*, 5; Cooper, *Statutes*, ii. 366, iii. 174, iv. 266.

[3] Trott, *Ecclesiastical Laws*, 83; *North Carolina Records*, vi. Preface, xxix–xxxiii and 10, 714, 720; vii. 150.

[4] Bacon, *Laws*, 1702, ch. 1.

[5] Sharpe's Correspondence, *Maryland Archives*, vi., ix., *passim*, especially vi. 15, ix. 369 and index under "Livings."

[6] *North Carolina Records*, vii. 150; Hening, *Statutes*, iii. 289; *Dinwiddie Papers*, ii. 695; Bacon, *Laws*, 1702, ch. 1.

cases to exert a considerable influence for better or for worse upon the growth of the church within his province.[1]

In addition to all these specific powers enumerated in the commission and instructions, the governor was authorized to take provisional action in matters not covered by his commission, though in such cases the consent of the council must always be had, and immediate notice must be given to the home government. He was, however, specifically forbidden to declare war, except against the Indians in emergencies.[2] This provisional authority seems to be quite inadequately defined; but, according to a judicial interpretation, it applied only to cases in regard to which the instructions, as well as the commission, were silent, and could therefore not stand against any express directions of the instructions.[3] It was simply a provision for unforeseen contingencies, guarded from possible abuse by the requirement of immediate notice to the home government.

---

[1] In Georgia also there was an establishment, and the governor had the right of collating to benefices (Stokes, *Constitution of the British Colonies*, 120; Jones, *History of Georgia*, i. 524, act of 1758). Even in Massachusetts, among the traditions of the Puritan commonwealth, there was a curious illustration of one aspect of the king's ecclesiastical prerogative. In 1725 the Congregational ministers of Massachusetts desired to hold a synod, and presented a petition to the governor, council, and assembly for their sanction. The House and the council were willing to grant the petition, but action was postponed. The case was then laid before the home government, which held that the application to the General Court, instead of to the governor alone, was an infringement of the royal prerogative, inasmuch as the king's supremacy, being a branch of the prerogative, was applicable in the colonies as well as at home. It was accordingly decided that it was not lawful for synods to meet in Massachusetts without the royal license (Chalmers, *Opinions*, 44–53, and *Revolt*, ii. 31).

[2] See instructions to Bernard of New Jersey, 1758, § 88; to Dudley of Massachusetts, 1702, p. 115; to Dobbs of North Carolina, 1754, § 129; to Dunmore of Virginia, 1771, § 87.

[3] Opinion of Chief-Justice Morris of New Jersey, in Chalmers, *Opinions*, 203.

CHAPTER VII.

THE GOVERNOR'S RELATION TO THE JUDICIARY.

IN the study of the governor's powers, no systematic consideration has hitherto been given to his authority and duties in connection with the judicial and legislative departments of the provincial government. The question as to the relative importance of these different forces in the constitutional life of the province is of the highest consequence to a true conception of the governor's actual position. Of the two powers, the judiciary and the assembly, the latter was by far the stronger, the more nearly independent, and therefore from the present point of view the more important.

The governor in his relation to the judicial system of the province may first be considered. Here again the analogy of the royal prerogative proves useful. In the English constitutional tradition, the king was "the fountain of justice and general conservator of the peace of the kingdom"; hence he had the right to erect courts, the processes of which ran in his name and were executed by his officers; he was moreover the prosecutor in criminal cases, because all such offences were committed "against the king's peace, or his crown and dignity." In course of time, however, practice had seriously modified this traditional theory. The king had originally possessed judicial power in himself; but gradually the actual administration of justice had passed into the hands of courts, the jurisdiction of which could not be changed without act of Parliament, and the independence of the judges had come to be secured by commission not as before during the king's pleasure, but during good behavior.[1] In practice, therefore, the English judiciary had gained a degree of independence of the crown quite inconsistent with the ancient tradition.

[1] Blackstone, *Commentaries*, i. 266–268.

In the commissions of the royal governors is found an interesting survival of the old theory. The governor, for example, was empowered by his commission to erect courts of justice; as has been already seen, he also had the appointment of judicial officers; and, finally, he formed with the council the highest court of appeal in civil cases. At first these powers, like those of the king, were much more extensive; but the organization of inferior courts and other legislation of the assembly soon brought them within narrower limits. Since the question as to the appointment of judicial officers has already been considered under the general head of the appointing power, it will be enough here simply to state the general rule, namely, that judges and justices of the peace were appointed by the governor with the consent of the council.[1] The question as to the tenure of judicial offices deserves somewhat more particular attention, in that it affected the relation of the governor to the judiciary.

It is obvious that a system of appointments during good behavior is far more favorable to the independence of the judiciary than appointment during pleasure. The early instructions were not clear on this point, directing merely that there should be no removals without just cause, which was to be made known to the home government, and that there should be no limitation of time in the commissions issued to judicial officers. These provisions were made, as the instructions declared, in order to prevent arbitrary removals, though it is not clear how this result was to be produced unless offices were to be held during good behavior.[2] Whatever the intention may have been, there seems to have been no uniform practice, though it is certain that in many of the colonies judges were appointed to serve during good behavior, and that in some colonies acts were passed to enforce this principle.[3]

[1] See above, p. 111. An exception must be made in the case of the provincial chief-justice, who during the latter part of the colonial era was appointed by the crown.

[2] Instructions to Dongan of New York, 1686, § 26; to Hunter of New York, 1709, § 43; to Cornbury of New Jersey, 1702, § 41.

[3] See additional instruction to governors of Nova Scotia, New Hamp-

The home government, however, stated distinctly its dis-
approval of the practice. In 1751 the assembly of Jamaica
passed an act providing that all judges of the supreme court
should hold office during good behavior, and the act was referred
to the law officers of the crown for their opinion. The latter
held that the provision seriously affected the royal prerogative,
and that under the circumstances it was not "advisable, either
for the interest of the plantations themselves, or of Great
Britain," that the colonial judges should hold office during
good behavior.[1] In 1754 the instructions to Governor Dobbs
of North Carolina contained distinctly the requirement that
commissions should be granted during pleasure only.[2]

Nevertheless, judicial commissions continued to be given
during good behavior, and acts were passed in Pennsylvania in
1759 and in North Carolina in 1760 definitely prescribing that
form of tenure. Early in the year 1761 the New York assembly
also passed a bill for the same purpose, but it was defeated by
the opposition of the governor. The Pennsylvania and North
Carolina acts were disallowed by the crown. In passing upon
the New York case, the Board of Trade insisted on the enforcement of the royal instructions on this point.[3] The result
was that an additional instruction was issued in December,
1761, reciting the previous neglect of the royal orders, and
charging the governors, on pain of removal from their posts,
to assent to no acts regulating in any way the tenure of judicial officers, and to issue all commissions during pleasure only,
"agreeable to what has been the Ancient Practice and Usage
in our said Colonies and Plantations."[4]

This decision of the home government was still strongly
resisted. The assemblies of New Jersey and New York
declared their intention of granting no salaries to judges

shire, New York, New Jersey, Virginia, the Carolinas, Georgia, etc., *New
Jersey Documents*, ix. 329. Cf. *Ibid.*, vii. 651, ix. 312, 346; *North Carolina Records*, vi. 255.

[1] Chalmers, *Opinions*, 433.   [2] § 62.

[3] *New Jersey Documents*, ix. 312 *seq.*; *Pennsylvania Colonial Records*,
viii. 543; *North Carolina Records*, vi. 587 *seq.*; *New York Documents*, vii.
462, 470, 484.

[4] *New Jersey Documents*, ix. 329.

unless the commissions were during good behavior.[1]   Nevertheless, the Board of Trade determined to enforce the rule; and accordingly in 1762 Governor Hardy of New Jersey was removed for disobedience in this respect, even though, before his actual removal, he had reversed his former action and had succeeded in getting the justices to accept commissions during pleasure.[2]   By the year 1765 Lieutenant-Governor Colden was able to report that the rule was enforced in New York also.[3] The popular feeling of opposition continued, however, and finally found expression in the well-known clause of the Declaration of Independence, which states, as one of the grievances against the king, the fact that "he has made judges dependent on his will alone for the tenure of their offices."

The arguments by which the home government justified its action deserve some attention.   In answer to the declaration of the people of New York, that such commissions in England were granted during good behavior and that sound policy required the same action in the colonies, the Board of Trade insisted that colonial appointments stood on an entirely different footing, saying that in England the principle of tenure during good behavior had been adopted on account of the arbitrary action of the crown prior to the revolution of 1688, and apparently assuming that no such danger existed in the colonies.   A special reason assigned for making appointments in the colonies during pleasure only was that there the material available for such offices was of poor quality; it was believed to be desirable that, when a man of superior talents was once found, the removal of inferior men who stood in the way of his appointment should be as easy as possible.

Another reason assigned for the adoption of a different rule in the colonies was that by the general practice of the colonial assemblies salary grants were made temporary, whereas in England they were fixed by permanent appropriations.   It was claimed that, without this unlimited right of removal, the crown or its representative would be forced to see the

<hr />

[1] *New Jersey Documents*, ix. 346; *New York Documents*, vii. 489.

[2] *New Jersey Documents*, ix. 361, 364, 368.

[3] *New York Documents*, vii. 796–797.

judiciary become completely subservient to the assembly; the Board, therefore, condemned the rule of tenure during good behavior as destructive of the interests of the subject and as "tending to lessen that just Dependance which the Colonies ought to have upon the Government of the Mother Country."[1] It may fairly be assumed that in this last clause we have the real secret of the royal opposition to the permanence of judicial appointments.

In addition to this means of influencing the judiciary, the governor was assigned by his commission the right, with the advice and consent of the council, to erect courts of justice, though limited in the exercise of this power by his instructions, which usually forbade him to erect new courts without a special order from the crown. He was further directed to see that in these courts justice was impartially administered.[2] This power of erecting courts was the subject of a very vigorous controversy. The practice in the different colonies, and even in the same colony at different times, varied so much that it is impossible to make any accurate generalization; but it is easy to find numerous instances in which courts were established by the action of the governor and council. Thus, chancery courts were in most cases established without any legislative process;[3] and in New Jersey the early judicial system was based mainly upon ordinances of the governor and council.[4] There are instances, too, in which, in the absence of any legislation, the governor was expressly directed to pro-

---

[1] Representation of the Board of Trade, *New Jersey Documents*, ix. 312 *seq.*

[2] Commission to Bernard of New Jersey, 1758, § 15; to Allen of New Hampshire, 1692, p. 59; to Dobbs of North Carolina, 1761, p. 528. Instructions to Bernard, §§ 33, 34; to Allen, p. 66; to Dunmore of Virginia, 1771, §§ 38, 39.

[3] *New York Documents*, iv. 914, 929; *Pennsylvania Records*, iii. 105. See also the opinion of Attorney-General Northey, in 1704, to the effect that the queen could by her prerogative erect a court of equity in Massachusetts, and that the General Court could not do so according to the terms of the charter: Chalmers, *Opinions*, 195.

[4] Field, *Provincial Courts of New Jersey*, App. C, D (ordinances establishing courts). Later ordinances run in the king's name (*Ibid.*, App. E, F).

vide for the necessary courts. This was the case in North Carolina, where in 1754 the instructions to Governor Dobbs, after declaring the repeal of the judiciary act of 1746, provided for deficiencies by directing the governor with his council to establish courts of justice. In Pennsylvania similar action was taken in 1707.[1]

On the other hand, acts of assembly were constantly passed, erecting courts and defining their jurisdictions; in fact, it may be said that, as a rule, courts were established and organized by such acts, and not by ordinances of the governor and council.[2] Yet this circumstance did not necessarily imply a denial of the legality of the latter method. For example, in 1705 Virginia passed an act establishing the General Court of that province, and declaring also that the courts therein named should be the only courts of record in the province; in order to avoid misunderstanding, however, an explanatory act expressly recognized the right of the crown to erect courts.[3]

Nevertheless, it must be said that there was also very general opposition to the exercise of this power by the governor, a very widespread feeling that such action was illegal. In Pennsylvania, where ordinances of this sort were several times passed, the assembly denied the governor's right to take such action.[4] In South Carolina also, the court of exchequer erected by Governor Nicholson was regarded as exercising an illegal jurisdiction;[5] and the New York assembly, in 1727, condemned the action of the governor in erecting a court of chancery without the consent of the assembly.[6] In short, so good an author-

[1] Instructions to Dobbs of North Carolina, 1754, § 41; *Charter and Laws of Pennsylvania*, 319.

[2] *North Carolina Records*, iv. 337; Martin, *Iredell's Public Acts*, i. 40, 74, 112, 117; Cooper, *Statutes of South Carolina*, iii. 179, vii. 163 *seq.*; *New Hampshire Provincial Papers*, iii. 183, 218; *Acts and Laws of New Hampshire* (1771), ch. 4; *Charter and Laws of Pennsylvania*, 395 *seq.*; Allinson, *New Jersey Acts of Assembly*, chs. 172, 193; Hening, *Statutes of Virginia*, iii. 95-96, 287, 489.

[3] Hening, *Statutes*, iii. 489.

[4] *Votes of Pennsylvania*, i. pt. ii. 158.

[5] Chalmers, *Revolt*, ii. 166.

[6] Smith, *History of New York*, 229-230.

ity as Thomas Pownall declares that the right of the governor to erect courts was "universally disputed."[1] The home government, too, seems to have recognized the propriety of action by the assembly; for the instructions to Governor Lovelace of New Jersey, in 1708, contained a clause directing him to recommend to the assembly the passage of an act creating a court for the trial of small causes.[2] It appears therefore that, although the governor was authorized by his commission to erect courts with the consent of the council, he was by his instructions restricted in the exercise of this power; that courts were regularly established and organized by acts of assembly; and that the right of the governor to erect courts by ordinance was very generally disputed.

A third method by which the governor made his influence felt upon the provincial judiciary was a necessary consequence of his position as chief executive. As such it was his duty to see that the laws were duly enforced; with him, or with agents appointed by him, lay the enforcement of judicial decisions; and with him also rested in part the duty of prosecution. The attorney-general of the province, though not always appointed by the governor, was subject to his orders; and prosecutions might be ordered by the governor and council, or, when once begun, might be suspended by their order.[3] It is clear that in these various ways the governor had an important influence for good or evil upon the administration of justice.

Hitherto attention has been given only to the action of the governor upon the judiciary power from without, through his influence in the constitution of the courts and in the enforcement of judicial decisions, — powers which, with the exception of the right to erect courts, are normal functions of the executive. The governor was more than an executive officer,

[1] *Administration of the Colonies*, 75 seq.

[2] Instructions, § 53, *New Jersey Documents*, iii. 322. Cf. instructions to Bernard, 1758, § 33.

[3] See *New Jersey Documents*, ix. 482, xiv. 486; Allinson, *Acts of Assembly*, ch. 23; Bacon, *Laws of Maryland*, 1715 ch. 48, 1722 ch. 5.

however: he was himself a part of the judicial system.   In the early days of the colonies there was, as has been seen, very little scientific definition of powers; the administration of justice was then in some cases almost entirely in the hands of the governor and council.   As time went on, the organization of courts, by acts of assembly or otherwise, naturally brought the governor's activity within much narrower limits; but in nearly all the colonies something of his old judicial power survived.

The governor's criminal jurisdiction seems for the most part to have passed away; but in Virginia the governor and council, under the name of the "General Court," continued to be the highest court in all cases, criminal as well as civil.[1]

The most important judicial function of the governor and council was the hearing of appeals in civil cases in which the value in question exceeded a certain fixed sum.[2]   This amount varied in different provinces: in the instructions to Lord Cornbury, in 1702, the right of appeal to the governor and council was limited to cases involving more than one hundred pounds sterling;[3] a Maryland statute of 1713 directed that appeals should lie from the provincial court to the governor and council only in cases involving more than fifty pounds;[4] an additional instruction of 1753 raised the minimum value for which a suit might be carried to the governor and council to three hundred pounds.[5]   In order to guard against abuses, a further right of appeal to the Privy Council was instituted by which appeals were allowed in cases involving from two hundred to five hundred pounds.   Appeal to the home government was

---

[1] Hening, *Statutes*, ii. 532 (charter of 1676), iii. 287, 489; Hartwell, Blair, and Chilton, *Present State of Virginia*, 20.

[2] See instructions to Bernard of New Jersey, 1758, §§ 39, 40; to Allen of New Hampshire, 1692, p. 68; to Dobbs of North Carolina, 1761, §§ 60, 61; to Dunmore of Virginia, 1771, §§ 41, 42.   Exception must be made of the colonies of Massachusetts, Pennsylvania, and Delaware.   Cf. *Laws of Delaware* (1797), i. 374; Proud, *History of Pennsylvania*, ii. 286.

[3] § 85.   [4] Bacon, *Laws*, 1713, ch. 4.

[5] *New Jersey Documents*, viii. (1) 188.

thus ordinarily possible only when very considerable sums of money were involved.[1] There were also several other conditions tending to discourage the reference of suits to the crown, one of which was the requirement that the appellant should give notice of appeal within fourteen days and furnish bonds to answer the charges in case the sentence should be confirmed; and still another lay in the fact that the process of appeal to a distant tribunal necessarily involved great inconvenience and expense. The result was that the governor and council were inadequately checked in the exercise of their judicial functions.[2]

The governor was furthermore the keeper of the province seal, and as such was, in theory at least, chancellor with jurisdiction in equity cases, for the trial of which courts were set up in nearly all the colonies. In some provinces the governor himself constituted the chancery court; in others the governor and council were judges, each with an equal vote in the decision of the court.[3] That this equity jurisdiction of the governor was generally distrusted is plainly seen in the popular view of the matter as given by Douglass in his "Summary": "It is said that a Governor and such of the Council as he thinks proper to consult with, dispense with such Provincial Laws as are troublesome or stand in their Way in Procedures of their

[1] Instructions to Bernard, §§ 39, 40; to Cornbury, §§ 85, 86. It should be said, however, that in answer to petitions in special cases the crown might and did allow appeals involving smaller amounts. See opinion of Attorney-General Northey, in Chalmers, *Opinions*, 490.

[2] Cf. Hartwell, Blair, and Chilton, *Present State of Virginia*, 26, 46.

[3] *New Hampshire Provincial Papers*, iii. 186; *Massachusetts Province Laws* (i.), 1692-3 ch. 33, § 14, 1693-4 ch. 12; Pownall, *Administration of the Colonies*, 80; *Pennsylvania Records*, iii. 105; Hartwell, Blair, and Chilton, *Present State of Virginia*, 20; Hening, *Statutes of Virginia*, iii. 291; Bacon, *Laws of Maryland*, 1721, ch. 14; Cooper, *Statutes of South Carolina*, vii. 163, 191; *North Carolina Records*, iii. 123, 150; Field, *Provincial Courts of New Jersey*, 113-114; *New Jersey Documents*, xiii. 553, xiv. 521; ordinance of 1753, in Allinson, *Acts of Assembly*, Appendix; *History of the British Dominions in North America*, ii. 120; Douglass, *Summary of the First Planting of the British Settlements in North America*, ii. 256-257. The governor's chancery court in Massachusetts seems to have been abandoned (cf. Douglass, as above).

Court of Equity, so-called."[1] This popular distrust of the chancery court without doubt impaired its efficiency in no small degree. In Pennsylvania it met with serious opposition from the assembly, which soon refused to recognize its authority.[2] In New York the governor's equity jurisdiction, though denounced by the assembly, was able to maintain a somewhat precarious existence; but it was held in contempt and was generally avoided, as indeed, according to Governor Pownall, seems to have been the case in other colonies in which such courts had been established.[3]

Other judicial powers of the governor may be considered very briefly. As a part of his ecclesiastical jurisdiction, he had the probate of wills and the issue of marriage licenses;[4] either alone or with the council he usually acted as a court of probate;[5] in Massachusetts and New Hampshire at least the governor and council constituted a court for the decision of questions of marriage and divorce.[6] The governor was also named in the royal commission for the trial of piracy cases, which usually included the governors of a few adjacent colonies, with some other officers of the colonial service.[7]

Thus the governor, besides having an indirect influence upon the administration of justice through his control over the

---

[1] II. 33, 49.

[2] *Pennsylvania Records*, iii. 617, iv. 38–46. Note the absence of reference to the chancery court in Proud's account of the courts, *History of Pennsylvania*, ii. 86.

[3] Smith, *History of New York*, 230; Pownall, *Administration of the Colonies*, 81.

[4] See instructions to Bernard of New Jersey, 1758, § 64; to Dobbs of North Carolina, 1754, § 105; to Dunmore of Virginia, 1771, § 72.

[5] Hening, *Statutes of Virginia*, iv. 16; Bacon, *Laws of Maryland*, 1715, ch. 39, § 27; South Carolina Historical Society, *Collections*, ii. 286; Massachusetts charter of 1691, in Poore, *Charters and Constitutions*, i. 942; *Massachusetts Province Laws* (i.), 1692–3, chs. 14, 46; *New Hampshire Provincial Papers*, ii. 500; *Laws of Delaware* (1797), i. 92, and cf. 427.

[6] *Massachusetts Province Laws* (i.), 1692–3, ch. 25; *New Hampshire Provincial Papers*, ii. 249, iii. 277.

[7] Stokes, *Constitution of the British Colonies*, 231–232; instructions to Bernard of New Jersey, 1758, § 80, and to Dunmore of Virginia, 1771, § 64; *New Jersey Documents*, ix. 282.

organization of the courts and the machinery of enforcement, was himself a part of the judicial system, in one important class of cases forming with the council the highest court of appeal within the province. It is clear that under such a system the independence of the judiciary must have been seriously impaired; indeed, so conservative a writer as Hutchinson speaks of the judges during one administration as distinctly dependent upon the governor,[1] referring specifically in this case to Belcher's frequent removals of judicial officers.

Furthermore, numerous cases might be cited of gross abuse by the governor of his influence upon the administration of justice. A classic illustration of such abuse is seen in the judicial murders of Berkeley's time; and another striking example of the same improper influence appears in the case of Nicholas Bayard of New York, who was tried and convicted of high treason by a packed court and jury, and sentenced to be hung and quartered, merely because he had made certain injudicious criticisms of the provincial administration.[2] Again, there is a case in which a governor grossly abused his power over the Supreme Court in order to gain his personal ends. Governor Cosby of New York had ordered a suit before the Supreme Court in a case involving the payment of his salary. The court ruled that this was a case in equity of which it could not take cognizance; whereupon the governor sent an abusive message to Chief-Justice Morris, declaring him unfit for his position, and shortly appointed in his place one of the judges who had given an opinion favorable to himself. Cosby declared that the removal of Morris was necessary in order to discourage the advocates of "Boston principles," which was a general term for opposition tendencies. In the famous Zenger case, Cosby used all his influence to bring about the conviction for libel of the man who published Morris's criti-

---

[1] *History of Massachusetts,* ii. 336–337, notes.
[2] Howell, *State Trials,* xiv. 471; *New York Documents,* iv. 945–974 *passim,* 1023.

cism of the governor's action; and he was defeated only by the bold appeal of Zenger's counsel to the jury.[1]

Clearly, a judiciary so constituted and so controlled could hardly have exercised any effective check upon the governor; and furthermore the process of appeal to the home government was so difficult as to be worth little as a restraint upon his action.

[1] See *New Jersey Documents*, v. 327, 340, 343, 356; also report of the case in Howell, *State Trials*, xvii. 675; *New York Documents*, vi. 4.

CHAPTER VIII.

THE GOVERNOR'S POWER OVER THE ASSEMBLY.

ATTENTION may now be turned to the governor's relation to a body which had a far more important influence in the constitutional history of the colonies, namely, the General Assembly, or General Court, as it was variously called.

A word must first be said as to the constitution of the assembly. In all the royal and proprietary governments, except Pennsylvania, it consisted of two houses, — the council appointed on the governor's recommendation, and a lower representative house. In Pennsylvania, as has already been seen, the councillors were excluded from direct participation in legislation, though the governor was required to take their advice. This requirement was very unpopular with the assembly, which naturally felt that in this way the council became practically an upper house.

The governor, by his commission, had other important powers in the constitution of the assembly. In the first place, the calling of the assembly was left in his hands, subject, however, to the advice and consent of the council: no assembly could even come into existence without his action.[1] This power was limited in two ways, however, first by specific requirements of charter or statute, and secondly by the practical necessity of calling assemblies in order to get supplies. In two colonies, Pennsylvania [Delaware] and Massachusetts, the charters, though giving to the governor the right of summons, required annual elections and sessions at

---

[1] Commission to Bernard of New Jersey, 1758, § 7; to Allen of New Hampshire, 1692, p. 58; to Dobbs of North Carolina, 1761, p. 526.

fixed dates.[1] In a few other colonies there were triennial or septennial acts, which required the calling of a new assembly at the end of a fixed period of time, but still left the governor comparatively free.[2] By far the more important check, however, from a practical point of view, was to be found in the financial necessities of the provincial governments. An assembly which held the purse-strings could not be dispensed with; and the result was that annual sessions became the rule in nearly all the colonies, though there were some exceptions. The Virginia statutes, for example, show several considerable gaps: from 1686 to 1691 there was no legislation and apparently no legislature, also from 1715 to 1718, and finally from 1748 to 1752, periods of three and four years.[3] It will be remembered that in Virginia official salaries were paid out of a permanent fund.

The right of summons has another aspect in its bearing upon the election of members of the lower house, or House of Representatives. Elections to this body were held regularly in accordance with writs issued by the governor to the sheriffs directing the choice of a certain number of representatives from each district.[4] The question then arises as to whether the governor had any discretion in the issue of the writ, so far, for example, as to determine the number of members who should be returned from a particular district, or to grant the right of representation to a new district. To this it may be said that in general the writ of summons was purely formal, though sometimes the question was raised in a practical form. An example is seen in a petition of the Maryland House, in 1676, protesting against the proprietor's abuse of the right of summons; the petition admitted the right of the proprietor (then governor) to determine the number to be elected, but

---

[1] Pennsylvania "charter of privileges," in Poore, *Charters and Constitutions*, ii. 1536; Massachusetts charter of 1691, *Ibid.*, i. 942.

[2] See below, pp. 155 *seq.*

[3] See Hening, *Statutes*, iii., iv., vi.

[4] See e. g. *Ibid.*, iii. 236; *North Carolina Records*, iv. 534; Cooper, *Statutes of South Carolina*, iii. 50–55. In South Carolina the churchwardens formed a part of this machinery of election.

there was dissatisfaction because, out of four persons elected, only two had been called out by writ to serve. The governor agreed at that time to summon four.[1] In 1681 and 1682 the lower house attempted to regulate the number of representa-tives by statute; but the proprietor resisted, and finally himself issued an ordinance regulating the representation. Thereupon the House demanded something more permanent, asking the passage of an act for that purpose; but the gov-ernor refused to surrender his prerogative. The appointment of delegates and the form of the writ were, however, finally settled by statute.[2]

A similar question arose in North Carolina, where com-plaint was made that Governor Burrington and his council ar-ranged electoral districts without the consent of the assembly in order to control elections. The governor insisted that he had precedents; but this claim the assembly denied, and finally went so far as to exclude members from new precincts not fixed by act of assembly. For a time the point was gained, and the representation was fixed by acts of assembly.[3] Finally, how-ever, the home government interfered: the acts of assembly creating electoral districts were disallowed, and the principle was laid down that the right to elect members ought to be con-ferred only by the crown, a principle which was carried out in the form of proclamations issued in the king's name by the governor.[4] In New Hampshire also the same point was the occasion of a contest, in which after long deadlocks the assembly was finally beaten.[5] A different position was taken in New

[1] *Maryland Archives*, ii. 507.

[2] *Ibid.*, vii. 118-125, 236, 333, 355, 452; Bacon, *Laws*, 1716, ch. 11.

[3] *North Carolina Records*, iii. 380, 383, 445, 576, 583, 611; Martin, *Iredell's Public Acts*, i. 67.

[4] Chalmers, *Opinions*, 271-292; *North Carolina Records*, v. 81-92, 341, 406; instructions to Dobbs, 1754, §§ 13-16. Cf. *North Carolina Records*, v. 767, and Iredell, *Laws of North Carolina*, 109.

[5] *New Hampshire Provincial Papers*, v. 260-265, 295, vi. 70-82, 125, 128-129, 138, 161, 840, 883. The additional instruction to Governor Ben-ning Wentworth, in 1748, took the ground that the right to send repre-sentatives was founded in the commission and instructions, and that it was the prerogative of the crown to extend the privilege as it chose (*Ibid.*, vi. 82).

Jersey, where the original apportionment of representatives was made in the governor's instructions. New assignments, however, were here fixed by acts of assembly, although these acts were passed with a clause suspending execution till the crown should give its assent.[1] In the other colonies the crown apparently made at first no objection to apportionment by acts of assembly; in fact, this method formed the general rule until the latter part of the colonial period, when the governors were specifically forbidden to assent to any act increasing the number of members of the assembly.[2]

Owing to the fact that elections were held in accordance with the governor's writs addressed to the sheriffs, who were his appointees, the governor had some opportunity to influence the election of members. Indeed, corruption of this kind was distinctly charged against several provincial governors; and in a report on the condition of the colonies, made to the Board of Trade in 1715, the governors generally were accused of influencing elections unlawfully.[3] It must be said, however,

[1] Allinson, *Acts of Assembly*, chs. 44, 125, 160, 207, 474; instructions to Cornbury, 1702, § 15.

[2] Bacon, *Laws of Maryland*, 1716, ch. 11; Hening, *Statutes of Virginia*, iii. 414; Cooper, *Statutes of South Carolina*, iv. 37; *Massachusetts Province Laws, passim*. By the Massachusetts charter the General Court had the right to apportion the representation of the towns; by ch. 38 of the acts of 1692-3 each town of forty qualified voters was required to send one representative; towns having one hundred and twenty qualified voters might send two members. For acts creating towns with full privileges, see *Massachusetts Province Laws* (ii.), 1724-5, ch. 13; 1728-9, ch. 20; 1735-6, ch. 10. For later rules on this point, see instructions to Dunmore of Virginia, 1771, § 14; to Dobbs of North Carolina, § 16; circular instruction, 1767, in *New Jersey Documents*, ix. 637.

[3] *North Carolina Records*, ii. 159. For charges brought against Moore of South Carolina in 1701, see Oldmixon, *British Empire in America*, i. 475; *Party-Tyranny in Carolina*, 13; *Case of the Dissenters*, 18. See the suggestions of Chalmers in the case of Governor Bellomont of New York, Chalmers, *Revolt*, i. 289-290. Bellomont himself says that he removed the sheriffs appointed by his predecessor and chose new men "well affected to the King," a phrase which seems sometimes to be used as if synonymous with "well affected to the governor." Similar charges were brought against Lord Cornbury in New Jersey; and the feeling in this province is further illustrated by the passage of an act, in 1725, designed to prevent improper

that this charge is supported by comparatively little direct evidence during the latter part of the colonial period.

After the assembly had once met, the governor of the colony claimed some control over the organization of the House. The royal commission contained the apparently innocent provision that the regular oaths of allegiance and fidelity should be administered by the governor to the members of the assembly, and that no one should be permitted to sit until he had taken the oath.[1] This practice seems generally to have been a mere formality; but in two colonies the governor attempted to make such use of the function as to impair the ancient parliamentary privilege of the right of the assembly to judge of the election of its members. For example, Governor Belcher of New Hampshire claimed that he had the right to judge what members were duly elected; the House took a decided stand against this assumption, and refused to proceed to business till the members in question were qualified; whereupon the governor yielded and administered the oath.[2] Similarly, Governor Cornbury of New Jersey refused, at the suggestion of his council, to swear certain members whom the council declared not qualified; and though he succeeded in having his way for the time being, yet he was censured by the Board of Trade, which wrote that his lordship would "do well to leave the Determination about Elections of Representatives to that House, and not to intermeddle therein."[3] It is clear, then, that the governor's interpretation was not sanctioned by the home government.

In nearly all the colonies it was customary, in accordance with the usage of the mother country, to present the newly-elected speaker to the governor for the latter's approval. In England this presentation had become a mere formality, and

action at elections on the part of sheriffs and others. See *New York Documents*, iv. 508; *New Jersey Documents*, iii. 87; Allinson, *Acts of Assembly*, ch. 116.

[1] Commission to Bernard of New Jersey, 1758, § 8; to Allen of New Hampshire, 1692, p. 58; to Dobbs of North Carolina, 1761, p. 526.

[2] *New Hampshire Provincial Papers*, iv. 680–684.

[3] *New Jersey Documents*, iii. 87 *seq.*, 100.

it appears to have been so in most of the colonies; the governor seems usually to have given his approval as a matter of course, even when, as in one instance in North Carolina, the choice must have been extremely distasteful to him.[1] There were, however, a few cases in which this usually formal procedure became of practical importance. In 1707, Governor Cornbury of New Jersey strongly objected to the assembly's choice of Samuel Jennings, a Quaker, as speaker, and was at first inclined to reject the appointment; but in order to avoid trouble, he finally decided to approve it, though he seems to have had no doubt of his legal right to negative the choice of the assembly.[2]

In Massachusetts the presentation of the speaker seems at first, as in most of the other colonies, to have been regarded as a mere formality.[3] When, however, in 1705, the House chose as speaker one Oakes, to whom Governor Dudley strongly objected, the latter refused to give his approval; whereupon the House ignored the governor's action and proceeded to business. Dudley finally yielded, but with a formal protest that he did so with a saving of his prerogative and owing to the pressure of the war.[4] The claim was revived under more favorable circumstances in 1720, when Governor Shute negatived the speaker chosen by the House, supporting his action by the opinion of the home government given at the time when the question was referred to it by Dudley. Shute advised the House to choose a new speaker, and to appeal to the home government for an explanation of that part of the charter which referred to the governor's negative upon all acts of the General Court. The House, however, held its ground,

---

[1] *Maryland Archives*, i. 397, 460; *Votes and Proceedings of the Lower House*, Dec. 12, 1754, and Sept. 28, 1757; *Votes of Pennsylvania*, i. pt. i. 44, 102, 108; Stokes, *Constitution of the British Colonies*, 127. Note especially the North Carolina case, *North Carolina Records*, iii. 540. Cf. *Ibid.* 360, 431.

[2] *New Jersey Documents*, iii. 224.

[3] See e. g. *Massachusetts Province Laws*, i. 90, note; Hutchinson, *History of Massachusetts*, ii. 17.

[4] Hutchinson, *History of Massachusetts*, ii. 17, 137; *Sewall's Diary*, ii. 130, 132.

refusing to choose a new speaker, and was dissolved. In 1721 the assembly chose another speaker. The governor declared his approval, which the House then pronounced unnecessary.[1] The dispute was finally settled by the so-called "explanatory" charter, which decided the question against the assembly.[2] In New Hampshire also the same point was successfully asserted by the governor, and his veto was sometimes used with effect.[3]

After the House had thus been summoned, had met, and had organized itself, the governor still had great power over it, inasmuch as the continuance of its sessions depended entirely upon his will, at least so far as the terms of the royal commission could confer that power. The governor was authorized by his commission to adjourn, prorogue, and dissolve all general assemblies as he might think necessary; and by a later instruction he was directed not to allow the assembly to adjourn itself except from day to day. To this general rule two exceptions must be noted. In Pennsylvania the charter provided for annual elections, and directed also that the assembly should sit on its own adjournments; but these provisions did not at first prevent the governor from exercising

---

[1] Hutchinson, *History of Massachusetts*, ii. 211, 214–215, 226, 241.

[2] Poore, *Charters and Constitutions*, i. 954.

[3] *New Hampshire Provincial Papers*, iv. 485–488. The veto was first used in 1728, when the House submitted, but declared the wisdom of their first choice. Governor Benning Wentworth made effective use of this power in his disputes with the assembly concerning the governor's right of summons. In 1749 began a deadlock, which lasted till 1752, when the assembly was dissolved; whereupon the new assembly chose another speaker, who was acceptable to the governor (*Ibid.*, vi. 70–82, 125, 129–130). Frequently the clerk of the assembly was appointed by the governor (Hening, *Statutes of Virginia*, iii. 41; Hartwell, Blair, and Chilton, *Present State of Virginia*, 28; *North Carolina Records*, iii. 354, 576; *Maryland Archives*, i. 261, ii. 63, 439, v. 505–506, vii. 3, 523; Stokes, *Constitution of the British Colonies*, 127; *New Jersey Documents*, iii. 226–227). In South Carolina the assembly's choice of a clerk was regularly at least subject to the governor's approval. In 1732 the governor was ordered to commission a particular person as clerk. (South Carolina Historical Society, *Collections*, ii. 119, 134; Chalmers, *Revolt*, ii. 170).

his powers of prorogation and dissolution. In Massachusetts there was a similar charter provision for annual elections and annual meetings; but the power of prorogation and dissolution remained within these limits.[1]

In regard to the question of prorogation, it was held by the crown law officers that the governor might prorogue to any time or to any place, that he might even prorogue an assembly when not in session.[2] How was this power actually exercised? In the first place, assemblies that proved refractory were often prorogued, in the hope that a short interval of consideration might bring them to a more favorable mood.[3] Furthermore, it was charged by the assemblies, and probably with some truth, that the governor also used this power merely as a means of harassing the assembly in the hope of forcing it to accede to his demands.[4] This view seems to be taken for granted by Douglass in his "Summary," where he says that the governor "calls, dissolves, prorogues, adjourns, removes, and other ways harasses the General Assembly at Pleasure."[5]

There can indeed be no doubt that assemblies were sometimes prorogued in order to prevent them from taking action not in accordance with the governor's wishes. A serious charge of this sort was brought against Governor Belcher when he was governor of both Massachusetts and New Hampshire. The crown, it seems, had recommended that the assembly of each province appoint commissioners to present its boundary

[1] See the charters of Massachusetts and Pennsylvania respectively, in Poore, *Charters and Constitutions*, i. 942, ii. 1536. Cf. *Votes of Pennsylvania*, i. Appendix, xv, and i. pt. ii. 16; commission to Bernard of New Jersey, 1758, § 12, and to Dobbs of North Carolina, 1761, p. 527; instructions to Dunmore of Virginia, 1771, § 15.

[2] Chalmers, *Opinions*, 239–243, 249. These rights were disputed in Massachusetts and North Carolina (Hutchinson, *History of Massachusetts*, ii. 241, 245; *Massachusetts Province Laws*, i. 363, ii. 234; *North Carolina Records*, ii. 576).

[3] See e. g. *North Carolina Records*, vi. 243–244, 828; *New Hampshire Provincial Papers*, i. 545.

[4] *New York Documents*, vi. 626; *New Jersey Documents*, xiv. 177.

[5] *Summary of the First Planting of the British Settlements in North America*, i. 474.

claims; and it was charged against Governor Belcher, who was a Massachusetts man by birth and whose sympathies were strongly on the side of that province, that he prorogued the assembly till some days after the date fixed for the meeting of the arbitrators; it was also charged that he afterwards prevented the assembly from meeting in time to appeal from the decision as reported by these arbitrators. For this conduct he was severely censured by the home government.[1] Other instances occurred in 1765 and 1768, when the governors of New York and Georgia used their right of prorogation in a similar way to prevent action by their assemblies on the Stamp Act Congress and the Massachusetts circular letter.[2] It must be remembered, too, that this control over adjournments worked both ways: if the governor might adjourn or prorogue the assembly against its will, he might also keep it in session equally against its will.[3]

The question in regard to dissolution now occurs. Prorogation merely ended a particular session; dissolution terminated the life of an assembly: it is therefore not difficult to see that the governor, with this power of dissolution in his hands, had a very effective hold upon the assembly. This right belonged to the governor in every colony except Pennsylvania where it was disputed and seems finally to have been abandoned.[4] Dissolution was a common method of getting rid of an obstinate assembly, in the hope of securing one which would prove more tractable. For example, Governor Shute dissolved the Massachusetts General Court in 1720, with the announcement that he would serve out a new summons speedily, when he

---

[1] *New Hampshire Provincial Papers*, iv. 864, v. 921–923; report of Lords of Council, in Belknap, *History of New Hampshire*, ii. 168. Cf. Hutchinson, *History of Massachusetts*, ii. 349–350.

[2] Almon, *Prior Documents*, 36, 217.

[3] See e. g. Hutchinson, *History of Massachusetts*, ii. 306–309, notes.

[4] " We sit upon our own adjournments, when we please, and as long as we think necessary; and we are not to be sent a packing, in the middle of a debate, and disabled from representing our just grievances . . . which has often been the fate of Assemblies in other places ": speech of Andrew Hamilton, in Proud, *History of Pennsylvania*, ii. 217. Cf. *Votes of Pennsylvania*, i. pt. ii. 16.

hoped that representatives would be chosen "that should fear God, and honour the King"; and Governor Johnston of North Carolina declared that the assembly had failed to "mend" and that he had therefore dissolved it.[1] The assembly was sometimes dissolved because the governor feared action inconsistent with his own interests. Thus, Governor Reynolds of Georgia was charged with having dissolved an assembly, with the taxes of the coming year unprovided for, in order to prevent an inconvenient inquiry into the conduct of one of his favorites.[2] Of course the dread of dissolution must have had some influence upon the action of members who were by no means sure of being returned at a new election; but on the whole it may be questioned whether the dissolution of a refractory assembly brought the governor any very great advantage in the long run, especially during the latter part of the colonial era, when the issue between local interests as represented by the assembly and royal interests as represented by the governor became more clearly marked, and when an abrupt dissolution would have tended to emphasize that issue more sharply. The result of such action might very well have been that a new election would be fatal to many of the governor's supporters, and that the new house would be more decided in its opposition than its predecessor.

Another feature of the right of dissolution, and perhaps on the whole a more dangerous one, was the power to refuse dissolution. If it was desirable to dissolve an unfavorable assembly, it was just as clearly desirable to keep a compliant one when once chosen, a consideration which often caused assemblies to be kept in existence for several years. For example, in Virginia the assembly which was first called in February, 1727, held its second session in May, 1730, its third session in May, 1732, and its fourth session in August, 1734. Another striking case is that of the assembly of 1742,

---

[1] *Sewall's Diary*, iii. 255; *North Carolina Records*, iv. 243. In New Hampshire the frequent dissolutions under Governor Belcher gave great dissatisfaction. They were due chiefly to failure to agree upon supply bills (*Provincial Papers*, iv. 679, 688).

[2] Jones, *History of Georgia*, i. 512.

which held its second session in 1744, its fourth in 1746, and its fifth in 1747.[1] The New Hampshire assembly of 1722 presented as a grievance the fact that it was five years since it first met, and prayed for a dissolution.[2] In another case in the same province, the governor refused to dissolve the assembly till the king's business was done, that is, till an appropriate supply was granted.[3] Hamilton, in his famous speech in defence of Zenger, referred to the case of a governor in his time who had kept an assembly for "near twice seven years together."[4]

That the necessity of limiting the action of the governor in the exercise of his functions of summons, prorogation, and dissolution was strongly felt, is seen in the large number of triennial and septennial acts passed in the different colonies. Reference has already been made to the charter provisions in Pennsylvania and Massachusetts. In some of the other provinces there survived traditions of a freer practice before the days of the royal government. Thus, South Carolina during the proprietary period had passed a statute limiting the life of an assembly to two years, and providing that sessions should be held at least once a year, closing, however, with a saving of the proprietors' prerogative to adjourn, prorogue, and dissolve any assembly "when and as often as they shall think fit."[5] In 1721, the second year of the royal government, a similar act was passed, requiring dissolution once in every three years.[6] Under the act of 1745 an annual dissolution was required; but this action seems to have been regarded as radical, for two years later a provision was made for dissolution only once in two years.[7] In North Carolina there had been a biennial assembly act during the proprietary period, but it was disallowed by the crown.[8] In East and West Jersey under

---

[1] See Hening, *Statutes*, iv., v.
[2] *New Hampshire Provincial Papers*, iv. 24.
[3] *Ibid.*, v. 562.
[4] Howell, *State Trials*, xvii. 708.
[5] Cooper, *Statutes*, ii. 79.   [6] *Ibid.*, iii. 135.
[7] *Ibid.*, 657, 692.
[8] Martin, *Iredell's Public Acts*, i. 9; *North Carolina Records*, ii. 213.

the proprietors, provisions for annual elections had been made; and in West Jersey the assembly adjourned itself.[1]

These precedents naturally had their influence upon the action of the assemblies. In 1723 the New Hampshire assembly passed a triennial act with a suspending clause; the bill was not favorably received by the home government, however, and it became evident that the royal assent was not likely to be given. In 1728 a new bill was brought in and passed; but this time the assembly prudently omitted the suspending clause, declaring with questionable logic that failure to disallow the act proved that it was not offensive to the crown.[2] Other attempts to enact triennial laws proved less successful. New Jersey passed a triennial act in 1728, but it was disallowed by the crown; and a similar bill passed the assembly in 1739, only to be vetoed by the governor.[3] In New York a triennial act was passed in 1737, and a strong message was sent home by the assembly urging the royal assent. In this appeal, reference was made to the long continuance of the last two assemblies as a serious grievance, and particular emphasis was laid on the fact that the corrupting influence of patronage upon the assembly was so great that "in some Counties," to use the words of the message, "even their very Representatives have become themselves their greatest Grievance." The Board of Trade, on consultation with its counsel, declared the act an infringement of the royal prerogative, and recommended its disallowance; a few years later, however, a poor substitute was secured in a septennial act, limiting the continuance of the assembly to seven years.[4] Virginia passed a septennial act in 1762, requiring that a session should be held at least once in three years.[5] Finally, in 1767, the home government declared itself definitely on the whole subject of such limita-

---

[1] Leaming and Spicer, *Grants, Concessions*, etc., 368, 423-424.

[2] *New Hampshire Provincial Papers*, iv. 114-115, 117, 126-127, 146, 468-469, 472, 489, 492; *Acts and Laws of New Hampshire* (1771), ch. 107.

[3] Allinson, *Acts of Assembly*, ch. 133; *Morris Papers*, 74, 124.

[4] *Documentary History of New York* (1849-51), iv. 245-256; *New York Documents*, vii. 353, viii. 444; *Laws of New York*, 1691-1773, ch. 746.

[5] Hening, *Statutes*, vii. 517.

tions of the governor's power, by a general instruction of that year directing the governors not to assent to any act fixing the duration of the assembly.[1]

As the motives that led to the passage of these acts are plainly apparent, so those which animated the opposition to them seem equally clear. It was believed that such acts tended to weaken the dependence of the colonial legislature upon the governor, and therefore its dependence upon the crown, whose representative he was. .Governor Montgomerie of New York and New Jersey probably stated accurately the feelings of many of his fellow-governors when, in urging the disallowance of the New Jersey triennial act, he said that his predecessors "could not have carried on the publick business so quietly and Successfully as they did, if they had been obliged to call a new Assembly every three years."[2]

In addition to these constitutional means of influence, there was another effective method by which the governor acted on the assembly, namely, through his power of dispensing patronage, a function that in many of the provinces was undoubtedly an element of considerable importance. Thus, according to a contemporary writer, the independence of the Virginia assembly was seriously impaired by the assignment of offices to various members of the lower house.[3] Similar charges were made in Massachusetts; in a pamphlet issued in this province in 1708, entitled "The Deplorable State of New-England," is an interesting passage which shows at least something of the state of popular feeling at the time.[4] The writer attributes the gover-

---

[1] *New Jersey Documents*, ix. 637. A year later the New Jersey assembly passed a septennial act with a suspending clause. In Allinson's collection of New Jersey statutes (ch. 473), the text of this act is followed by a note explaining that the act had never received the royal assent, but was inserted on the " Probability that so reasonable a law will be regarded." Whether this expectation was reasonable may well be doubted; on the other hand, the limitation imposed was so slight that the temptation to violate it could hardly have been serious.

[2] *New Jersey Documents*, v. 236.

[3] Hartwell, Blair, and Chilton, *Present State of Virginia*, 27–28.

[4] " It must needs be a Mortal Sin, to Disoblige a Governour, that has

nor's influence over the representatives to his distribution of official patronage. Allowance must of course be made here for extreme partisanship; but much the same view is gained from more trustworthy sources.[1] The New York assembly, in urging the passage of the triennial act, had emphasized the corrupting influence of official patronage upon the members of the assembly.[2] Maryland furnishes an extreme illustration of the same point. It was at one time a favorite policy of the proprietor, and of his secretary, to win over the members of the opposition by appointing them to provincial offices. At one time, indeed, an elaborate system of corruption was proposed, by which the assembly was to be kept permanently under control.[3]

Something should be said in regard to the attempts made by the various assemblies to check this dangerous abuse. In 1678 the question was raised in the Maryland assembly as to whether the proprietary sheriffs or law officers should be allowed to sit in the assembly. Soon afterwards an act was passed disqualifying sheriffs and ordinary-keepers (who received their licenses from the governor); and three years later the assembly enforced its view by throwing out all sheriffs who had been elected members.[4] In 1716 an act was finally passed disqualifying for membership in the assembly ordinary-keepers and all other persons disqualified to sit in the British Parliament.[5] In 1757 the lower house passed a radical measure, disqualifying for election to the assembly all holders of proprietary offices; providing, furthermore, that if any person

Inabled a Man to Command a *whole Country Town,* and to Strut among his Neighbours, with the Illustrious Titles of, *Our Major,* and, *The Captain,* or, *His Worship " : The Deplorable State of New England* (1708), 21.

[1] For example, Hutchinson says of both Shirley and Pownall that they used official patronage as a means of influencing the assembly : *History of Massachusetts,* iii. 57.

[2] *Documentary History of New York* (1849–51), iv. 245. Clarke of New York seems to have been a serious offender (see *New Jersey Documents,* vi. 75).

[3] *Maryland Archives,* vi. 183, ix. 331, 375 *seq.,* 423.

[4] *Ibid.,* vii. 17, 63, 114.

[5] Bacon, *Laws of Maryland,* 1716, ch. 11.

within six years after ceasing to be a member of the assembly should hold any office of trust or profit, or receive any pension, he should be fined one thousand pounds; and, finally, forbidding members to solicit offices for their friends under penalty of a fine of the same amount.[1] This was an extreme measure, and was of course rejected by the upper house;[2] but it is interesting, because it shows that civil service reform had made some progress in Maryland even at that early date.

A Virginia act of 1730 disqualified sheriffs absolutely, and provided that members accepting other offices of profit should resign their seats, though they might be re-elected. A similar act was passed in 1762.[3] A South Carolina statute of 1745 disqualified salaried officers of the province for membership in the assembly.[4] The New York assembly, after an attempt to disqualify all officers, finally in 1770 passed an act disqualifying judicial officers for sitting in the assembly; but the act was disallowed by the crown.[5] These are comparatively insignificant results, but they are at least interesting as showing an appreciation of the evils which they were designed to correct.

Thus far attention has been given to the indirect action of the governor upon legislation through his influence over the assembly. But the governor was not limited to this indirect influence: he was himself a part of the legislative system. Some of the early governors had been invested with legislative authority, either independently or with the coöperation of the council; but, as has been seen, this abnormal condition gradually passed away, leaving to the governor only a limited right of issuing ordinances and the power to approve or veto the legislation of the assembly.

Reference has already been made to the governor's right of issuing ordinances or proclamations of two classes, namely,

---

[1] *Votes and Proceedings of the Lower House*, Dec. 8, 1757.
[2] *Ibid.*, Dec. 16, 1757, May 4, 1758.
[3] Hening, *Statutes*, iv. 292, vii. 529.
[4] Cooper, *Statutes*, iii. 657.
[5] *New York Documents*, viii. 206–207, 215.

those for the regulation of fees and those for the erection of courts. It will be remembered also that in both of these cases his use of this authority gave rise to serious disputes.[1] With these exceptions, however, the issue of ordinances by the governor seems as a rule to have been kept within reasonable bounds, and complaints of his exercise of the power are comparatively rare. The most common of the ordinances issued by him were proclamations enforcing the provisions of statute or treaty, and regulations regarding subjects that might fairly be considered matters of executive concern. Some instances may be taken almost at random. Thus, in the Virginia statutes is a proclamation regarding settlement on the outlands in time of danger; another forbidding the seating of certain lands near the North Carolina border; a third establishing regulations for trade with the westward Indians.[2] Again, the governor of North Carolina is recommended by his council to issue a proclamation regulating the sale of liquor to Indians.[3] A Maryland proclamation of 1672 prohibits the export of sheep, a measure intended to check evasion of the statute prohibiting the export of wool.[4] During the French and Indian troubles the New Hampshire council, at Governor Dudley's direction, issued an ordinance requiring the registration of all Frenchmen within the province.[5] In 1721 the governor of Massachusetts, anticipating war with the Indians, issued an order to the frontier settlers directing them to remain on their estates and keep possession of the country; and though his authority was questioned, yet some extension of the power to issue ordinances may be justified by the stress of military necessity.[6] Another case, which seems more distinctly an encroachment upon legislative ground, is the ordinance issued by the governor of New Jersey in 1717 in regard to the regulation of ferriage.[7] On the whole, however, it may fairly be

[1] See above, p. 118 *seq.*, 137 *seq.*
[2] Hening, *Statutes*, iv. 546, 552–553.
[3] *North Carolina Records*, iv. 45, and cf. 41–42.
[4] *Maryland Archives*, v. 105.
[5] *New Hampshire Provincial Papers*, ii. 429.
[6] Hutchinson, *History of Massachusetts*, ii. 236.
[7] Allinson, *Acts of Assembly*, ch. 78.

said that there is no evidence of general or serious abuse of the power of issuing ordinances.

The governor was furthermore, as has been said, a part of the regular legislative system of the province, acting with the coöperation of the council and assembly: the commission empowered him, with the consent of the council and assembly, to make laws not repugnant but, as nearly as might be, agreeable to the laws of England.[1] In theory this power seems considerable. How much did it actually mean in practice?

In some of the colonies during the earliest period there had been, as has been seen, an effort to secure for the governor the right of initiative in legislation. All such attempts had failed, however; and during the later period also any attempt on the part of the governor to initiate legislation was regarded with great suspicion. This feeling was so strong, indeed, that when Governor Wentworth of New Hampshire sent down the draft of two orders on money matters, to be passed upon by the House, his action was resented as tending to impair the independence of the assembly.[2] In reality, the governor had the bare right of recommending legislation; and this he usually did in his speech delivered before the assembly at the beginning of its sessions. In this speech he ordinarily gave some account of the condition of the province, and, in time of war, of the conduct of military operations or of negotiations with the Indians; he then advised the passage of laws necessary to meet the needs of the province, usually urging as his most prominent recommendation the passage of a supply act.[3] The governor was also made the medium through which the home government communicated with the assembly, receiving always in his instructions a number of articles directing him to recommend the passage of particular legislation desired by the crown.[4]

[1] Commission to Bernard of New Jersey, 1758, § 9; to Allen of New Hampshire, 1692, pp. 58–59; to Dobbs of North Carolina, 1761, p. 527.

[2] *New Hampshire Provincial Papers*, vi. 64.

[3] For an illustration of a governor's speech, see that of Governor Wentworth in 1752, *Ibid.*, 130.

[4] For example, Governor Bernard of New Jersey was in 1758 required to recommend acts for the following purposes: for the prevention of the in-

Since the right of recommendation necessarily carried with it very little actual power, the governor was left to find his really important legislative function in his right to approve, or to refuse to approve, bills passed by the council and the representative house. The commission gave him a negative vote on all laws, statutes, and ordinances, "to the end that nothing may be passed or done by Our said Council or Assembly, to the Prejudice of us, Our Heirs and Successors."[1] Furthermore, this veto was not merely suspensive: there was no such thing as passing a bill over the governor's head.

On the other hand, the governor's right of assent to legislation was neither final nor unrestricted, inasmuch as bills approved by him were still liable to disallowance by the crown at any time. The home government required that all acts passed by the provincial assemblies be sent over, within three months after their passage for approval or disallowance by the crown;[2] and although such acts were in force until actually disallowed by the crown, yet this disallowance might take place at any time without any limitation. When, however, an act was once confirmed by the crown, it could not be repealed except in the regular course of legislation.

In the second place, the governor was restricted in his right of assent to legislation, in that there were certain kinds of

human treatment of servants and slaves; for the enforcement of the marriage discipline of the church of England and of military discipline; and for the maintenance of schools. See instructions, §§ 37, 66, 67, 73.

[1] Commission to Bernard of New Jersey, 1758, § 11; to Allen of New Hampshire, 1692, p. 59; to Dobbs of North Carolina, 1761, p. 527.

[2] Instructions to Bernard, §§ 28–30 (cf. commission, §§ 9, 10); to Allen, p. 64 (cf. commission, p. 58); to Dobbs, 1754, § 37 (cf. commission, 1761, p. 527). For the proprietary governments, see above, pp. 13 *seq.* The Massachusetts charter of 1691 specified that disallowance must be declared within three years; otherwise repeal might take place only by act of assembly. This provision was sometimes evaded by the practice of not beginning to count the three years until the time when the bills were actually laid before the Privy Council. They were often withheld by the Board of Trade (*Massachusetts Province Laws*, i. 486, notes). Acts of the Pennsylvania assembly might be disallowed within six months of their delivery to the Privy Council (Chalmers, *Opinions*, 336).

bills that he was forbidden to approve, a precaution intended
in particular to protect imperial or British interests against
injurious local legislation. He was not, for example, to allow the final enactment of bills for the issue of paper money,
or to approve acts imposing discriminating duties on British
ships or manufactures.[1] Some of these acts might be passed
with the so-called "suspending clause," by which execution
was suspended until the royal consent could be given; but
others were forbidden absolutely. Sometimes a penalty was
annexed; that is, the governor was forbidden to pass particular
acts on pain of the royal displeasure and of recall from his
province.[2]

These restrictions, however, were much more easily imposed
than enforced. The colonists generally believed that they
were unreasonable, that they were infringements of the inherent legislative independence of the assemblies, and consequently they usually resisted instructions of this kind. Thomas
Pownall, who was certainly entitled to speak with some authority, declared: "In some cases of emergency, and in the cases
of the concerns of individuals, the instruction has been submitted to, but the principle never."[3] The instructions prohibiting the issue of paper money, or, in the proprietary
colonies, those forbidding the taxation of proprietary estates
presented peculiar difficulties. If, as sometimes happened, an
assembly absolutely refused, unless such acts were passed, to
appropriate military supplies urgently needed for the conduct
of the war, what was the governor to do? It was almost in-

[1] Instructions to Bernard, §§ 22, 25. Other instructions forbade the
governor to pass, without a suspending clause, statutes repealing laws then
in force. He was to pass no private acts without a saving of the queen's
rights and those of other persons, and no temporary acts unless for distinctly temporary ends. See *Ibid.*, §§ 14, 15, 17. Cf. also §§ 16, 20, 21,
23, 26.

[2] See e. g. the instruction in regard to paper money, *New Jersey Documents*, vi. 95–96. Cf. instructions to Bernard, § 22.

[3] Pownall, *Administration of the Colonies*, 39–47. Cf. *Votes of Pennsylvania*, iv. 571 : the assembly, in 1756, resolved that the deputy-governor
"has, or ought to have, full Powers to give his Assent to all such Bills as
we have an undoubted Right to offer."

evitable that he should do what in the majority of cases he actually did, that is, yield to the pressure thus put upon him.

The assemblies soon learned to make the most of these difficulties and to increase them by various expedients, one of which was the practice, pursued in direct defiance of the royal instructions, of inserting items entirely foreign to the main body of the bill, of attaching legislative riders to bills appropriating money. Thus in an act for the inspection of tobacco the Maryland assembly inserted sections limiting officers' fees;[1] and in the supply bill of 1759 the North Carolina assembly inserted a provision for the appointment of an agent.[2]

Another device was that of coupling the supply bill with some other act desired by the assembly, and refusing to pass the one till the other had received the governor's assent. Thus, the North Carolina assembly of 1760 refused to pass the aid bill until certain other measures were approved by the governor.[3] In 1715 Governor Hunter of New York wrote that the revenue act had been passed in return for his assent to the naturalization act.[4] Again, in 1741, the assembly of the same province resolved that it would not raise any support for the government unless the governor first assented to all the bills that it had sent or should send up to him.[5] In 1759 the governor of New Hampshire presented to the House an additional instruction, directing the assembly to settle salaries on the judiciary; whereupon the House replied that it would settle suitable salaries on the justices when the province was divided into three counties, and not before.[6] Furthermore, the assembly, through its control of the governor's salary, was able to appeal to more selfish motives.

Under these circumstances, what wonder is it that instructions were constantly violated? That they were so violated is proved by abundant evidence. In 1749 Governor Johnston

---

[1] Bacon, *Laws*, 1763, ch. 18.
[2] *North Carolina Records*, vi. 34.   [3] *Ibid.*, 402 *seq.*
[4] *New York Documents*, v. 416.
[5] *Morris Papers*, 142.
[6] *New Hampshire Provincial Papers*, vi. 718, 726.

of North Carolina apologized for assenting to a paper-money bill, urging that only in this way could he raise the necessary supplies; and the first royal governor of South Carolina violated his instructions by passing a similar act.[1] New Hampshire also furnishes a striking illustration of the governor's difficult position. In 1745, in response to a request from the assembly asking the passage of a bill for the issue of paper money, Governor Wentworth of that province referred to his instructions prohibiting such action, and refused to pass the desired bill. He afterwards yielded, on condition that a committee of the assembly should instruct its agent to implore the crown to excuse his action.[2]

These few illustrations, which might easily be multiplied, are in accord with the general testimony of the home government; indeed, the order requiring that laws should be sent to England for approval was so often evaded that the crown had frequently no opportunity whatever to pass upon the legislation of a provincial assembly.[3] It is clear, then, that the royal restrictions upon the governor's power of assent to provincial legislation were by no means universally observed, that they often proved ineffective against a strong popular sentiment.

[1] *North Carolina Records,* iv. 922; Chalmers, *Revolt,* ii. 97.

[2] *New Hampshire Provincial Papers,* v. 279, 336, 338. For other illustrations, cf. *Ibid.,* vi. 513 *seq.; North Carolina Records,* vi. 589–591; *New Jersey Documents,* ix. 332; Pownall, *Administration of the Colonies,* 41 *seq.*

[3] See the circular of the Lords of Trade in 1752, reciting the general neglect of royal instructions, *New York Documents,* vi. 760; see also above, pp. 66, 67.

CHAPTER IX.

THE POWER OF THE ASSEMBLY OVER THE GOVERNOR.

Two aspects of the governor's relation to the legislature have now been considered: first his influence in the constitution of the assembly and upon its individual members, and secondly the part assigned him in the direct work of legislation. It is now time to pass to a consideration of the other side, to a study of the control which the assembly was able to exercise over the governor and of the use which it made of that control in its gradual assumption of executive powers properly belonging to the governor.

In the first place, the assembly was a check upon the governor through its very existence as a critical body empowered to inspect accounts and eager to detect abuses in the provincial administration; furthermore, it gave to the public sentiment of the province a constitutional means of expression; it organized public sentiment and thus made it effective. The value of such influence is easily underrated: an assembly which performs this function, even though it be without any power of legislation or without the control of the purse, has yet in its hands a weapon against arbitrary government which is not to be despised.

The assembly might control the executive by legislation directly limiting the governor's powers, although such legislation was ineffective unless it received the governor's assent. It is true that laws might be enacted with the consent of a weak or short-sighted governor, the repeal of which his successor would find it difficult, perhaps impossible, to secure; still, in order to be effective, this line of attack required some means of forcing the governor's assent.

By far the most important check upon executive action possessed by the assembly was certainly that exercised through its power over the purse. Inasmuch as no government can maintain itself without money, it is evident that a body which has the power to grant or refuse supplies holds the key to the situation. Such was the case in all the colonies, as has been already noticed. No principle was more firmly held than this, that no taxation within the province was legal without the consent of the assembly, and this doctrine came more and more to mean the domination of the lower house in all financial legislation.

Inasmuch as the general question of supply has already been treated somewhat fully in connection with the governor's financial powers, it will be enough here to state the main conclusions there reached. These were, that in nearly all the colonies even the bills for the support of the ordinary administration of government were temporary, often indeed for a space of only one year; that even in those colonies in which there was a permanent civil list it was constantly necessary to make demands for other purposes; and that these demands were often, as in time of war, of the most urgent kind. In the last chapter was seen something of the way in which this power of granting supplies was used by the assemblies.

There is one phase of the general subject regarding the assembly's control of the purse which requires a special treatment, namely, that which may for convenience be called the salary question. A consideration of this topic involves, in the first place, a study of the process by which temporary and even annual salary grants became established in most of the colonies, with some consideration of the arguments advanced on both sides of the controversy. In the second place, the effect of the practice will be noticed.

The crown very early adopted the policy of throwing the support of the provincial governments, including the granting of official salaries, upon the provincial assemblies. Until the institution of the royal government in Georgia, there was but one government, royal or proprietary, — that of North Carolina, — in which the civil list was not provided for by either temporary or permanent acts of assembly.[1] It soon became clear, however, that, if salaries were to be granted by the assembly, this body must in the long run control the amount of those salaries, and must even have the power to withhold them if it should see fit. This was a dangerous situation from the standpoint of the home government, which soon awoke to an appreciation of the fact that, with a governor dependent for his support upon the temporary grants of the assembly, the crown would lose one very strong hold upon the colonies. In two provinces, Maryland and Virginia, the issue was decided very early, in favor of the proprietor and the crown respectively, by the settlement of definite funds for this purpose.[2] Elsewhere the result was very different, though the same demand was made in all the other colonies.

By the earlier instructions it was required of all the assemblies that no money should be granted to the governor directly, but that the grant should be made to the crown with the request that it be appropriated to the governor's use if her majesty thought fit, otherwise to some other purpose stated in the act of grant; until the royal pleasure should be known the money was to remain in the hands of the royal receiver.[3] The governor was further directed to recommend a permanent settlement of salaries.[4] It would appear, however, that the requirement of royal assent to salary grants was almost universally ignored, and that the recommendation to settle salaries fell upon unwilling ears. In 1703 the crown therefore found it necessary to issue special instructions on this subject, reciting the evil effects of temporary grants in the colonies and urging the necessity of fixed salaries; the assembly was called upon to settle a salary upon the governor without limitation of time; and, when that was once done, no governor was to accept a present from the assembly on pain of the royal

---

[1] See above, p. 59.　　　　[2] *Ibid.*

[3] Instructions to Allen of New Hampshire, 1692, p. 65; to Cornbury of New Jersey, 1702, § 21.

[4] Instructions to Cornbury, § 22. For permission formally given to Lord Bellomont in Massachusetts to receive £1000, see *Massachusetts Province Laws*, i. 419.

displeasure and of recall from his province.[1] Some other instructions even went so far as to insist that the governor should
accept nothing less than a permanent settlement.[2]

These demands were easily made; but how were they received
by the assemblies? This question, involving a consideration
of the general controversy that sprang up throughout the
colonies, may perhaps be studied to best advantage by following the course of the contest in the provinces of New York and
Massachusetts.

In New York the policy of making temporary salary grants
appears plainly as early as 1707. An interesting letter of that
year pointed out that the revenue of the province was to expire
in 1709 and that although some of the opposition were resolved
not to renew it, yet a more far-sighted party proposed to make
grants, though only from year to year in order to insure the
dependence of the governor upon the assembly. Governor
Hunter then appealed to the crown to settle a salary upon
the governor, and in 1711 the Board of Trade went so far as to
recommend, but without success, that a parliamentary revenue
be established in New York.[3] Then followed a succession of
grants for fixed terms of years;[4] but finally the House resolved to grant revenue for one year only, and from that time
the government had to put up with annual grants.[5] The
crown still persisted in its demands, but without success:
the assembly declared that it would never give more than temporary support.[6] When in 1755 these repeated demands met
with another determined refusal, the Board of Trade appeared
at last to recognize the hopelessness of its task, declaring that
it was advisable to allow the governor to accept temporary

---

[1] *New Hampshire Provincial Papers*, iii. 251; cf. *New York Documents*, iv. 1040.

[2] See e. g. Hutchinson, *History of Massachusetts*, ii. 301 *seq.*, 333 *seq.*
Cf. *New Jersey Documents*, iii. 99; *Massachusetts Province Laws*, ii. 633.

[3] *New Jersey Documents*, iii. 238; Chalmers, *Revolt*, i. 365-366.

[4] *New York Journal of Assembly*, i. 375, 448, 580, 585, 646; *New York
Documents*, v. 877-882.

[5] *New York Journal of Assembly*, i. 700, 734.

[6] Chalmers, *Revolt*, ii. 315-316.

grants, and, though it held the refusal of the assembly to be unwarrantable, instructing the governor not to press the matter.[1] Clearly this step was hardly less than an unconditional surrender.

In Massachusetts, as has already been noted, the issue was very early defined. According to Chalmers, there was in this province a very considerable party composed of those who were dissatisfied with the new charter, and who hoped to find some compensation in a policy of temporary salary grants.[2] Under the first two governors, Phips and Bellomont, these temporary grants, or presents, were all that the assembly could be induced to vote.[3] In 1703 came the additional instruction already cited, calling upon the assembly to grant a settled revenue, in reply to which Governor Dudley wrote that for the present nothing could be done.[4] Again, in 1705, the General Court was urged to make a permanent settlement; but the House in its reply argued that, since the ability of the province varied at different times, it was not expedient that salaries should be permanently fixed.[5]

The efforts of Dudley's successor, Governor Shute, met with no better success. In despair of accomplishing any result with the assembly, he recurred to the idea previously acted upon by Governor Hunter of New York, and petitioned the king to settle a permanent salary upon the present governor and upon all succeeding governors in New England.[6] The Board of Trade reported that a salary ought to be settled and paid by the crown to the governor until the people of New England could be induced to make permanent grants; but this recommendation was not adopted, and Governor Shute was again instructed to recommend in strong terms the settlement of a fixed salary.[7]

---

[1] Chalmers, *Revolt*, ii. 318–320; *New York Documents*, vii. 32, 39.

[2] *Ibid.*, i. 234.

[3] *Ibid.*, 236. Cf. *Massachusetts Province Laws*, i. 109, 174, 394, 419, 437.

[4] Chalmers, *Revolt*, i. 330.

[5] Hutchinson, *History of Massachusetts*, ii. 137, 139.

[6] *Townshend Papers*, 272.   [7] *Ibid.*, 273.

The crisis of the struggle came under Shute's successor, Governor Burnet, who was instructed to insist on a permanent settlement, and who declared his determination to adhere strictly to his instructions.[1] Both parties in the struggle were now equally determined to hold their ground, and both stated their positions with perfect definiteness. The governor pointed to the precedent of the British constitution, with its careful provisions for the independence of each department of the State, calling attention especially to that one which secured the independence of the crown by a permanent civil list. He urged that the dependence of the executive was the weak point of the colonial constitution, and that the remedy lay in placing the office on an independent footing, claiming that the avowed purpose of keeping the governor dependent upon the assembly by means of temporary salary grants was not honorable, inasmuch as such a course prevented him from acting freely and according to his own judgment upon matters of legislation coming before him. As evidence that this was the real intention of the House in refusing permanent grants, he reminded it that it had often kept back the governor's allowance until other bills had been approved.[2]

The popular argument, on the other hand, is best stated in a message of the House in August, 1728.[3] As against the governor's reference to the British constitution, the Representatives urged that that argument could not be regarded as conclusive, claiming furthermore, that even on the analogy of the British constitution no part of the government ought to be wholly independent, since it was only by mutual dependence that the proper balance could be preserved. They called attention to the fact that, although the governor was dependent on the assembly for his salary, the assembly was in many ways dependent on the governor. In reply to the governor's suggestion that the temporary salary granted to the governor, in contrast with the permanent provision made by Parliament

[1] Hutchinson, *History of Massachusetts*, ii. 301 *seq.*
[2] Speech and messages of Governor Burnet, in *House Journal*, 1728, July 24, August 9, September 3.
[3] Message of the House, August 31.

for the support of the crown, showed a lack of proper confidence in the governor, they urged, while maintaining that their policy implied no lack of confidence, that the governor's tenure was too uncertain to give him any strong interest in the prosperity of the province such as the king had in the mother country. In another resolution the House laid down the same principle, declaring that, after a salary was settled, the governor's particular interest would be very little affected by serving or neglecting the interest of the people.[1] This one statement contains the gist of the whole controversy, giving essentially the argument of the assembly and indicating the argument of the crown.

The two positions were now frankly stated, and they were irreconcilable. In the meantime the assembly had all the advantage on its side, insisting that the governor should take a temporary salary or none at all. Burnet maintained a gallant and honorable but hopeless struggle until the time of his death, constantly refusing, at great personal sacrifice, the most liberal propositions if only the principle were conceded.[2]

It would seem that by this time the hopelessness of attempting to force the royal policy upon the assembly must have been clear; but the instructions to the next governor give no evidence that the home government was inclined to yield. Nevertheless, the contest was practically over. Burnet's successor, Belcher, was obliged at first to get special leave from the crown to assent to particular grants, and finally to obtain a general permission to accept temporary support.[3] The Board of Trade, though it recommended this surrender, urged that it would be better for the crown to establish a standing salary; but again its recommendation failed of any practical results. Shirley, who succeeded Belcher, was directed to recommend a permanent settlement, but, if that could not be secured, to

[1] Address of the House of Representatives, cited in Hutchinson, *History of Massachusetts*, ii. 319.

[2] *Townshend Papers*, 273 *seq.*

[3] Hutchinson, *History of Massachusetts*, ii. 333, 338. *Massachusetts Province Laws*, ii. 632–635; Chalmers, *Revolt*, ii. 139; *Townshend Papers*, 274 *seq.*

accept annual grants.[1] Thus in Massachusetts, as in New York, the contest ended in the victory of the assembly.

The struggle in the other provinces presents no peculiar features, unless in the case of New Hampshire, whose assembly was several times induced to settle a salary upon the governor during his term of service. Even this measure of success was finally lost, and New Hampshire followed the example of her neighbors in making annual grants.[2]

There can be no doubt that the House used its power to extort legislation from the governor even in violation of his instructions, as a few examples will plainly show. For example, Clarke of New York was charged with having passed the triennial act in return for his salary, which was not always voted as a matter of course.[3] Again about 1765 the South Carolina assembly, irritated by a real or supposed breach of its privileges, withheld the governor's salary altogether;[4] and at an even earlier date the council of the same province had declared that the acceptance of temporary grants by the governor was "the great bane" in the province.[5] In 1721 the Massachusetts House resolved that it would not consider grants and allowances until the governor had passed upon the acts of that session.[6] In 1727, when a bill for the emission of paper money, presented by the House, was vetoed by the governor on the ground that it was contrary to his instructions, the House again withheld salaries; whereupon a new bill of similar purport sent up to the governor received his approval.[7] Lewis Morris, while president of the New Jersey council, wrote: "The rendring governors and all other officers intirely dependant on the people is the generall inclination and endeavour of all the plantations in America, and nowhere pursued with more Steadinesse and less decency than in New

---

[1] *Massachusetts Province Laws*, iii. 450.

[2] *New Hampshire Provincial Papers*, iii. 260, 308, iv. 543, 550, 760, vi. 674, 676, 696, 716, vii. 179, 227.

[3] *New York Journal of Assembly*, i. 735; Chalmers, *Revolt*, ii. 149–150.

[4] South Carolina Historical Society, *Collections*, ii. 189.

[5] *Ibid.*, i. 299.

[6] Hutchinson, *History of Massachusetts*, ii. 230.

[7] *Ibid.*, 296.

Jersie."[1] Morris himself afterwards became governor, and confirmed his previous statement by his own experience.[2]

Nowhere, however, was the policy of keeping the governor under control by temporary grants, of granting money in exchange for legislation, more frankly and more cynically avowed than in Pennsylvania. In 1709 the assembly declared that the duty of supporting the government was grounded upon the "condition precedent" that grievances should be satisfied;[3] and the governor was informed that the House had voted him two hundred pounds, and that the speaker would present him a bill for that amount when he had passed the acts referred to him.[4] On another occasion the assembly thanked the governor for passing certain bills, and then gave him an order on the treasurer for his salary.[5] Under Governor Keith the principle of bargain and sale seems to have been carried to an extreme point; indeed, so largely a matter of course did this system become that the assembly in 1744, in giving Governor Thomas his annual salary at one time instead of granting it as usual in two instalments, alluded to its action as a special "Mark of Confidence."[6]

Another notorious offender in this respect was Governor Denny. In 1759, in violation of his instructions, he signed an act for the issue of bills of credit. The councillors in their formal protest insinuated improper motives, and immediately after his approval of the bill he was presented by the speaker with an order on the treasurer for one thousand pounds. In the following year the proprietary protested against several acts passed by Denny, for each of which, according to Chalmers, he had received a distinct sum from the delegates, with an "indemnification" against the forfeiture of his bond.[7] The

---

[1] *New Jersey Documents*, v. 315.

[2] For the New Jersey practice, see *Ibid.*, vi. 259, 421, vii. 251, xiv. 177; *Morris Papers*, 154.

[3] Proud, *History of Pennsylvania*, ii. 36–37.

[4] *Ibid.*, 32–33; *Pennsylvania Records*, ii. 492–493.

[5] *Pennsylvania Records*, iii. 174.

[6] *Ibid.*, iv. 688. Cf. *Historical Review of the Constitution and Government of Pennsylvania* (1759), 72–73.

[7] *Pennsylvania Records*, viii. 357–362; Chalmers, *Revolt*, ii. 344. See

demoralizing influence exerted upon the public conscience by such practices is well illustrated by the cynical declarations in a publication sanctioned by no less distinguished a patriot than Benjamin Franklin. "Every proprietary Governor," it was said, "has two Masters; one who gives him his Commission, and one who gives him his Pay," adding, "the Subjects Money is never so well disposed of as in the Maintenance of Order and Tranquility, and the Purchase of good Laws."[1]

It is easy to see that this method of controlling the executive was in many respects thoroughly vicious. It proved the danger of having an executive dependent for support "upon the temporary and arbitrary will of the legislature," inasmuch as this body often used its power improperly; and it gave rise to constant bargaining between governor and assembly, often on terms dishonorable to both. Nevertheless, the force of the popular argument, as stated by men like Franklin, cannot be denied. Here, it was said, were strangers, with no permanent stake in the province which they were sent to govern, often men of vicious character or mercenary motives, with little sense of personal responsibility, and officially accountable only to a distant authority across the sea: hence, if there was to be any effective popular control of the executive, it must be exercised by making the governor feel his dependence for support upon the assembly.[2]

It is worth noting that the men of the constitutional period, who had seen the working of the system in the colonies, even extreme radicals like Jefferson, were able to see that, although the method was perhaps inevitable under the circumstances of the colonial era, it was yet inherently vicious; they saw that such a policy could have no justification in an elective system in which the executive, just as truly as the legislature, was the representative of the people. In Jefferson's draft of a constitution for Virginia there was a provision that the gover-

also the statement of Governor Sharpe tending to support the charge made by Chalmers, *Maryland Archives*, ix. 351.

[1] *Historical Review of the Constitution and Government of Pennsylvania* (1759), 72, 73.

[2] Almon, *Prior Documents*, 229.

nor's salary should be unchanged during his whole term of office;[1] and the same principle was laid down by the framers of the constitution of the United States, in the clause providing that the salary of the President is not to be increased or diminished during his term of office and that during that period he is not to receive "any other emoluments from the United States, or any of them."[2]

[1] Jefferson, *Writings* (*Ford's edition*), iii. 326.
[2] Constitution, Art. II., § 1, ¶ 7.

CHAPTER X.

THE ENCROACHMENTS OF THE ASSEMBLY UPON THE EXECUTIVE.

IT has been seen that, although on the one side the governor had in various ways considerable power over the assembly, the latter on the other hand had a still more effective weapon in its control of the purse. At first the assembly used this power merely to check abuse of executive functions, but it did not stop there: its next step was to deprive the governor even of the actual executive power itself in certain important cases.

There can be no doubt that it is the tendency of the legislature, when once firmly established, to encroach upon the proper functions of the executive, especially by minute supervision and control; and that in the case of the colonial assemblies this tendency was greatly strengthened by the misconduct of governors.[1] The corruption in the provincial governments also served to call the attention of the people to the usages in the charter colonies of New England, where the executive as well as the legislature was representative, and where a very important part of the executive business was performed by committees of the assembly. It is true that much of the New England republican system was in the nature of the case impracticable in the provincial governments, since in these colonies the governor himself could not be got rid of, but had to be accepted as the agent of the crown, and as such constantly in opposition to local interests. The popular policy was, therefore, first to insure as far as possible the governor's

---

[1] Pownall, *Administration of the Colonies*, 50; *New York Journal of Assembly*, i. 170–171.

dependence upon the assembly by the system of temporary grants, and secondly to weaken the executive as far as possible by the transference of many of its proper functions to the assembly.

Of the reality of this New England influence upon the other colonies there can be no doubt. New Englanders very early pushed out into the other colonies. The New England element in Long Island made itself felt in the earliest politics of New York; and to other provinces also these transplanted New Englanders were likely to carry with them the political spirit of the Puritans. It seems to have been very early recognized that these settlers could best be attracted by liberal political institutions. There is evidence, too, that the practice of one colony was occasionally cited by the assembly of another.[1] In the New Hampshire records of 1755 are recorded the votes of the Massachusetts General Court appointing a committee of war.[2] In 1743 Governor Morris of New Jersey wrote of the members of the assembly: "They are gen^{lly} so fond of the example of the parliament of 1641 & that of their neighbours in Pensilvania & New England, that until some measures are taken in England to reduce them to propper limits I suspect they will not mend much."[3] Governor Sharpe said of the Maryland assembly in 1758 that their minds were "infected with the Disputes of the Pensilvanians."[4]

These are only a few chance illustrations, but they leave no room for doubt that the constitutional life of the different colonies was not isolated and independent, that tendencies which made themselves felt in Massachusetts or Pennsylvania had a very real influence in New York and Maryland. By the formation of Massachusetts into a royal government the

---

[1] This comparison of practice in different colonies was not confined to the assemblies. For example, there is a letter written by James Alexander of New Jersey to Joseph Murray of New York, inquiring as to the custom in other colonies in regard to the governor's sitting with the council in its legislative sessions. The query was to be extended to correspondents in Virginia, South Carolina, and the West India governments. See letter of December, 1747, *New Jersey Documents*, vii. 77–81.

[2] *New Hampshire Provincial Papers*, vi. 366.

[3] *Morris Papers*, 162.   [4] *Maryland Archives*, ix. 177–178.

republicanism of that colony lost something of its complete-
ness; but on the other hand it gained in influence, since now
for the first time the traditions of the old republican system had been placed upon a substantial footing and received
legal recognition within a royal government. The example of
Massachusetts might now be cited with greater force by the
popular party in other governments; and Massachusetts thus
became the natural medium through which these New England ideas were communicated to the other colonies. The
influence of Pennsylvania made itself felt in a lesser degree
but in much the same direction, since here also under the
liberal charter of the founder, the people and the assembly
had made serious inroads upon the executive authority of the
governor.

Among royalists the leadership in these democratic tendencies was very generally attributed to New England. Chalmers
says of the policy of temporary grants: "That profound
determination the New-English imparted, with other lessons,
to every colony."[1] Governor Cornbury wrote of the preva-
lence of republican ideas in New York and New Jersey,
especially in the east end of Long Island, "where they are
generally Commonwealths men."[2] Governor Nicholson of
South Carolina wrote in 1724 that the "spirit of common-
wealth-maxims, both in church and state, increase here daily,"
chiefly, as he supposed, by the influence of the New Englanders.[3] Governor Cosby of New York, writing in 1732,
said: "Yᵉ example and spirit of the Boston people begins to
spread amongst these Colonys In a most prodigioùs maner."[4]

---

[1] *Revolt*, i. 224.   [2] *New Jersey Documents*, iii. 78.

[3] Chalmers, *Revolt*, ii. 99; South Carolina Historical Society, *Collections*,
i. 283.

[4] *New Jersey Documents*, v. 321. Cf. *Ibid.*, iii. 283. An extreme royalist view of this New England influence is given by Chalmers, who, speaking particularly of the colonists of North Carolina at the close of the
seventeenth century and at the beginning of the eighteenth, says: "During
that gloomy period, New England alone cultivated her former commercial
connection with them; supplying their inconsiderable wants, and carrying
their tobacco and their corn without restraint wheresoever interest directed
her traders. When the original planters . . . had engrafted New-English

There can thus be no doubt of the reality of this New England influence or of its character.

The assembly had gained its power over the governor chiefly through its control of the purse: it was therefore natural that the first assumption of executive powers by the assembly should be in the department of finance. The assembly, and within the assembly the House in particular as the body invested with the exclusive right of granting the people's money, felt that it had also the right in its representative character to determine how that money should be spent. The representatives claimed the right not merely to appropriate money in general terms, but to define narrowly and in detail the uses to which it was to be put, holding that it was their right and duty to provide all necessary safeguards for a proper application of the money to the purposes for which it was intended. It is clear that this view might easily have led to an assumption of powers properly executive.

Reference has already been made to the fact that the governor's financial powers had been brought within very narrow limits by the practice of appropriation in detail, by reason of which he had come to have hardly more than the power of an accounting officer, issuing his warrants in accordance with the detailed appropriations made by the assembly, and having very little real discretion. It will now be seen that even this function was in some cases taken from him by the assembly, though it is hardly safe to say that this transference was general; in fact, though there are many illustrations of such action, the practice was nevertheless in all probability usually regarded as exceptional and irregular. It is important to note, however, that this part of the governor's prerogative was under some circumstances invaded in almost all the colonies. In New York at one time the assembly appropriated salaries to be paid without any warrant from the governor, though it seems finally to have retired from this position and to have

maxims upon their stock of native principles, such specimens of turbulence were given by them to the other provinces, during the reign of Anne, as may be conceived but cannot be described " (*Revolt*, i. 398–399).

allowed salaries to be issued by the governor's warrant.[1] Governor Dobbs of North Carolina complained that payments were made without his warrant; and even in Virginia Governor Dinwiddie felt himself obliged to assent to a bill intrusting the disposition of funds to commissioners.[2] In Pennsylvania it was a common practice for the speaker to issue orders upon the treasurer for the payment of money; in the case of the governor's salary this was regularly done.[3]

The governor's power of issuing warrants was reduced to a mere formality by the requirement that money, even when duly appropriated, should not be drawn out of the treasury without a special vote of the assembly. South Carolina, for example, imposed this restriction.[4] In Massachusetts the General Court assumed the right of examining the muster rolls, passing upon each item, and voting an order on the treasurer for its payment if approved. The governors protested against this practice, but the House persisted in it for many years, until finally the crown instructed the governor not to allow such provisions in future acts of supply; whereupon the House, after a vigorous contest, yielded under protest.[5] In New Hampshire the assembly claimed and exercised the same power, though it was denounced by Governor Wentworth as an invasion of the prerogative.[6]

Thus the assembly had in many cases deprived the governor of even that limited control over provincial finance involved in the requirement of his warrants for the payment of public

[1] *New York Documents*, iv. 1146, vi. 353, 820–821; Chalmers, *Revolt*, ii. 315. For practice in New Jersey, see *New Jersey Documents*, ix. 154–155; Allinson, *Acts of Assembly*, ch. 301.

[2] *North Carolina Records*, vi. 320; *Dinwiddie Papers*, i. 161.

[3] See e. g. *Pennsylvania Records*, ii. 412. Pownall notes the fact that in many colonies the governor's warrant was not always required: *Administration of the Colonies*, 52.

[4] Cooper, *Statutes*, iii. 191, 481–484 (acts of 1722 and 1737).

[5] *Massachusetts Province Laws*, ii. 219–222, 235–236, 278–280, 574, 593, 596, 702 ; Hutchinson, *History of Massachusetts*, ii. 266, 338. Cf. *Province Laws*, 1730–31, ch. 17, 1733–34, ch. 7.

[6] *New Hampshire Provincial Papers*, v. 283, vi. 343. For similar action taken by the New York assembly, see " Representation of the Board of Trade," 1751, *New York Documents*, vi. 616.

money. In other financial matters also the House, either directly or through its committees, assumed functions properly executive in their character.[1]

From the fundamental assumption that the assembly as the representative of the people was the constitutional guardian of the people's money, there was only a short step to the claim by that body of the right to appoint those officers who were charged with the collection, custody, and disbursement of the public funds. The prevailing doctrine of the colonial assemblies upon this point is briefly summed up in the following resolutions passed in 1753 by the assembly of Jamaica: "Resolved, That it is the inherent and undoubted Right of the Representatives of the People to raise and apply Monies for the Service and Exigencies of Government, and to appoint such Person or Persons for the receiving and issuing thereof as they shall think proper, which Rights this House hath exerted, and will always exert, in such manner as they shall judge most conducive to the service of His Majesty, and the Interest of His People."[2]

The most important exercise of this assumed right was the appointment by the assembly of the provincial treasurer, a practice which prevailed in a majority of the provincial governments. In New Hampshire, New Jersey, and Georgia it would seem that the assembly had not succeeded in wresting from the executive this appointing power.[3] In Maryland, there

---

[1] In New Hampshire the assemblies appointed committees to farm out the excise (*Provincial Papers*, iv. 204, v. 660). The Virginia assembly in 1701 appointed a committee to oversee the building of the Capitol (Hening, *Statutes*, iii. 214).

[2] *North Carolina Records*, v. 758.

[3] See *New Hampshire Provincial Papers*, iv. 6, 533, vi. 860. Governor Belcher of New Jersey in his report gave an account of the offices in the province, naming some which were filled in a different way, and adding that all other civil officers were appointed by the governor (*New Jersey Documents*, viii. (2) 86). In 1762 Governor Hardy appointed a treasurer for the eastern division of the province during the royal pleasure. In 1774, on Skinner's resignation, the House undertook to nominate his successor, and finally the same person who had been so nominated was appointed by the governor and council (New Jersey Historical Society, *Proceedings*, v. 59-

appears to have been a conflict of precedents.[1] When the assemblies had gained this power, it seems to have been usual to make the appointment by formal act of assembly; sometimes, however, it was done by simple resolution of the House of Representatives.[2]

Even when the appointment was made by act of assembly the lower house clearly had the real choice; for such a bill, like all others having to do with the raising of money, would originate in the House, and amendments by the council would be sure to meet with resistance. In North Carolina in 1760 the council ventured to change the name of the treasurer as given in the bill of the House, and the House agreed to make the change in this case, saving "the inherent right of this House, to nominate Persons to be appointed to the office of Public Treasurers."[3] In South Carolina the Representatives, or "House of Commons," as they styled themselves, at first nominated the treasurer, but they were forced to consent to appointment by act of the governor, council, and assembly.[4] In Virginia there was for a time a rule which kept the treasurership practically in the hands of the House exclusively; this was the provision that the speaker should be *ex officio* treasurer.[5]

Something should be said as to the process by which the appointment of treasurer came into the hands of the assembly. In Massachusetts the charter itself gave a constitutional sanc-

61; *New Jersey Documents*, ix. 366, x. 420 note, xiv. 249–250). For Georgia, see Jones, *Colonial Acts of Georgia*, 23, 49, 145–146, 157, 166, 168, 179, 212; note the references to "his majesty's treasurer." Cf. Stokes, *Constitution of the British Colonies*, 120, 184. Stokes, in his general account of the royal governments, was undoubtedly thinking particularly of Georgia.

[1] *Maryland Archives*, viii. 352; *Votes and Proceedings of the Lower House*, April 18, 1758. For the opinion of Attorney-General Willes in 1737, who held that, in spite of precedents for the appointment of the treasurer by the assembly, the proprietor still had the right of nomination, see Chalmers, *Opinions*, 179.

[2] See e.g. *New York Journal of Assembly*, i. 197; *Votes of Pennsylvania*, iv. 271, 490.

[3] *North Carolina Records*, vi. 508.

[4] Cooper, *Statutes*, ii. 299, iii. 148.

[5] Hening, *Statutes*, v. 64, 173.

tion to the practice, by the provision that all civil officers, with the exception of those connected with the administration of justice, should be appointed by the General Court.[1] In New York the issue arose during Lord Cornbury's corrupt administration, when the assembly of 1703 passed resolutions requesting, in view of previous misapplication of public money, that some person might be commissioned as treasurer by the governor, "for the receiving and paying of such Monies now intended to be raised for the publick Use, as a Means to obstruct the like Misapplication for the future."[2] In 1705 the assembly passed a vote declaring its intention of appointing a treasurer "for receiving and paying the publick Monies to be raised by this House.'"[3] By 1715 the House had apparently carried its point, for in that year Governor Hunter wrote that by the new supply act the funds were lodged with the treasurer, adding that "no Act could lodge them otherwise."[4] In 1768 the matter had gone so far that the treasurer of that year was invested with his commission by the speaker and gave bond to the speaker, a circumstance indicating to what an extreme point had been carried the conception of the treasurer as peculiarly an officer of the lower house and almost independent of the crown.[5]

In Virginia the treasurer was regularly appointed by act of assembly from the year 1704 until 1738, when the office was attached to the speakership of the House.[6] This system proved a failure, however, and the treasurer was again appointed as before by act of assembly, in which the lower house probably had the right of nomination.[7] In South Carolina, acts were passed appointing receivers of public taxes. In 1707 it was enacted that the "Commons" should have the right to nominate the public receiver of the province; and although this act was repealed by the proprietors, yet in 1721 it was

[1] Charter of 1691, in Poore, *Charters and Constitutions*, i. 942.
[2] *New York Journal of Assembly*, i. 170.
[3] *Ibid.*, 197.
[4] *New York Documents*, v. 416–417.   [5] *Ibid.*, viii. 61.
[6] Hening, *Statutes*, iii. 225, iv. 135, 150, 433, v. 64.
[7] *Ibid.*, viii. 210, 211.

decreed that the treasurer should thereafter be appointed by
the general assembly.[1] This appointment was made by ordinances, which like statutes required the concurrence of governor, council, and assembly. The movements in the other
provinces present no peculiar features which require discussion here. In one colony at least, that of North Carolina, the
home government made a virtue of necessity by instructing the
governor that, although the appointment of treasurers by act
of assembly was irregular, yet it would be improper to set
aside a usage of so long standing.[2]

The appointment of the treasurer by the assembly took the
control of provincial finance almost entirely out of the governor's hands and placed it in those of an officer who was
generally regarded as "solely and entirely a servant of the
assembly."[3] The treasurer was often a person of considerable
importance. In Virginia, as has been seen, the speaker was
for a time treasurer also, and consequently possessed great
influence, which he was charged with using in improper
ways.[4] In 1731 Governor Burrington of North Carolina wrote
that the treasurer Edward Moseley was speaker and manager
of the assembly.[5] Chalmers charges the treasurer of North
Carolina, John Starkey, with having, like the Virginia treasurer, made a corrupt use of the power he possessed over the
members of the assembly.

This union of legislative leadership with financial admin-

---

[1] Cooper, *Statutes*, ii. 16, 41, 65, 299, iii. 148.

[2] For usage in North Carolina and the other colonies, see *North Carolina Records*, iii. 291, 299, 302, iv. 1006, 1020, vi. 55 (note the appointment
of a treasurer for life, vi. 218); *Votes of Pennsylvania*, i. 88, 117, iv. 271,
490; Proud, *History of Pennsylvania*, ii. 60, 218; *Pennsylvania Archives*,
1st Series, iv. 600.

[3] Pownall, *Administration of the Colonies*, 52.

[4] Hening, *Statutes*, viii. 210; *Dinwiddie Papers*, i. 307, 312; Chalmers,
Revolt, ii. 354.

[5] *North Carolina Records*, iii. 151, 265.

[6] It is not certain that the charge was well founded. There is a letter
of the royal receiver-general, who in asking a leave of absence proposed
Starkey as his substitute, commending him as a man of unspotted integrity
and honor. See *Ibid.*, v. 589. Cf. Chalmers, *Revolt*, ii. 358–361; also
North Carolina Records, vi., Prefatory Notes, xxxiii–xxxiv.

istration suggests an interesting comparison with the parliamentary system; but the combination in one person of the three functions of leader of the House, speaker, and minister of finance is perhaps without precedent. If it were profitable to dwell upon what might have been, it would be interesting to consider how this development might have worked itself out had it been uninterrupted by the Revolution; not improbably it might have led ultimately to a modified form of parliamentary government.

The interference in appointments on the part of the assembly was not confined to the choice of treasurer, but extended to a large number of other offices, chiefly those concerned with the collection or payment of public money. It has been noticed that in Massachusetts the assembly had a constitutional right to appoint administrative officers, and the example set by Massachusetts was followed in nearly all the colonies. In New York, collectors, excise-commissioners, and commissioners for various other purposes were appointed by act of assembly; indeed, it was a standing ground of complaint on the part of the New York governors that the assembly constantly assumed this right of exercising executive functions.[1] In New Jersey, during Queen Anne's War, the assembly passed an act for raising three thousand pounds, naming in this act two treasurers, commissioners for managing the expedition against Canada, and a commissary.[2] Again, during the last French war commissioners were appointed by the assembly to carry out the provisions of the military supply acts; but the home government objected strongly to this action and forbade the governor's assent to future acts of that character. Governor Bernard, however, failed to comply with his instructions on that point.[3]

---

[1] *New York Acts of Assembly,* 1691–1718, 97; *Laws of New York,* 1691–1773, chs. 934, 935, 1598; *New York Documents,* vi. 285; Chalmers, *Revolt,* ii. 315.

[2] *New Jersey Documents,* xiii. 415.

[3] *Ibid.,* ix. 154, 158, 170. The assembly also appointed county collectors, boundary commissioners, commissioners of river navigation, of roads and

Outside of Massachusetts the two provinces which carried this policy to the greatest extreme were South Carolina and Pennsylvania. In South Carolina the practice had grown up under the weak proprietary administration and had secured a hold too strong to be shaken off. Here in 1721 it was enacted that the treasurer, comptroller, powder-receiver, and all other civil officers paid out of the public funds should be appointed by the assembly.[1] Among other officers appointed in the same way were commissioners for military supplies, Indian agents, and Indian commissioners.[2] In 1729 an effort was made to stop the practice: Governor Johnson was directed not to give his assent to any law for the appointment of officers, and he declared his intention of insisting on a strict compliance with his instructions.[3] The effort had little effect, however; for Johnson's successor, James Glen, wrote in 1748: "Almost all the places of profit or of trust are disposed of by the General Assembly. . . . The executive part of the government is lodged in different sets of Commissioners. . . . The above officers and most of the Commissioners are named by the General Assembly, and are responsible to them alone. . . . Thus the people have the whole of the administration in their hands."[4]

In Pennsylvania the assembly assumed the appointment of nearly all administrative officers. In passing an act for any purpose it was customary for the assembly not only to provide the necessary official machinery for its enforcement, but also to make the actual appointment of the officer. Thus, for example, in the loan acts the assembly appointed trustees of the loan office;[5] in an act levying taxes, special commissioners were named to enforce its provisions.[6] Naturally

bridges, and of barracks. See Allinson, *Acts of Assembly*, ch. 77, § 6, ch. 93, § 12, chs. 319, 320, 370, 396, 407, 418, 541.

[1] Cooper, *Statutes*, iii. 148.

[2] *Ibid.*, ii. 158, 176, 183, 189, 311, 315, 624, 654, iv. 4, 9, 14, 45, 52, 154, 157, 166.

[3] South Carolina Historical Society, *Collections*, ii. 119, 134.

[4] *Ibid.*, 303–304; cf. Carroll, *Historical Collections*, ii. 220–221.

[5] *Statutes at Large of Pennsylvania* (1896), iii. 325, 391.

[6] *Ibid.*, ii. 389.

therefore it became customary for persons desiring such appointments to apply not to the governor but to the assembly; an example is the petition, in 1750, of R. Shewell of Philadelphia, baker, praying to be appointed flour-brander for the city and county of Philadelphia.[1] In 1757, after the assembly had declared that the nomination of Indian commissioners was its "settled right," as it was the right of the British House of Commons, the governor's message objected only to the choice of commissioners from the members of the assembly, not to that body's exercise of the right of nomination.[2] Andrew Hamilton, speaker of the assembly, on retiring from public life in 1739, made a speech in which he congratulated the province on the fact that it had no officers except those who were necessary and who earned their salaries, and that these were generally either elected by the people or appointed by their representatives.[3]

These are the most striking cases; but in all the colonies the assemblies had, to a greater or less extent, assumed the exercise of the appointing power.

From the administration of finance and the appointment of officers, the assembly was naturally led to encroachments upon another department which may with even greater propriety be regarded as the exclusive right of the chief executive. If there is any function which especially requires a concentration of authority in a single head, it is certainly the command of military forces and the conduct of military operations. Yet even into this field the assembly forced its way,

---

[1] *Votes of Pennsylvania*, iv. 143.   [2] *Ibid.*, 747, 750.

[3] Proud, *History of Pennsylvania*, ii. 217. For the practice in the other colonies, see Chalmers, *Opinions*, 361; *New Hampshire Provincial Papers*, iii. 761, v. 177, 191, 207, 220, vi. 140, 232; Jones, *Colonial Acts of Georgia*, 37, 47, 63, 102; Martin, *Iredell's Public Acts*, i. 110; *North Carolina Records*, vi. 660; *Maryland Archives*, vii. 610. In regard to a Maryland statute Attorney-General Pratt gave his opinion that "the sole nomination of those commissioners who are new officers, appointed by this bill, belongs neither to the proprietary, nor the lower house; but, like all other regulations, must be assented to by both, but can be claimed by neither": Chalmers, *Opinions*, 264.

availing itself of the exceptional opportunities for such en-croachments afforded by the frequent French and Indian wars of that period. The urgent need of supplies for military purposes occasioned by these wars enabled the assembly, in making its grants of money, to impose the most arduous con-ditions. This power it used in three general ways. In the first place, in granting military supplies it prescribed in detail the purposes for which they were to be expended, dictating the course of military operations and the disposition of troops. Secondly, it left in the hands of committees of the assembly, or of commissioners appointed by act of assembly, the dispo-sition of these funds, often too with a very considerable con-trol of the conduct of military enterprises. Finally, through the appointment and removal of officers, it went so far as to interfere with the discipline of troops.

Of all these ways in which the assembly infringed upon the military prerogative of the governor there are abundant illus-trations. Take, for example, the first instance, — the power assumed by the assembly of regulating the employment of military forces. The Pennsylvania assembly voted in 1757 that of fourteen hundred men to be enlisted, three hundred should be employed in garrison and the remaining eleven hun-dred in ranging and scouting parties.[1] Again, an order of the Massachusetts General Court in 1722 provided for the raising of a certain number of men for a military expedition, direct-ing that three hundred of these should be posted at Penobscot and the rest at different places on the frontier. The governor insisted that by the charter he had the sole direction of mili-tary forces; but he was compelled to submit in order to get the necessary supplies.[2] Under Governor Shirley, who was anxious to keep the assembly in good humor, this tendency to dictate in military affairs worked itself out almost without restraint and was the cause of serious embarrassment to his successor.[3] Thus in 1758 the House, following precedents established under Shirley, undertook in voting pay for the

---

[1] *Votes of Pennsylvania*, iv. 717.
[2] Hutchinson, *History of Massachusetts*, ii. 252.
[3] *Ibid.*, iii. 66.

forces on the frontier to specify the number of men to be employed at each point. Governor Pownall declared this an infringement of his rights under the charter; but he finally gave his assent under protest, declaring that he did so only on account of the pressing necessity of the situation.[1]

Of the second class of encroachments, namely, of the practice of controlling the conduct of military operations by committees of the assembly or through commissioners appointed by the assembly, there is equally good evidence. In 1709 and 1711 the New York assembly was allowed to name commissioners to take charge of the commissariat; and, later, commissioners of fortifications were appointed in the same way.[2] In 1722 the representatives in the provinces of Massachusetts and New Hampshire passed votes providing for the appointment of committees of war to concert plans for the conduct of the war and to exercise a certain supervision; and although in each case the plan was then blocked by the opposition of the council, yet in 1745 both assemblies appointed committees of war, which assumed the management of the commissariat.[3] The practice was most general during the last French war. The New Jersey military supply acts were regularly executed by commissioners named in the acts. The home government, it is true, forbade the governor's acceptance of such acts, but it was unable to enforce its prohibition.[4] A similar course was taken in Pennsylvania, where serious difficulties arose on one occasion from the failure of the commissioners to agree with the governor as to the proper course to be pursued.[5] With reference to a Maryland bill of the year

[1] *Massachusetts Province Laws*, iv. 94, 95; Hutchinson, *History of Massachusetts*, iii. 66–67. For New York, see Chalmers, *Revolt*, ii. 229–232; *New York Documents*, vi. 616. For South Carolina, see Cooper, *Statutes*, iii. 179.

[2] Chalmers, *Revolt*, i. 361–362, 367, ii. 224–228.

[3] Hutchinson, *History of Massachusetts*, ii. 257, 370; *New Hampshire Provincial Papers*, iv. 49, 325, v. 293, 329. Cf. the action of the New Jersey assembly in 1740, *New Jersey Documents*, vi. 99.

[4] *New Jersey Documents*, ix. 154, 158, 170, 225.

[5] *Votes of Pennsylvania*, iv. 717; *Historical Review of the Constitution and Government of Pennsylvania* (1759), 440–441.

1757, the governor declared that according to its provisions the troops were to be "under the Command of no Body but the Agents," who were appointed by the assembly.[1]

Nowhere was this policy carried farther than in Massachusetts and New Hampshire. In Massachusetts a committee was appointed by the General Court to consider projects for carrying on the war, with instructions to report to the assembly; another was named to take charge of provisions and other supplies. A committee of war consisting of five members was also chosen, to sit at or near Albany and to follow instructions from the General Court "for the more effectual carrying into Execution the intended Expedition against Crown Point."[2] Similar action was taken in New Hampshire, where perhaps the most extreme measure was that adopted in 1756, when agents were appointed to repair to Albany and to transact there any affairs relating to the expedition, following "such Instructions as they may Receive from time to time from the Generall Assembly."[3]

Finally, the assembly was disposed to interfere with the discipline of the army in the matter of appointment and removal of officers. An indication of this tendency has already been seen in the appointment of special commissioners by acts of assembly, which sometimes appointed paymasters and commissaries, and apparently such officers as chaplains and surgeons.[4] It did not often, if ever, claim the right directly to appoint military officers in the strict sense of the term, but it sometimes interfered seriously with the discipline of the troops by attempting to enforce the removal of such officers. Thus in 1722 the Massachusetts assembly summoned the commanding officer of the army to appear before it and explain why certain orders voted by the House had not been executed;

[1] *Maryland Archives*, ix. 100. Cf. Bacon, *Laws of Maryland*, 1756, ch. 5.

[2] *Massachusetts Province Laws*, iii. 940–963.

[3] *New Hampshire Provincial Papers*, vi. 368–371, 506–520. For a somewhat similar case in Virginia, see Hening, *Statutes*, vi. 524, vii. 13.

[4] Chalmers, *Revolt*, i. 361–362, ii. 229–232; *New York Documents*, vi. 616; *New Jersey Documents*, ix. 225; *New Hampshire Provincial Papers*, v. 296, 299–300, 376, 438, vi. 368–371, 376.

and it finally compelled his discharge by refusing to vote his pay.[1] The South Carolina assembly passed a very extreme measure in 1721, by appointing Indian commissioners, who among other duties were to inspect forts and garrisons and to give any necessary orders for the reform of abuses. The military officers were bound to carry out orders of this kind; and if they failed to do so, the commissioners were empowered to suspend them and to make temporary appointments in their places.[2]

From these facts it is clear that in military affairs the assembly had seriously encroached upon the governor's prerogative. Indeed, this statement of the evidence gathered from the practice of the different provinces may be summed up with the remark of the historian Chalmers in regard to the conduct of the last of the French wars: "The king's representative acted merely as the correspondent of his ministers. The war was conducted by committees of assembly."[3]

In regard to the interference of the assembly with external relations a few words will suffice. These external relations, it will be remembered, were chiefly of two kinds, — intercolonial interests and Indian affairs. As to questions arising between the colonies, it may be said that the appointment by the assembly of commissioners to deal with boundary disputes is frequently recorded by nearly every colony, and was finally sanctioned in some cases by the authority of the crown itself.[4] In regard to relations with the Indians, the assembly showed a similar disposition to assert its control, as a few illustrations taken almost at random will sufficiently indicate. In 1722 the Massachusetts House voted that the speech to be made by the governor at a meeting with delegates of the Iroquois nation should be spoken in the name of the assembly, and that the House of Representatives should be present. The governor at first refused, but he was finally obliged to submit.

---

[1] Hutchinson, *History of Massachusetts*, ii. 254–260, 265–266.
[2] Cooper, *Statutes*, iii. 142; cf. 230, 329, 333.
[3] *Revolt*, ii. 300–301.
[4] See above, p. 109, and Allinson, *Acts of Assembly*, ch. 396.

The House had in the first place proposed that the speech should be composed by a joint committee of the two houses; and although this was not done, yet the speech was actually submitted to the assembly for its approval.[1] Again, in 1723, the House is found sending instructions to the commissioners appointed to confer with the Five Nations at Albany.[2] In South Carolina and Pennsylvania Indian commissioners were appointed by the assembly.[3] In 1755 the South Carolina assembly voted that the governor and council should take the counsel of several members of the assembly in their negotiations with the Creeks.[4]

It has now been seen, perhaps in wearisome detail, to how great an extent the assembly had in various ways encroached upon essentially executive functions of the governor. These usurpations, or whatever else they may be called, probably reached their height during the last of the Indian wars, when the pressure upon the governors was of course stronger than at any other time. It is probable, however, that if the political development of the colonies had not been in a sense interrupted by the events of the revolutionary period, the assemblies would have made even greater advances. Already indeed in some of the provinces the governor's power had been reduced within very narrow limits. Governor Glen's statement in regard to South Carolina, to the effect that the executive power was very largely in the hands of commissioners appointed by the assembly, applies fairly well to Pennsylvania also.[5] In regard to the Massachusetts government the Board of Trade wrote in 1757: "Almost every act of executive and legislative power, whether it be political, judicial or military, is ordered and directed by Votes and Resolves of the General

[1] Hutchinson, *History of Massachusetts*, ii. 254.

[2] *House Journal*, 1723, pp. 5–8.

[3] See above, pp. 187, 188.

[4] Cooper, *Statutes*, iv. 19. In 1758 the Maryland assembly appointed agents to provide presents for the Indians, though the money was to be expended only with the approval of the governor. See Bacon, *Laws of Maryland*, 1758, ch. 1.

[5] South Carolina Historical Society, *Collections*, ii. 303.

Court, in most cases originating in the House of Representatives."[1] A similar statement in regard to New York was made by the Board in 1752.[2] Even at the close of Queen Anne's reign, Chalmers said of the New York government that it "was really changed; from being monarchical, it had already become democratical."[3]

Without undertaking to pass a final judgment upon the policy of the assembly or the opposition of the home government, some conclusions may fairly be drawn. In the first place, it is clear that such a policy was not likely to bring about the most effective administration of public affairs, involving, as it did, the practical breaking off of large or small fragments of the governor's prerogative, some of which were given either to committees of the assembly or to the assembly itself, and others to officers more or less responsible to the assembly. The policy, it is true, accomplished the end which it had in view, namely, the weakening of the governor, who, if not personally an object of distrust and suspicion, was at least looked upon as the representative of interests at variance with those of the colonies. Certainly, however, the result was a system of administration far from ideal. There was no concentration of responsibility, no unity of administration; and yet whether these evils were any greater than those which would have grown up, which indeed had already made themselves felt, under the old system contemplated by the commission and instructions, is a question not to be hastily decided.

Though it be admitted that any lack of administrative efficiency was more than made good by the enforcement of the principle of popular control over the executive, yet the fact must be recognized that the system was intrinsically corrupt, corrupt not only in its immediate results but in the vicious traditions which were left behind. This influence was manifest in the first constitutions of the independent States, as

[1] Board of Trade to Governor Pownall, Dec. 8, 1757, *Massachusetts Province Laws*, iv. 95–96.
[2] Chalmers, *Revolt*, ii. 255.
[3] *Ibid.*, 53.

shown in the very general distrust of the executive expressed in those instruments, in the tendency to make the governor so far as possible dependent upon and subordinate to the legislature.

The experience of a few years, however, proved the folly of this narrow course. It became evident that jealousy of the executive had no place in a system in which the executive as well as the legislature was the representative of the people; and gradually the vicious traditions of the old régime gave way to the sounder principles of the Federal constitution.

CHAPTER XI.

THE GOVERNOR'S LEGAL AND POLITICAL ACCOUNTABILITY: CONCLUSION.

THE governor's accountability, like his whole official character, was two-fold: he was held by legal and administrative checks to his accountability to the home government, and by various practical and political checks to his responsibility to the people of his province.

His accountability to the crown for the loyal support of British and royal interests was enforced by the liability to removal for serious violations of his trust. Some of the specific penalties attached to breach of particular instructions have already been noticed. Another method of enforcing responsibility lay in the requirement of bonds for the due observance of instructions. Such security was first demanded by the crown from the proprietary governments. In Pennsylvania it was exacted from the governor by the proprietor himself.[1]

In addition to these checks, which may perhaps be called administrative, the governor had also a certain legal accountability in the courts, though he was answerable only at the King's Bench, and not in any court within his province. This principle was clearly stated by Chief Justice Mansfield in his decision in the case of Fabrigas *vs.* Mostyn, which came before him in 1773.[2] Indeed, as early as 1700 the jurisdiction of the King's Bench in case of criminal misconduct on the part of

[1] Above, p. 68; *New Jersey Documents*, ii. 141, 142; Proud, *History of Pennsylvania*, ii. 182, 188.

[2] He declared that the governor must be accountable in the court of King's Bench, for otherwise he could be held to account nowhere. See Howell, *State Trials*, xx. 231.

colonial governors was defined by act of Parliament.[1] Suits for damages might be brought against the governor in the same court.[2] Instances of the actual prosecution of governors in this way are, however, hard to find. Douglass in his "Summary" mentions only two cases of actual trial before the court of King's Bench, those of Douglass, governor of the Leeward Islands in 1716, and Lowther of Barbadoes in 1720. The only instances found in the old thirteen colonies are those of Lord Bellomont, governor of New York at the close of the seventeenth century, against whom suit for false imprisonment was brought, and Sir William Phips, who was sued for illegal interference with a collector of customs.[3]

According to two important witnesses, these legal checks were nevertheless very far from giving perfect security against misconduct. One testimony, from an official or semi-official source, certainly not from the standpoint of a colonist, is a report presented through Secretary Stanhope to the Board of Trade in 1715. This writer declares that "on Complaints of grievances, and of many great oppressions, which have not been done in a Judicial way, and where the proceedings were not of record, and consequently could not be proved so fully before the King, as in the aforesaid case of Appeals, the persons injured meet with unsupportable difficulties and have seldom bin relieved on their complaints."[4] The other witness is Hamilton, who, in his famous speech delivered in defence of Zenger in the year 1735, based his argument for freedom of speech largely upon the fact that other means of holding the provincial governor to his accountability were ineffective. "We are indeed told," said he, "and it is true they are obliged to answer a suit in the king's courts at Westminster, for a wrong done to any person here: But do we

[1] *Statutes at Large*, 11 & 12 Will. III. c. 12.

[2] See case of Fabrigas *vs.* Mostyn, in Howell, *State Trials*, xx. 81.

[3] For Douglass and Lowther, see Douglass, *Summary*, i. 217. The case of Bellomont is cited by Mansfield in his decision in the case of Fabrigas *vs.* Mostyn (Howell, *State Trials*, xx. 217–218, 232). The decision of Mansfield referred to arose in Minorca, and at the very end of our colonial era. For Phips, see Hutchinson, *History of Massachusetts*, ii. 74–75, 82.

[4] *North Carolina Records*, ii. 161–163.

not know how impracticable this is to most men among us, to leave their families, (who depend upon their labour and care for their livelihood) and carry evidences to Britain, and at a great, nay, a far greater expence than almost any of us are able to bear, only to prosecute a governor for an injury done here? But when the oppression is general, there is no remedy even that way." [1]

Since the restraints imposed upon the governor by the home government are seen to have been practically inadequate, more effective checks must be sought within the province. It is true that one branch of the provincial government, the judiciary, was largely ineffective for this purpose, since it was too much under the control either of the crown or of the governor, and was therefore not sufficiently representative of public opinion. This public opinion of the province was after all the strongest restraining influence upon the governor; to it, indeed, even the royal administrative control owed a large share of such efficiency as there was in the system. Of course the great organ of public opinion was the provincial assembly; and yet, underlying the need of an organic embodiment of public opinion, there is a need yet more necessary and fundamental, — the necessity of a free and open interchange of ideas on political subjects, of freedom to criticise the acts of any public officer, even the highest. In times like those of the colonial era, when redress from the home government could be had only with difficulty, when judges were subservient, when even assemblies might be corrupted, this was the last resort, the only ground of hope for a sound political life.

In the early years of the colonial era the right of free speech was not always well guarded. There was frequent legislation, for example, against "seditious utterances," a term which might mean almost anything. In 1639 the Maryland assembly passed an act for "determining enormous offences," among which were included "scandalous or contemptuous words or writings to the dishonour of the lord proprietarie or his lieutenant generall for the time being, or of any of the council." [2]

---

[1] Howell, *State Trials*, xvii. 707.
[2] Bozman, *History of Maryland*, ii. 603.

By a North Carolina act of 1715 seditious utterance against the government was made a criminal offence, and in 1724 Joseph Castleton, for malicious language against Governor Burrington and for other contemptuous remarks, was sentenced by the General Court to stand in the pillory for two hours and on his knees to beg the governor's pardon.[1] A New Jersey act of 1675 required that persons found guilty of resisting the authority of the governor or councillors "either in Words or Actions . . . or by speaking contemptiously, reproachfully, or maliciously, of any of them," should be liable to fine, banishment, or corporal punishment at the discretion of the court.[2] In Massachusetts even during the eighteenth century the right of free political discussion was denied by the House of Representatives as well as by the royal governor, though often unsuccessfully.[3]

The history of the liberty of speech and of the press in the colonies does not lack its *causes célèbres*. One of the most striking is that of Nicholas Bayard in 1702. Under a statute declaring that persons endeavoring "by force of arms, or other ways, to disturb the peace, good, and quiet of this their majesties' government, as it is now established," should be deemed rebels, Bayard, on a warrant of the governor and council, was committed on a charge of high treason. The grand jury, which was said to have been packed, brought in an indictment charging the prisoner with circulating, particularly among the soldiers, libels declaring the existing government oppressive, and thus inciting the king's subjects "to disown the present authority." These alleged libels were embodied in an address to Lord Cornbury, the newly-appointed governor, who had not yet arrived in the province, — a course of action on Bayard's part which was held to be in contempt of the governor then in office, — in a second address to the king and in a third to the House of Commons.

The trial took place before commissioners who were specially

---

[1] Iredell, *Laws of North-Carolina*, 17; *North Carolina Records*, ii. 546.
[2] Leaming and Spicer, *Grants, Concessions*, etc., 99. Cf. *Ibid.*, 77.
[3] See on this subject, C. A. Duniway, *History of Restrictions upon the Freedom of the Press in Massachusetts*, chs. 3, 4.

appointed for the purpose by the governor, and who throughout the trial displayed a marked bias against the prisoner.   It
was claimed that the jury was packed.   According to some of
the most damaging charges preferred by the prosecuting witnesses, Bayard had asserted that "the hottest and ignorantest of
the people were put into places of trust," and that the assembly
had given the governor money to induce his approval of certain bills.   In the course of the trial one of the commissioners
even made the astonishing statement that it might be a crime
"to petition the House of Commons in the plantations, where
the king governs by prerogative."   On such charges Bayard
was found guilty, and was sentenced to be hung, drawn, and
quartered.   This extreme sentence was not carried out, however; with difficulty he obtained a reprieve, and on Cornbury's
arrival the attainder was reversed by an act of assembly, which
was confirmed by Queen Anne.[1]

Another method of restraining the liberty of public speech
has already been noticed in the unsuccessful attempt to give
to the governors a censorship of the press.[2]   Apart from these
extreme methods, an attempt was also made to curb the expression of political opinions by the application of the law of libel.
The classic illustration of this class of efforts is the case of
John Peter Zenger, who was tried for publishing a libel against
Governor Cosby of New York.[3]   Lewis Morris, chief justice
of the Supreme Court, had rendered a decision unfavorable to
the governor in a suit involving the latter's salary.   Cosby
thereupon removed Morris and appointed a new chief justice,
De Lancey, who, as associate justice, had dissented from the
opinion rendered by Morris.   Morris then wrote several papers
criticising the governor's course, which were published in
Zenger's "Journal."   These the governor straightway denounced as false and scandalous libels; whereupon Chief Justice De Lancey charged the grand jury, dwelling upon the

---

[1] See the report of the case in Howell, *State Trials*, xiv. 471.   Cf.
Chalmers, *Opinions*, 340 ; Smith, *History of New York* (1776), 141–144.

[2] See above, p. 127.

[3] For an earlier case in Maryland, see Hamilton's speech in the Zenger
trial (Howell, *State Trials*, xvii. 717).

peculiar danger of libels on the governor, arguing that they endangered the peace and created a distrust of government; but the jury failed to respond to his appeal. The council then sent a message to the House of Representatives urging that body to take action; but the House laid the message on the table. The council then ordered that the papers should be burned; Zenger was arrested on an order of the governor and council; and an unsuccessful effort was made to pack the jury. Andrew Hamilton of Pennsylvania, the leading colonial lawyer of the time, undertook the defence without any retainer.

The issues were drawn very distinctly. The prosecuting attorney argued that government was a sacred thing; that if persons high in office were exposed to censure by private individuals, government could not maintain itself. Hamilton, on the other hand, rested his argument for the defence largely on the principle that falsity is necessary to constitute a libel. The court refused to admit the question of truth; whereupon Hamilton made his appeal to the jury with a strong argument for free criticism as the only safeguard against abuses in government. This appeal won the day, and the prisoner was discharged.[1] The outcome of this case had a marked influence in other colonies. It is true that in 1768 Chief Justice Hutchinson, in his charge to the grand jury, urged action on certain articles reflecting upon the governor's conduct which were published in the "Boston Gazette"; but the grand jury ignored the suggestion.[2]

It is no exaggeration to say that without at least partial freedom of speech and of the press the restraining influence of the representative system upon the governor would have been impossible. In the face of open public criticism, the governor could no longer secure the election of representatives who would carry out his policies without question. Subservient representatives knew that they would have to face the

---

[1] On this whole affair, see the report of the case in Howell, *State Trials*, xvii. 675, and the letter of Governor Cosby to the Lords of Trade, *New York Documents*, vi. 4.

[2] Quincy, *Massachusetts Reports*, 262 *seq.*

wrath of their constituents, whereas opposition to the governor might be one of the shortest roads to popularity.

Furthermore, the free expression of public opinion in the press and in the assembly had an important result in strengthening the efficiency of the English system of control. The public sentiment of the colony was thus enabled to make itself felt not only by the governor but also by those authorities to which alone the governor was strictly and legally accountable. Indeed, the assemblies, through their regularly-appointed agents, came to have a very considerable influence in London, and were sometimes even strong enough to secure the recall of obnoxious governors.[1] The name of Benjamin Franklin will at once suggest itself as that of the most successful, or at least the most eminent, of these representatives of colonial opinion.

This study of the provincial governor may be properly closed by a brief survey of the main conclusions which have been reached.

The royal or provincial government was not a system which came full-armed into existence at the beginning of our colonial history, but it had been preceded by other systems, among which it had gained a place which gradually became the dominant one. Direct control by the crown, for example, had been preceded by various arrangements under which government was left in the hands of private persons or of corporations. Again, the ultimate form of the executive in the royal provinces, that of a governor checked by an executive council, had been preceded by experiments, now with a collegiate executive, or again with a single head unchecked by any council. The powers of the governor had also gradually undergone important limitations, as is shown by comparing the elaborate instructions of later days with the brief, indefinite grants of power which had gone before them. In a word, the old confusion of functions had been forced to give way to a partial separation of powers. In the provincial governments, then, — a term including proprietary as well as royal govern-

---

[1] See above, p. 51.

ments, — the executive finally took the form of a governor appointed either by the crown or by the proprietor as the case might be, checked and assisted by an executive council appointed commonly on the governor's recommendation.

The governor's powers and duties were defined by a great variety of instruments, of which the most important were the commission and instructions, issued either by the crown or by the proprietor. These instruments were modified to an important extent by the local usages of the different provinces. The main outlines of the governor's office were determined by his vice-regal character: as the representative of the king, he succeeded with certain inevitable limitations to the powers of the royal prerogative. He was in the first place invested with certain powers which may be regarded as essentially executive, such as the command of the military, the determination of questions of war and peace within narrow limits, the representation of the colony in its external relations, the appointing power, a certain limited control of provincial finance, and finally the power of pardon.

The governor also stood in close and important relations with the other departments of the provincial system, the judiciary and the legislature. Over the former branch he exercised a strong influence through his right of appointing judges and through a limited control of the provincial courts; furthermore, with the council he was in most of the colonies himself a part of the judicial system, whose independence and consequent value as a check upon the executive were seriously impaired. Over the assembly, too, the governor had very considerable influence. He had generally its very existence in his hands; in most provinces he might determine its sessions at will; its upper house was a body of men chosen for the most part on his recommendation, and he had also in his power of distributing patronage a very important instrument for undermining the independence of the representative house; finally, he was himself, through his power of approving or vetoing the acts of the assembly, a part of the legislature of the province.

On the other hand, the assembly through its mere existence as a critical body was the organized expression of the public opinion of the province, and through its power over the purse was able to control the governor's action to an extent which more than counteracted the measure of power which he possessed over the assembly. In this control of the financial situation the assembly had a formidable weapon, which it used not merely as an instrument of security against abuse of executive power, but also as a means of extorting from the governor important powers properly belonging to the executive. The result was that in some of the colonies a very large share of the executive power fell into the hands of the assembly or of their appointees.

But the governor was more than the head of a local system: he was also the agent of the crown, bound to maintain its interests; he was the regular medium of communication between the colonies and the home government, and the executor of acts of Parliament relating to the colonies. Naturally this double nature of the office was often the source of serious embarrassment when royal or British interests came into conflict, or apparent conflict, with the interests of the province.

The governor had also a double responsibility, owing a legal and official accountability to the home government, and a moral and practical one to the people of the province and their representative, the assembly. The first obligation was imperfectly enforced by judicial and administrative processes; the second was more effectively secured by the hold of the assembly on the public purse.

Throughout this study the conflict of opposing principles has been apparent. In the first place, there was the inevitable conflict between legislative and executive departments, marked by the almost universal tendency of the legislature first to check and finally to usurp executive powers. This issue was complicated by the conflicts between two other pairs of opposing principles. The governor, as the representative of the monarchical idea, stood over against the assembly, which represented the people. Finally the governor, as the agent of the crown and therefore the representative of imperial or perhaps more accurately British interests, came in conflict with the assembly which embodied the local forces, the local interests of the province, and sometimes at least broader colonial or American interests. In all of these contests the governor stood for a losing cause.

Rightly then to understand the deeper forces which produced the war of independence, one must understand the gradual growth of that sense of divergent interests without which all the political agitation of Samuel Adams, the eloquence of Patrick Henry, and even a few injudicious measures of British statesmen from 1760 to 1774, could hardly have led to revolution. Nowhere can this gradually awakening consciousness of divergence, so far as it reveals itself prior to what is commonly called the revolutionary era, be better studied than in the conflicts between the provincial governor and the provincial assembly. It is the significance of these issues which has given to this study its chief importance. The questions involved are not of merely antiquarian or temporary or local interest: they are vital, permanent, and fundamental.

APPENDICES.

———•———

APPENDIX A.

REPRESENTATIVE COMMISSIONS AND INSTRUCTIONS.

I. COMMISSION TO SIR THOMAS WEST, LORD LA WARR,
AS GOVERNOR OF VIRGINIA, 1610.

[From Whitelocke Papers, vol. i. No. 38; printed in Alexander Brown, *Genesis of
the United States*, i. 375.] *

THE COPPIE OF THE COMMISSION GRANTED TO THE RIGHT HONORABLE
SIR THOMAS WEST, KNIGHT, LORD LA WARR.

To all unto whome theis presents shall come, We the Lords and others
of his Majesties Councell for the Company of Adventurers and Planters
of the first Collonie in Virginia, resident in England, and We the Treasurer and Companie of the said Adventurers do send greeting in our Lord
God Everlasting. —

Whereas the King's most royall Majesty, that now is, by his Highnes
Letters Pattents under the Great Seale of England, bearing date at
Westminster the three and twentith day of May now last past, before
the date of these presents, hath given unto us his Majesties said Councell full power and authority as well at this present tyme as hereafter
from tyme to tyme, to nominate make constitute ordaine and confirme
by such name or names, stile or stiles as to us his Majesties said Councell shall seeme good, and likewise to revoke discharge, change and alter
all and singular Governors, Officers, and ministers, which have been
made, as also, which should be by us his Majesties said Councell there
after thought fitt and needfull to be made and used for the Government
of the said Collonie and Plantation, and the same at all tymes thereafter

* Reprinted by permission of the author and Messrs. Houghton, Mifflin and
Company.

to abrogate, revoke or change, not only within the precincts of the said Collonie but also upon the seas in going and coming to and from the said Collonie, as we the said Councell in our discretions shall thinke to be fittest for the good of the Adventurers and Inhabitants there.

And Whereas his Majestie by his said Letters Pattents hath declared that for divers reasons and considerations him thereunto especially moveing, his will and pleasure is, and by his said letters patents he hath ordained, that immediately from and after such tyme that any Governor, or principall Officer so to be nominated by us his Majesties said Councell for the government of the said Collonie aforesaid, shall arrive in Virginia and give notice unto the Collonie there resident of his Majesties pleasure in this behalf, the Government, power and authoritie of the President and Councell then to be there established and all Laws and Constitutions by them formerly made shall utterlie cease and be determined, and all officers, Governors and ministers formerlie constituted or apointed shalbe discharged anything in any of his Majesties Letters Pattents concerning the said Plantation contained in anywise to the contrary notwithstanding.

And Whereas, also his said Majestie by his said Letters Pattents hath ordained and graunted that such Governers, officers and ministers as by us his Majesties said Councell shall be constituted and apointed, according to the natures and limitts of their severall offices and place respectivelie should and might from tyme to tyme forever thereafter, within the precincts of Virginia or in the way by the sea thither and from thence, have full and absolute power and authoritie to correct, punish, pardone, governe and Rule, all such the subjects of his Majestie, his heirs and successors in any voyage thither, or that should at any tyme there inhabite in the precincts and Territorie of the said Collonie, as is aforesaid, according to such ordinances, orders, directions, constitutions and Instructions, as by us his Majesties said Councell for the tyme being shalbe established, and in defect thereof in case of necessitie according to the good discrecions of the said Governors and Officers respectively, as well in cases Capitall and Criminall as civill, both Marine and others, so allwaies as the said statutes, ordinances and proceedings as neere as convenientlie maybe, be agreeable to the Laws, Statutes, Government and Policie of this his Majesties Realme of England.

And Whereas likewise his said Majestie hath by his said Letters Pattents, graunted, declared and ordained that such principall Governors as from tyme to tyme should dulie and lawfullie be authorized and appointed in manner and forme as by the said Letters Pattents be expressed, should in cases of Rebellion and Muteny have power and authoritie to use and exercise Marshall Law in as large and ample manner and forme as his Majesties Lieftenants in his highnes counties within the Realme of England, have or ought to have, by force of their Commissions of Lieftenancie, as in and by the said Letters Pattents amongst other things in them contained more at large doth and may apeare.

Now KNOW YEE that We his Majesties said Councell upon good advise and deliberation and upon notice had of the Wisedome, valour, circumspection, and of the virtue and especiall sufficiencie of the *Right Honourable Sir Thomas West, Knight Lord La Warr* to be in principall place of authoritie and Government in the said Collonie, and finding in him the said Lord La Warr propensness and willingness to further and advance the good of the said Plantation, by virtue of the said authoritie unto us given by the said Letters Pattents have nominated, made, ordained and apointed and by these presents do nominate make ordaine and apointe the said Sir Thomas West, Knight Lord La Warr to be principall Governor, Commander and Captain Generall both by Land and Sea over the said Collonie and all other Collonies planted or to be planted in Virginia or within the limitts specified in his Majesties said Letters Pattents and over all persons, Admiralls Vice-Admiralls and other Officers and Commanders whether by sea or land of what quallitie soever for and during the term of his natural life, and do hereby ordaine and declare that he the said Lord La Warr during his life shall be stiled and called by the name and title of *Lord Governor* and *Captain General of Virginia* and of the Collonie and Collonies there now planted or to be planted, and do by these presents revoke and change all and all manner of former constitutions, ordinancies, apointments and authorities by us his Majesties said Councell or any of us given, made, nominated, constituted ordained or apointed to any to be President, Chief Governor or principal Officer in Virginia aforesaid or to use or exercise the authority jurisdictions or offices 'herein limitted graunted or apointed or mentioned to be graunted or apointed to the said Lord La Warr and of and from the same and everie of them do hereby discharge all and everie persone and persones heretofore authorized, nominated or apointed to use execute or exercise the same or any of them and that the said Lord La Warr, Lord Governor and Captain Generall as is aforesaid in all cases of Rebellion and Mutenie happening or which shall happen, either within the precincts of Virginia limited or specified in his Majesties said Letters Pattents or in the present intended passage and expedition thither, shall have such power and authoritie to use, exercise and put in execution

Marshall Law as in the said Letters Pattents is mentioned, and upon all other cases as well Capitall as Criminall and upon all other accidents and occasions there happening, to rule, punish, pardone and governe according to such directions orders and instructions as by his Majesties said Councell, or the greater part thereof here resident in England shall from tyme to tyme, be in that behalf made and given with the consent of Henrie Earle of Southampton, William Earl of Pembroke, Philip Earle of Mountgomerie, Robert Lord Viscount Lisle, Theophilus Lord Howard of Walden, Edmond Lord Sheffield and George Lord Carew, or any two of them, and in defect of such informations he the said Lord Governor and Captain Generall shall and may rule and governe by his owne discretion or by such lawes for the present government as he with such councell as he shall take unto him, or as he the said Lord Governor and Captain Generall shall think fitt to make and establish for the advancement of the publique weale and good of the said Collonie with as full and absolute power authority and commaund as either we by virtue of his Majesties said Letters Pattents have power to derive and graunt to him or as he the said Lord Governor and Captain Generall by his Majesties said Letters Pattents in any sort is authorized to use and exercise.

AND FURTHER KNOW YEE that we his Majesties said Councell by these presents as much as in us lieth do give and graunt full power and authoritie to the said Lord Governor and Captain Generall, of his free will and pleasure to call unto his assistance and to choose for Councellors such and so many persons of the said Collonie now planted in Virginia or hereafter to be planted there as he shall think fitt and meete, and to displace such from being Councellors whose demerit he shall conceive to give cause thereof. And likewise to place for Councellors and Officers such persons as he from tyme to tyme during his government there shall think fitt. And also at all tymes at his will and pleasure, to discharge, displace and put from the execution of all, every or any such Officer or Officers as he shall think meete, such personns as now be there in office, or which shall hereafter be in any office in the said Collonie now planted or hereafter to be planted in Virginia during his life as he the said Lord Governor and Captain Generall shall deeme worthie to be displaced or put from any such his office or place, which any such person doth or shall so hould : The Office of Lieftennant Governor, Marshall, Admirall and Vice-Admirall, and all governors of Provinces and Townes which shalbe made or constituted by us, the said Councell resident here in England, allwaies excepted, which said officers and governors so excepted, it shall and may nevertheles be lawfull to and for the said Lord Governor and Captain Generall to suspend and put from the execution of all and everie their said office and offices and governments, and others in their places, offices and governments to constitute and apoint at his pleasure, untill further order shalbe therein taken by us his Majesties said Councell resident here in England. And in like manner we his Majesties said Councell, Treasurer and Companie do by these presents as much as in us lieth, give and graunte full power and authoritie to the said Lord Governor and Captain Generall at his will and pleasure from tyme to tyme, and at all tymes hereafter during his life, by or with any office or place in Virginia aforesaid, for increase of any man's person, by bill of adventure for land, onelie not to exceede a four fould proportion of the first rate of his adventure, or of the Office which he shall beare, unless the same be by expresse consent of the said Councell and Companie, here resident, of Virginia and under their Seale, to reward and recompense the good and well deservinge of any person or personns what soever under his Government according as he the said Lord Governor and Captain Generall shall in his wisedome and discretion think such persons to have merited and deserved. To have, hould, use and exercise the stile and title of Lord Governor and Captain Generall of Virginia and all other the jurisdictions, powers and authorities aforesaid, to him the said Sir Thomas West, Knight, Lord La Warr, for and during the tearme of his naturall life, without any revocation or restraint by us the said Councell or any of us in any wise to be made otherwise than before is excepted : —

AND KNOW YEE further that we his Majesties said Councell have made, ordained and constituted and by these presents do make, ordaine and constitute the said Lord La Warr, Admirall of the whole Fleete of such shipps and other vessels as are apointed and by the Grace of God shall be imploied and passe in this present intended expedition to Virginia aforesaid, giving him the said Lord La Warr full power and authoritie to exercise and put in execution in all cases and upon all occasions and accidents, upon all persons passing in the said Fleete full and absolute power, authoritie and command in this behalf as by his Majesties Letters Pattents we or any of us, have power to derive and graunt unto him : And for the more securitie and safetie as well of the said Fleete in their present passage as of the said Collonie and Plantation We his Majesties said Councell by virtue of the authoritie unto us in this behalf given or graunted Do hereby give full power and authoritie to the said Lord La Warr, at all tymes during his naturall life, to encounter, expulse, repell and resist by force of Arms, and by all wayes and meanes whatsoever, all manner of persons that shall at any time either by sea or land, enterprise or attempt the destruction, invasion, hurt, detriment or anoyance of the said Fleete, Collonies, or Plantation. We also hereby and in his Majesties name strictlie command and require, all and everie person and persons now inhabiting or which shall hereafter inhabite within the precincts of the said Collonie, and which shall passe in the said Fleete thitherward, in all things and upon all occasions, to yield unto the said Lord Governor and Captain Generall all due honour and respect, and dulie and willinglie to obey and execute the directions and commands of the said Lord Governor and Captain Generall according to the authoritie to him limited and given, as also to be unto him upon all occasions, to their powers and habilities, aiding and assisting, as they will to their utmost perills answere the contrary.

AND LASTLIE We his Majesties said Councell for us, and We the said Treasurer and Companie respectivelie, by these presents as much as in us or any of us lieth or shalbe, do respectivelie promise and graunt to the said Lord La Warr, Lord Governor and Captain Generall of Virginia, that if it shall hereafter apeare to his Lordship that it shall be meet for him to have any other Articles or Clauses to authorise him more then in these premises is mentioned, to rule, governe, do or execute any Act or Acts, thing or things, which may tend to the furtherance or benefite of the said Collonies or Plantations, or the good government thereof, or the rewarding of any persons as aforesaid, that then upon notice thereof and request made by or from his Lordship: to us the said Councell, Treasurer and Companie, and the successors of us the said Councell, Treasurer and Companie, for the tyme being, We his Majesties said Councell, Treasurer and Companie for the tyme being, shall and will, from time to tyme do our utmost Indeavour and as much as in us or any of us lieth, by graunt or otherwise to enlarge the same and to satisfie his Lordships reasonable desire therein. And lastlie, we his Majesties said Councell do condescend and agree, to and with the said Sir Thomas West, Knight, Lord La Warr, that in cases of necessitie, or upon any other occasion which shall happen, he may withdraw himself from being resident with or in the said Collonie or Collonies in Virginia and that it shall and may be lawfull to and for him the said Lord La Warr, to nominate, make, constitute, depute and apoint, such person or persons as he shall think meet to be his Deputie or Deputies and Lieftennant Governor in his absence to rule and governe the said Collonie and Collonies in Virginia, for, by and during the space of one whole year next after the said Lord La Warr his being absent from the Collonie and his deputing of any person or personns so to be by his Lordship constituted, deputed or apointed, for no longer tyme, unlesse authoritie and further warrant therein shalbe given unto such deputie and deputies by and from us his Majesties said Councell, under our Councell Seale and sent to him as a warrant for his or their continueing Deputie or Deputies or Lieftennant Governor over the said Collonie or Collonies: which Deputie or Deputies so to be made, constituted or apointed by the said Lord La Warr for the space of such whole yere as aforesaid shalbe in the absence of the said Lord La Warr Governor of the said Collonie or Collonies, and shall have such power and authoritie by and with all our consents, agreements and apointments to do and execute all things touching the said Government, as the said Lord La Warr shall unto such Deputie or Deputies, assigne, limitt and appoint.

In wittness wherof we his Majesties said Councell, apointed by his Majesties Letters Pattents, for so much in these presents as concerneth us and our graunt herein mentioned, by mutuall consent and agreement have sett hereunto our hands and the seale of us the said Councell: And likewise We the said Treasurer and Company for so much in these presents as concerneth us and our graunts herein mentioned, by mutuall consent and agreement have hereunto sett the seale of Our Corporation.

Given at his Majesties cittie of London aforesaid the 28th day of February in the 7th yere of his Majesties raigne of England, France and Ireland and of Scotland the 43.

SOUTHAMPTON.	PEMBROKE.
PHILIP, MOUNTGOMERIE.	THEOPHILUS HOWARD.
EDWARD CECILL.	WILLIAM WAAD.
WALTER COPE.	EDWARD CONOWAY.
THOMAS SMITH.	BAPTIST HICKS.
DUDLIE DIGGS,	ROBART MANSILL.
CHRISTOPHER BROOK.	WILLIAM ROMNEY.

2. COMMISSION TO SIR WILLIAM BERKELEY AS GOVERNOR OF VIRGINIA, 1641.

[From Rymer, *Fœdera*, xx. 484.]

De Constitutione Gubernatoris & Concilii pro Virginia.

Charles, by the Grace of God, King of *England*, *Scotland*, *France* and *Ireland*, Defender of the Faith, &c.

To our trusty and welbeloved,

Sir *William Berkeley* Knight, one of the Gentlemen of our Privy Chamber,

Sir *Francis Wyat* Knight,

John West Esquire,

Richard Kempe Esquire,

Samuel Matthews Esquire,

Nathaniel Littleton Esquire,

Christopher Wormely Esquire,

William Pierce Esquire,

Roger Windgate Esquire,

John Hopson Esquire,

Thomas Pawlet Esquire,

George Minify Esquire,

Henry Brown Esquire,

William Brocas Esquire,

Argol Yardley Esquire,

Thomas Pettus Esquire,

Thomas Willoughby Esquire,

Richard Bennet Esquire,

And *Humfrey Higgeson* Esquire, Greeting.

Whereas, by our Letters Patents under our Great Seal of *England*, bearing date the eleventh day of *January*, in the fourteenth year of our Reign, for the better maintenance and government of the Colony and Plantation in *Virginia*, [we] did nominate and appoint the said Sir *Francis Wyatt* Knight, to be the then present Governor thereof, and such other persons, as We in and by Instructions under our Sign Manual, had then named and assigned, or thenafter should name and assign, to be the then present Counsel, of and for the said Colony and Plantation of *Virginia;* Granting unto him or them, and the greater number of them, full power and authority to perform and execute the Places, Powers and Authorities, incident to a Governor and Counsel of *Virginia* respectively, as by the same Letters Patents of Commission, more at large may appear ; Which said Commission and all Places, Powers and Authorities, Matters and Things thereby granted or mentioned to be granted, We do to all Intents and Purposes, fully and absolutely revoke, determine and make void by these Presents ; Nevertheless, We being willing to give all encouragement to that Plantation, and minding that our Colony and People there, should be regulated as well in Ecclesiastical as Temporal Government, according to the Laws and Statutes of our Realm of *England*, which We purpose to have established there, and being resolved not to impeach or hinder, but to promote and advance the particular Interests of such of the Planters there, as shall conform themselves as loyal Subjects, in all due Obedience to our Government, and to discourage such, as shall be found Disturbers of the Peace and Impugners of the said Colony.

Know ye therefore, that We for the effecting of the Premises, and the better ordering, governing and managing, of the Affairs of the said Colony and Plantation in *Virginia*, and of the Persons now inhabiting, and which shall hereafter inhabit there, until We shall find some more convenient means, upon mature Advice, to give more ample Directions for the same ; And reposing assured Trust and Confidence, in the Understanding, Care, Fidelity, Experience and Circumspection, of you the said

Sir *William Berkeley*,
Sir *Francis Wyatt*,
John West,
Richard Kemp,
Samuel Matthews,
Nathaniel Littleton,
Christopher Wormley,
William Pierce,
Roger Windgate,
John Hopson,
Thomas Paulet,
George Minify,
Henry Brown,
William Brocas,
Argol Yardly,
Thomas Pettus,
Thomas Willoughby,
Richard Bennet,
And *Humfrey Higgeson*,

Have nominated and assigned, and by these Presents do nominate and assign you the said Sir *William Berkeley*, to be the present Governor, and you the said Sir *Francis Wyatt, John West, Richard Kemp, Samuel Matthews, Nathaniel Littleton, Christopher Wormeley, William Peirce, Roger Windgate, John Hopson, Thomas Paulet, George Minify, Henry Brown, William Brocas, Argol Yardley, Thomas Pettus, Thomas Willoughby, Richard Bennet,* and *Humfrey Higgeson,* to be the present Counsel of and for the said Colony and Plantation in *Virginia*, giving, and by these Presents granting unto you and them, and the greater number of you and them respectively, full Power and Authority, to perform and execute the Places, Powers, and Authorities, incident to a Governor and Counsel of *Virginia* respectively, and to direct and govern, correct and punish our Subjects, now inhabiting or being, or which hereafter shall inhabit or be in *Virginia*, or in the Isles, Ports, Havens, Creeks or Territories thereof, either in time of Peace or War, and to order and direct the Affairs, touching or concerning that Colony or Plantation, in those Foreign Parts only, and to execute and perform all and every other matters and things, concerning that Plantation, as fully and amply, as any other Governor and Counsel resident there, at any time, within the space of ten Years now last past, had or might perform or execute.

And because, by the experience of industrious and well-experienced Men, the limits and bounds of the said Plantation may be augmented, and Trade and Commerce, for the maintenance and enriching of the Inhabitants there, from time to time residing, much advanced; Our will and pleasure is, and We do by these Presents give and grant unto you the said Sir *William Berkeley*, and the rest of you our said Counsel beforementioned, or any four or more of you, (whereof the Governor for the time being to be always one) full Power and Authority, to grant one or more Commission or Commissions, unto any of our Subjects, addressing themselves unto our said Governor and Counsel, for the discovery of the same Country and Ports, Bounds, Limits and Extents thereof; And also for the finding out, what Trades shall be most necessary to be undertaken, for the benefit and advantage of the said Colony and Plantation, and the good of the People inhabiting, or which shall inhabit there, both by Sea and Land; And further, upon all occasions as you or any four or more of you (whereof you the Governor for the time being to be always one) shall see fit, to send out Forces, for the subduing of the *Indians* and Savages of the said Country; And likewise to make War and Peace with them, in all such cases as may stand with the safety of the said Colony and our Honour, keeping always sufficient Forces for the holding of the places now enjoyed.

And if it shall happen, you the said Sir *William Berkley* to die, or in case of your urgent occasions (allowed by four or more of our said Counsel there) shall call you thence at any time, then our Will and Pleasure is, and We do hereby give and grant to you the said Sir *William Berkeley*, and the rest of the Commissioners before named, or the greater number of you, full Power and Authority, upon the Death or in the absence of you the said Sir *William Berkeley*, to elect, nominate and assign one of our said Counsel, to be the present Governor for the said Colony and Plantation in *Virginia*, and so to do from time to time, as often as the case shall require ; And We do by these Presents assign and appoint, such Person, as by you our said Counsel or the greater number of you, from time to time shall be elected and chosen to be the present Governor, and the said Governor and the rest of our Commissioners, to be our present Counsel for the said Colony or Plantation for *Virginia;* Giving and by these Presents granting unto you, and the greater number of you respectively, full Power and Authority, to execute and perform the Places, Powers and Authorities, of a Governor and Counsel of *Virginia* respectively, in manner and form aforesaid ; Nevertheless our Will and Pleasure is, that you and every of you, from time to time proceed, according to such instructions as you or they, do now or hereafter shall receive from us, or the Lords and others of our Privy Council here ; And that you, our said Governor and Counsel there for the time being, shall be from time to time subordinate, subject and obedient, to the Lords Commissioners and Committees here for our Plantations, for the time being, touching the present Government of that Plantation, and according to such Orders and Directions, as they from time to time shall conceive and set down.

Provided always, and our express Will, Pleasure and Commandment is, and We do hereby give full Power and Authority unto you the said Sir *William Berkeley*, and such other Person as shall be Governor there, for the time being, according to the true intent of these Presents, and our intention herein before declared, that upon the death or discontinuance of any one of our Counsel there, you the said Sir *William Berkeley*, and such other Person as shall be Governor there, and our Counsel there for the time being, or the greater part of them, shall elect, nominate and appoint, such other sufficient, able and discreet Person or Persons, in the room or place of him or them so dying or discontinuing, during the continuance of this our present Commission ; And that you shall from time to time, return and certify the Names and Qualities of such Person or Persons, so by you to be nominated and appointed, in the

room of such of our Counsel, there dying or discontinuing as aforesaid, unto
Us and the Lords and others our Commissioners for Plantations here
to the end, such Person or Persons to be by you and them so elected
nominated and appointed, in manner aforesaid, may receive allowance
or disallowance, of such their election or choice, in the room of such of
our Counsel there, as shall either die or discontinue, as there shall be
cause, or to us or our said Commissioners for Plantations here, shall
seem meet.

And our further Will and Pleasure is, That you the said Sir *William
Berkeley* and *Richard Kemp,* before you or either of you depart out of
this our Kingdom of *England,* shall take such Oaths, before the Lord-
Keeper, Lord Privy Seal or either of them, for this our Kingdom, as the
Governor and Counsel for the said Plantation and Colony, have hereto-
fore taken, and after such Oaths, by you the said Sir *William Berkeley*
and *Richard Kemp* so taken as aforesaid, We do hereby charge and
command you, to administer unto the said Sir *Francis Wyatt Knight,
John West, Samuel Matthews, Nathaniel Littleton, Christopher Wormeley,
William Peirs, Roger Windgate, John Hopton, Thomas Paulet, George
Minify, Henry Brown, William Brocas, Argal Yardley, Thomas Pettus,
Thomas Willoughby, Richard Bennet,* and *Humfrey Higgeson,* and every
of them, the like Oath upon the Holy Evangelist, as you or either of you
have already taken, as Counsellor, of or for the said Colony or Plantation; Willing and requiring you and them, to be diligent and attendant
in the execution of this our Service and Commandment, and also requiring all our loving Subjects there, to be directed and governed by you,
or the greater number, of you and them our Commissioners aforesaid, in
all things, according to the intention and true meaning of these Presents;
And lastly, our Will and Pleasure is, that this our Commission shall
continue in force, until We, by some other Writing under our Signet,
Privy Seal, or Great Seal of *England,* shall signify our Pleasure to the
contrary.

In Witness &c.
Witness our self at *Westminster,* the ninth day of *August.*

Per ipsum Regem.

3. INSTRUCTIONS TO SIR WILLIAM BERKELEY AS GOVERNOR OF VIRGINIA, [1641].

[From the MacDonald Papers (pp. 376–388), in the Virginia State Library; printed in the *Virginia Magazine of History and Biography*, ii. 281.] *

Instructions to Sir William Berkeley, Knt., one of the Gentlemen of our Privy Chamber, Governor of Virginia, and to the Council of State there :

That in the first place you be carefull Almighty God may be duly and daily served according to the Form of Religion established in the church of England both by yourself and all the people under your charge, which may draw down a blessing on all your endeavours.   And let every congregation that hath an able minister build for him a convenient Parsonage House, to which for his better maintenance over and above the usual pension you lay 200 acres of Gleable lands, for the clearing of that ground every of his Parishoners for three years shall give some days labours of themselves and their Servants, and see that you have a special care that the Glebe Land be sett as neare the Parsonage House as may be and that it be of the best conditioned Land.   Suffer no invasion in matters of Religion and be careful to appoint sufficient and conformable Ministers to each congregation, that you chatechise and instruct them in the grounds and principles of Religion.

2. That you administer the Oaths of Allegiance and Supremacy to all such as come thither with intention to plant themselves in the country, which if he shall refuse he is to be returned and shipped from thence home and certificate made to the Lords of the Councill, the same oath is to be administered to all other persons when you shall see it fitt as Mariners, Merchants &c. to prevent any danger of spyes.

3. That Justice be equally administered to all his Majesty's subjects there residing and as neere as may bee after the forme of this Realm of England and vigilant care to be had to prevent corruption in officers tending to the delay or perverting of Justice.

4. That you and the Councellors as formerly once a year or oftener, if urgent occasion shall require, Do summon the Burgesses of all and singler Plantations there, which together with the Governor and Councill makes the Grand Assembly, and shall have Power to make Acts and Laws for the Government of that Plantation correspondent, as near as

* Reprinted by permission of the Editor.

may be, to the Laws of England, in which assembly the Governor is to have a negative voice, as formerly.

[5.] That you and the Councill assembled are to sett down the fittest Months of the Quarterly meeting of the Councill of State, whereas they are to give their attendance for one and consult upon matter of Councill and State and to decide and determine such Causes as shall come before them, and that free access be admitted to all Suitors to make known their particular grievances, being against what persons So ever wherein the Governor for the time being, as formerly, is to have but a casting voyce if the number of the councellors should be equally divided in opinion, besides the Quarterly Meeting of the Council it shall be lawful for you to summon, from time to time, Extraordinary meetings of the Councill according to emergent occasions.

6. In case there shall be necessary cause to pr'ceed against any of the Councill for their own persons they are in such cases to be summoned by you, the Governor, to appear at the next Sessions of the Councill, holden there to abide their Sensure or otherwise, if you shall think it may concern either the Safety or quiet of that State to proceed more speedily with such an offender. It shall be lawful to summon a councill extraordinary where at six of the council at least are to be present with you, and by the Major part if [of] their voyces comit my councillors to safe custody or upon Bayle to abide the order of the next quarter councill.

7. For the ease of the Country and quicker despatch of Business you, the Governor and Councill, may appoint in places convenient Inferior Courts of Justice and Commissioners for the Same, to determine of suits not exceeding the value of Ten Pounds and for the punishments of such offences as you and the Councill shall think fitt to give them the power to hear and determine.

8. The Governor shall appoint officers of sealing of writts and subponas and such officers as shall be thought necessary for the execution [of] orders.

And — also the acts and Laws of the Generall Assembly and for punishing any neglect or contempt of the Said Orders, Acts or Laws respectively. And shall nominate and appoint all other publique officers under the degree of the council, the Captain of the Fort, Master and Surveyor Generall excepted.

9. That since the Council attend his Majesties Service and the publique business to the great hindrance of the private, that they and ten servants for every Councellor be exempted from all publique charges

and contributions assessed and levyed by the Generall Assembly (a Warr defensive, assistance towards the Building of a Town or churches or the ministers' dues excepted).

10. To avoid all questions concerning the Estates of Persons dying in Virginia, it shall be lawfull as it hath been used heretofore to make probates of Wills, and default of a Will to grant Letters of Administration in ye Colony : Provided always that such to whom Administration is granted do put in sufficient security to be accomptable to such persons in England or elsewhere unto whom of right those Estates shall belong. And that such Probate of Wills and Letters of Administration shall be and abide in full force and virtue to all intents and purposes.

11. To the end the country may be the better served against all Hostil Invasions it is requisite that all persons from the age of 16 to 60 be armed with arms, both offensive and defensive. And if any person be defective in this kind, wee strictly charge you to command them to provide themselves of sufficient arms within one year or sooner if possible it may be done, and if any shall faill to be armed at the end of the Term limited we will that you punish them severely.

12. And for that Arms without the Knowledge of the use of them are of no effect wee ordain that there be one Muster Master Generall, appointed by us for the Colony, who shall 4 times in the year and oftener (if cause be) not only view the arms, ammunition and furniture of every Person in the Colony, but also train and exercise the people, touching the use and order of arms and shall also certify the defects if any be either of appearance or otherwise to you the Governor and Councill. And being informed that the place is vacant by the death of George Dunn we do nominate and appoint our trusty and beloved John West, Esq., being recommended unto us for his sufficiency and long experience in the country, to be Muster Master of the said Colony. And for his competent maintenance we will that you, the Governor and Councill, so order the business at a General Assembly that every Plantation be rated equally according to the number of persons, wherein you are to follow the course practised in the Realm of England.

13. That you cause likewise 10 Guarders to be maintained for the Port at Point Comfort. And that you take course that ye Capt[n] of ye said Port have a competent allowance for his services there. Also that the said ffort be well kept in Reparation and provided with ammunition.

14. That new Comers be exempted the 1st yeare from going in p'son or contributing to the wars Save only in defence of the place where they shall inhabit and that only when the enemies shall assail them, but all

others in the Colony shall go or be rated to the maintenance of the war proportionately to their abilitys, neither shall any man be priviledged for going to the warr that is above 16 years old and under 60, respect being had to the quality of the person, that officers be not forced to go as private soldiers or in places inferior to their Degrees, unless in case of supreme necessity.

15. That you may better avoid and prevent the treachery of the savages we strictly forbid all persons whatsoever to receive into their houses the person of any Indian or to converse or trade with them without the especiall license and warr^t given to that purpose according to the commissioner inflicting severe punishment upon the offenders.

16. For preventing of all surprizes as well as of the treacherous savages as of any fforaine enemy we require you to erect Beacons in severall partes of ye Countries by firing whereof the country may take notice of their attempts of their Beacons or their watching them to beare the charge of the country as shall be determined by a Generall Assembly or otherwise by the shooting off 3 Pieces whereby they may take the Alarum as shall be found most convenient.

17. That for raising of towns every one [of] ye [who] have and shall have a grant of 500 acres of land, shall, within a convenient time, build a convenient house of brick of 24 feet long and 16 feet broad with a cellar to it and so proportionately for Grants of larger or lesser quantity. And the grounds and platforms for the towns to be laid out in such form and order as the Governor and Councill shall appoint. And that you cause at ye publick charge of ye country a convenient house to be built where you and the councill may meet and sitt for the dispatching of publick affairs and hearing of causes. And because the buildings at Jamestown are for the most part decayed and the place found to be unhealthy and inconvenient in many respects. It shall be in the power of you and the council, with the advice of ye Generall Assembly, to choose such other seate for your chiefe Town and Residence of the Governor as by them shall be judged most convenient, retaining the ancient name of James Town.

18. That you shall have power to grant Patents and to assign such Proportion of Land to all adventurers and Planters as have been useful heretofore in the like cases, either for adventurers of money, [or] Transportation of people thither according to the orders of the late company and since allowed by his Majesty.

And that there likewise be the same proportion of Fifty acres of land granted and assigned for every p'son transported thither since Midsummer, 1625. And that you continue ye same course to all persons transported thither untill it shall be otherwise determined by his Maj⁺ʸ.

19. Whereas the greatest part of the Land on James River hath been formerly granted unto particular persons or public society but being by them either not planted at all or for many years deserted, divers planters have by orders and leave of the Governor and Councill of Virginia set down upon these lands or some part of them which was absolutely necessary for the defence and security of the Colony against the Indians, that the Governor confirm those Lands unto the present Planters and Possessors thereof. And that the like course be taken for Planting new Patents in any other places so unplanted and deserted as aforesaid where it shall be found necessary. And in case former proprietors make their claims thereunto that there be assigned to them the like quantities in any other part of the Colony not actually possessed where they shall make choice.

20. That you call for the Charter Parties that Masters of Ships bring along with [them] and strictly examine whether they have truly p'formed the condicons of their contracts. And further, diligently to inquire and examine whether they have given sufficient and wholesome food and drink with convenient room to the passengers during the voyage. And that no Servants be discharged the Ships and turned ashore as formerly untill their Masters have notice and sufficient time to send for them. And that upon complaint in any of these particulars you give such redress as justice shall require.

21. That in regard you may daily expect the coming of a fforaign enemy, Wee require you soon after the first landing that you publish by proclamation throughout the Colony that no person whatsoever upon the arrival of any ships shall dare to go on board without ye express warrᵗ from you the Governor and councill, least by the means they be surprized to the great prejudice if not the overthrow of the Plantation.

22. And to avoid that intolerable abuse of Ingrossing comodities of forestalling ye Market, That you require all Masters of Ships not to break Bulk until they arrive of Saint James City or otherwise without speciall orders from ye the Governor and Councill, and that care be taken that there be sufficient Storehouses and Warehouses for the same and convenient laying of their goods as they shall arrive.

23. That you endeavour by severe punishment to suppress drunkenness, And that you be carefull ye great quantity of wine and strong waters be not sold into the hands of those that be likeliest to abuse it, but that so near as you can it may be equally disposed of for the relief of ye whole Plantation. And if any Merchant or other for

private Lucre shall bring in any corrupt or unwholesome wines, waters or any other Liquors, such as may endanger the health of the people and shall so be found upon the oaths of sufficient p'sons appointed for the Tryall that the vessel be staved.

24. That especiall care be taken for ye preservacon of neat cattle and that the ffemales be not killed up as formerly, whereby the Colony will in short time have such plenty of victualls, yt much people may come thither for the setting up of iron works and other staple commodities. That you cause the People to plant great store of corne, as there may be one whole years provision before hand in the Colony least in relying upon one single Harvest, Drought, Blasting or otherwise they fall into such wants or Famine as formerly they have endured. And that the Plow may go and English [?] be sowed in all places convenient. And that no Corne nor Cattle be sold out of the Plantation without leave from the Governor and Councill.

25. That they apply themselves to the Impaling of Orchards and gardens for Roots and Fruits w'ch that country is so proper for, & that every Planter be compelled for every 500 acres granted unto him to Inclose and sufficiently ffence either with Pales or Quicksett and Dikes, and so from time to time to preserve, enclosed and ffenced a quarter of an acre of Ground in ye most convenient place near his Dwelling House for Orchards and gardens.

26. That whereas yoᵣ Tobacco falleth every day more and more unto a baser price, that it be stinted into a far less proportion then hath been made in ye last year 1637, not only to be accounted by the plants but by the quantity when 'tis cured. And because of Great Debts of the Planter in Tobacco, occasioned by the excessive rates of commodities have been the stinting thereof, so hard to be put into execution that the course commanded by his Majesty in his letter of the 22nd of April, in ye 13th year of His Reign for regulating ye debts of ye Colony be duly observed. And also not to suffer men to build slight cottages as heretofore hath been there used. And to remove from place to place, only to plant Tobacco. That Trademen and Handy Crafts be compelled to follow their severall Trades and occupations, and that ye draw you into Towns.

27. We require you to use yoᵣ best endeavᵣ to cause ye people there to apply themselves to the raising of more staple commodities as Hemp and Flax, Rope, Seed and Madder, Pitch & Tarr for Tanning of Hides and Leather. Likewise every Plantation to plant a proportion of Vines, answerable to their numbers, and to plant white Mulberry Trees, and attend Silk Worms.

28. That the Merchant be not constrained to take Tobacco at any Price, in Exchange for his wares. But that it be lawfull for him to make his own Bargain for his goods he so changeth notwithstanding any Proclamation here published to the contrary.

29. That no merchant shall be suffered to bring in Ten pounds worth of wine or strong waters that brings not one hundred pounds worth of necessary commodities and so rateably. And that every Merchant that deserveth a Warr^t for the recovery of his Debt shall bring in a bill of Parcells with the Rates of the severall Commodities, whereby ye certainty of the Debt and ye comodities thereof may ye better appeare.

30. That whereas many ships laden with Tobacco and other merchandize from thence, carry ye same immed^{ly} into fforraine countries, whereby his Maj^{ty} loseth ye custom and Duties thereupon due, nothing being answered in Virginia, You bee very carefull that no ship or other vessell whatsoever depart from thence, fraighted with Tobacco or other commodities w^h that country shall afford, before Bond w^h sufficient sureties be taken to Maties use to bring the same directly unto his Maj^{ties} Dominions and not else where, and to bring a Bill of Lading from home that the staple of those comodities may be made here, whereby his Maj^{tie}, after so great expence upon that Plantation and so many of his subjects Transported thither, may not be defrauded of what shall be justly due unto him for custom and other duties upon those goods. These Bonds to be transmitted to ye Councill here, and from thence to ye Exchequer, that ye Delinquent may be proceeded with according to due course of Law.

31. Next that you strictly and resolutely forbid all Trade or Trucking for any Merchandize whatsoever w^h any ship other then His Maj^{ties} subjects, that shall either purposely or casually come to any of y^r plantations. And that if, upon some unexpected occasions and necessity, the Governor and Councill shall think fitt to admitt such intercourse, wch we admitt not but upon some extremity, That good caution and Bond be taken, both of the Master and also the owner of the said Tobacco or other comodities so laden that they shall (Damages of the Sea Excepted) be brought to our Port of London, there to pay unto us such duties as are due upon the same.

And to conclude, That in all things accordingly to y^r best understanding ye endeavour the extirpation of vice and encouragement of Religion, virtue and goodness.

CHARLES.

4. COMMISSION TO FRANCIS BERNARD AS GOVERNOR OF NEW JERSEY, 1758. [Draft.]

[From the Public Record Office, Board of Trade, New Jersey Papers, vol. xvi. p. 25; printed in *New Jersey Documents,* ix. 23.]

1.* GEORGE THE SECOND by the Grace of God, of Great Britain, France and Ireland King, Defender of the Faith, &c.

To Our trusty and Wellbeloved Francis Bernard Esq.ʳ Greeting : We reposing especial Trust and Confidence in the Prudence, Courage and Loyalty of you the said Francis Bernard, of our especial Grace certain Knowledge and meer motion, have thought fit to constitute and appoint, and by these Presents do constitute and appoint you the said Francis Bernard to be Our Cap.ⁿ General and Governor in Chief in & over Our Province of Nova Cæsarea or New Jersey, Viz : the Division of East and West New Jersey in America, which we have thought fit to reunite into one Province and settle under one entire Government.

2. And We do hereby require and command you to do and execute all things in due manner, that shall belong unto your said Command and the Trust We have reposed in you, according to the several Powers and Directions granted or appointed you by this present Commission, and the Instructions and Authorities herewith given you, or by such further Powers, Instructions and Authorities as shall at any time hereafter be granted or appointed you under Our Signet and Sign Manual or by Our Order in Our Privy Council, and according to such reasonable Laws and Statutes, as now are in Force, or hereafter shall be made and agreed upon by you, with the Advice and Consent of Our Council and the Assembly of Our said Province under your Government, in such manner and form as is hereafter expressed.

3. And Our Will and Pleasure is, that you the said Francis Bernard, after the Publication of these Our Letters Patents, do in the first Place take the oaths appointed to be taken by an Act passed in the first Year of Our late Royal Father's Reign, entituled, *An Act for the further Security of His Majesty's Person and Government, and the Succession of the Crown in the Heirs of the late Princess Sophia being Protestants, and for extinguishing the Hopes of the pretended Prince of Wales and his open and secret Abettors :* As also that you make and subscribe the Declaration mentioned in an Act of Parliament made in the 25ᵗʰ Year of the

---

* The paragraphs are not numbered in the original ; the figures are inserted here for convenience of reference.

Reign of King Charles the Second, Entituled *an Act for preventing Dangers which may happen from Popish Recusants*, and likewise that you take the usual Oath for the due Execution of the office and Trust, of Our Captain General and Governor in Chief in and over Our said Province of Nova Cæsarea or New Jersey; as well with regard to the due and impartial Administration of Justice, as otherwise; and further that you take the Oath requir'd to be taken by Governors of Plantations to do their utmost, that the several Laws relating to trade and the Plantation be observed; which said Oaths and Declaration Our Council in Our said Province or any three of the Members thereof, have hereby full Power and Authority, and are required to tender and administer unto you, and in your Absence to Our Lieutenand[t] Governor, if there be any upon the Place; all which being duly performed. You shall administer to each of the Members of Our said Council, as also to Our Lieutenant Governor, if there be any upon the Place, the Oaths mentioned in the said Act, entituled, *an Act for the further Security of His Majesty's Person and Government and the Succession of the Crown in the Heirs of the late Princess Sophia being Protestants, and for extinguishing the hopes of the pretended Prince of Wales and his open and secret Abettors;* You shall also cause them to make and subscribe the aforemention'd Declaration, and administer to them the Oath for the due Execution of their Places and Trusts.

4. And We do hereby give and grant unto you full Power and Authority to suspend any of the Members of Our said Council, from sitting, voting and assisting therein, if you shall find just Cause for so doing.

5. And if it shall at any time happen, that by the Death, Departure out of Our said Province, or suspension of any of Our said Councillors or otherwise, there shall be a Vacancy in Our said Council, any three whereof We do hereby appoint to be a Quorum; Our Will and Pleasure is, that you signify the same unto us by the first opportunity, that We may under Our Signet and Sign Manual constitute and appoint others in their Stead.

6. But that Our Affairs may not suffer at that Distance, for Want of a due Number of Councillors, if ever it shall happen that there be less than seven of them residing in Our said Province; We do hereby give & grant unto you the said Francis Bernard full Power and Authority to chuse as many Persons out of the Principal Freeholders, Inhabitants thereof, as will make up the full Number of Our said Council to be seven, and no more; which Persons so chosen and appointed by you, shall be to all

intents and purposes Councillors in Our said Province, untill either they shall be confirmed by Us, or that by the Nomination of Others by Us under Our Sign Manual and Signet, Our said Council shall have seven or more Persons in it.

7. And We do hereby give and grant unto You full Power & Authority, with the Advice and Consent of Our said Council, from time to time as need shall require, to summon and call general Assemblies of the said Freeholders and Planters within your Government, in manner and form as shall be directed in Our Instructions, which shall be given you together with this Our Commission.

8. And Our Will and Pleasure is, that the Persons thereupon duly elected by the Major Part of the Freeholders of the respective Counties and Places, and so returned, shall, before their sitting, take the Oaths mentioned in the said Act, entituled, *an Act for the further Security of His Maj^{tys} Person and Government and the Succession of the Crown in the Heirs of the late Princess Sophia being Protestants, and for extinguishing the hopes of the pretended prince of Wales and His open and secret Abettors ;* as also make and subscribe the aforementioned declaration, or being of the people called Quakers, shall take the Affirmation, and make and subscribe the declaration appointed to be taken and made instead of the Oaths of Allegiance, Supremacy and Abjuration, by an Act passed within Our said Province of Nova Cæsarea or New Jersey, in the first Year of our Reign, entituled, *an Act prescribing the Forms of Declaration of Fidelity, the Effect of the Abjuration, Oath and Affirmation, instead of the Forms heretofore required in such Cases ; and for repealing the former Acts in the like Cases made & provided ;* which Oaths, Affirmation & Declaration You shall commissionate fit Persons under Our Seal of Nova Cæsarea or New Jersey to tender and administer unto them ; and until the same shall be so taken, made & subscrib'd, no person shall be capable of sitting though elected, And We do hereby declare that the persons so elected and qualifyed shall be call'd and deemed the General Assembly of that Our Province.

9. And you the said Francis Bernard, with the Consent of Our said Council, [and] Assembly or the Major Part of them respectively, shall have full Power and Authority to make, constitute and ordain Laws, Statutes and Ordinances for the publick Peace, Welfare & good Government of Our said Province and of the People and Inhabitants thereof, and such others as shall resort thereto, and for the Benefit of Us, Our Heirs and Successors ; which said Laws, Statutes and Ordinances are not to be repugnant, but as near as may be agreable unto the Laws and Statutes of

this Our Kingdom of Great Britain; provided that all such Laws, Statutes and Ordinances, of what Nature or duration soever, be, within three Months or sooner after the making thereof, transmitted unto Us under Our Seal of Nova Cæsarea or New Jersey, for Our Approbation or disallowance of the same, as also Duplicates thereof by the next Conveyance.

10. And in case any or all of the said Laws, Statutes and Ordinances (being not before confirm'd by Us) shall at any time be disallow'd and not approved, and so signified by Us, Our Heirs or Successors under Our or their Sign Manual and Signet, or by Order of Our or their Privy Council unto you the said Francis Bernard or to the Commander in Chief of Our said Province for the time being, then such and so many of the said Laws, Statutes and Ordinances as shall be so disallowed and not approved, shall from henceforth cease, determine and become utterly void and of none Effect, any thing to the contrary thereof notwithstanding.

11. And to the end that nothing may be passed or done by Our said Council or Assembly, to the Prejudice of us, Our Heirs and Successors, *We Will & Ordain*, that you the said Francis Bernard shall have and enjoy a Negative Voice in the making and passing of all Laws, Statutes and Ordinances, as aforesaid.

12. And you shall and may likewise from time to time, as you shall judge it necessary, adjourn, prorogue and dissolve all General Assemblies, as aforesaid.

13. *And Our further Will & Pleasure is,* that you shall and may use and Keep the Publick Seal of Our Province of Nova Cæsarea or New Jersey, for sealing all things whatsoever that pass the Great Seal of Our said Province under your Government.

14. And We do further give & grant unto you the said Francis Bernard full Power and Authority from time to time and at any time hereafter, by Yourself or by any other to be authorized by you in that behalf, to administer and give the abovementioned Oaths and Affirmations to all and every such Person and Persons as you shall think fit, who shall at any time or times pass into Our said Province or shall be resident or abiding there.

15. And We do further by these Presents give and grant unto you the said Francis Bernard full Power and Authority with the Advice and Consent of Our said Council, to erect, constitute and appoint such & so many Courts of Judicature and publick justice within Our said Province under your Government, as you and they shall think fit and necessary for the hearing and determining all causes, as well Criminal as Civil, according to Law and Equity, and for awarding of Execution thereupon,

with all reasonable and necessary Powers, Authorities, Fees and Privileges belonging thereto; as also to appoint and commissionate fit Persons in the several parts of your Government to administer the Oaths mentioned in the aforesaid Act, Entituled, *an Act for the further Security of Our Person and Government and the Succession of the Crown in the Heirs of the late Princess Sophia being Protestants, and for extinguishing the hopes of the pretended Prince of Wales and his open and secret Abettors;* as also to tender and administer the aforesaid Declarations and Affirmations unto such Persons belonging to the said Courts as shall be obliged to take the same.

16. And We do hereby authorize and impower You to constitute and appoint Judges (and in Cases requisite Commissioners of Oyer and Terminer), Justices of the Peace, and other necessary Officers and Ministers in Our said Province for the better Administration of Justice and putting the Laws in Execution, and to administer or cause to be administered unto them such Oath or Oaths as are usually given for the due Execution and Performance of Offices and Places, and for the clearing of Truth in Judicial Causes.

17. And We do hereby give and grant unto you full Power and Authority where you shall see Cause, or shall judge any offender or offenders in criminal Matters, or for any Fines or Forfeitures due unto Us, fit Objects of Our Mercy, to pardon all such Offenders, and to remit all such Offences, Fines and Forfeitures, Treason and Willful Murder only excepted, in which Cases you shall likewise have Power upon extraordinary Occasions to grant Reprieves to the Offenders, untill and to the Intent Our Royal Pleasure may be Known therein.

18. And We do by these Presents authorize and impower you to collate any Person or Persons to any Churches, Chapels or other Ecclesiastical Benefices within Our said Province, as often as any of them shall happen to be void.

19. *And We* do hereby give and grant unto you the said Francis Bernard by yourself or by your Captains and Commanders by you to be authorized, full Power and Authority to levy, arm, muster, command, and imploy all Persons whatsoever residing within Our said Province of Nova Cæsarea or New Jersey under your Government, and, as Occasion shall serve, to march from one place to another, or to embark them for the resisting and withstanding of all Enemies, Pirates and Rebels, both at Sea and Land, and to transport such Forces to any of Our Plantations in America (if necessity shall require) for the Defence of the same against the invasion or Attempts of any of Our Enemies, and

such Enemies, Pirates and Rebels, if there shall be occasion, to persue and prosecute in or out of the Limits of Our said Province and Plantations or any of them; and, if it shall so please God, them to vanquish, apprehend and take, and being taken either according to Law to put to Death, or Keep and preserve alive at your Discretion, & to execute Martial Law in time of Invasion or other times when by Law it may be executed, and to do and execute all and every other thing and things which to Our Captain General and Governor in Chief doth or ought of Right to belong.

20. And We do hereby give and grant unto you full Power & Authority, by and with the Advice and Consent of Our said Council, to erect, raise and build in Our said Province of Nova Cæsarea or New Jersey such and so many Forts and Platforms, Castles, Cities, Boroughs, Towns and Fortifications, as You by the Advice aforesaid shall judge necessary; and the same or any of them to fortify and furnish with Ordnance, Ammunition, and all sorts of Arms fit and necessary for the security & Defence of our said Province, and by the Advice aforesaid the same again or any of them to demolish or dismantle as may be most convenient.

21. And for asmuch as divers Mutinies and Disorders may happen by Persons shipped and imploy'd at Sea, during the time of War, and to the end that such as shall be shipped & imployed at Sea during the time of War, may be better govrn'd and order'd; We do hereby give and grant unto You the said Francis Bernard full Power and Authority to constitute and appoint Captains, Lieutenants, Masters of Ships and other Commanders and officers, and to grant unto such Captains, Lieutenants, Masters of Ships and other Commanders and officers, Commissions to execute the Law Martial, during the time of War, according to the Directions of an Act passed in the 22^d year of Our Reign, entitled, an Act for amending, explaining and reducing into one Act of Parliament the Laws relating to the Government of his Majestys' Ships, Vessels and Forces by Sea; and to use such proceedings, Authorities, Punishments, Corrections and Executions upon any offenders, who shall be Mutinous, Seditious, Disorderly or any way unruly, either at Sea or during the time of their Abode or Residence in any of the Ports, Harbours, or Bays of Our said Province, as the Cause shall be found to require, according to Martial Law and the said Directions, during the time of War, as aforesaid, Provided that nothing here in contain'd shall be construed to the enabling you, or any by your Authority, to hold plea or have any Jurisdiction of any offence, Cause, Matter or Thing committed or done upon the high Sea, or within any of the Havens, Rivers

or Creeks of Our said Province under your Government, by any Captain, Commander[,] Lieutenant, Master, officer, Seaman, Soldier or other Person whatsoever, who shall be in actual Service and pay, in or on Board any of Our Ships of War or other Vessels acting by immediate Commission or Warrant from our Commissioners for executing the office of Our High Admiral, or from Our High Admiral of Great Britain for the time being under the Seal of Our admiralty; but that such Captain, Commander, Lieutenant, Master, officer, Seaman, Soldier, or other Person so offending, shall be left to be proceeded against and tryed as their offences shall require; either by Commission under Our Great Seal of Great Britain, as the Statute of the 28th of Henry the eight directs; or by Commission from Our said Commissioners for executing the office of Our High Admiral; or from Our High Admiral of Great Britian for the time being, according to the afore-mention'd *Act for amending, explaining and reducing into one Act of parliament the Laws relating to the Government of His Majestys' Ships, Vessels and Forces by Sea,* and not otherwise.

22. Provided nevertheless that all Disorders and Misdeameanors committed on Shore by any Captain, Commander, Lieutenant, Master, officer, Seaman, Soldier or other Person whatsoever, belonging to any of Our Ships of War or other Vessels acting by immediate Commission or Warrant from Our said Commissioners for executing the office of Our High Admiral, or from Our High Admiral of Great Britain for the time being under the Seal of Our Admiralty may be tryed and punished according to the Law of the place where any such Disorders, offences and Misdemeanours shall be committed on Shore, notwithstanding such offender be in Our actual Service and born in Our Pay on Board any such Our Ships of War or other Vessels acting by immediate Commission or Warrant from Our said Commissioners for executing the office of Our High Admiral or from Our High Admiral of Great Britain for the time being as aforesaid, so as he shall not receive any protection for the avoiding Justice for such offences committed on Shore, from any pretence of his being imployed in Our Service at Sea.

23. Our further Will & Pleasure is, that all publick Money raised or which shall be raised by any Act hereafter to be made within Our said Province, be issued out by Warrant from You, by and with the advice & Consent of Our Council, and disposed of by you for the Support of the Government, and not otherwise.

24. And We do hereby give you the said Francis Bernard full Power and Authority to order and appoint Fairs, Marts and Markets, as also

such and so many Ports, Harbours, Bays, Havens and other Places for the Convenience and Security of Shipping and for the better Loading and unloading of Goods and Merchandize, as by you, with the Advice and Consent of Our said Council, shall be thought fit and necessary.

25. And We do hereby require and command all Officers & Ministers Civil and Military, and all other Inhabitants of Our said province to be obedient, aiding and assisting unto you the said Francis Bernard in the execution of this Our Commission, and of the Powers and Authorities herein contain'd; And in Case of your Death or Absence out of Our said Province, to be Obedient, aiding and assisting unto such Person as shall be appointed by Us to be Our Lieutenant Governor or Commander in Chief of our said province, to whom We do therefore by these presents give and grant all and singular the powers and Authorities herein granted to be by him executed & enjoyed during Our pleasure, or until your arrival within Our said province.

26. And if upon your Death or Absence out of Our said province there be no person upon the place commissionated or appointed by us to be Our Lieutenant Governor or Commander in Chief of Our said province, Our Will & Pleasure is, that the eldest Councillor whose name is first placed in Our said Instructions to you, and who shall be at the time of your Death or Absence residing within Our said province of New Jersey, shall take upon him the Administration of the Government, & execute Our said Commission and Instructions and the several Powers and Authorities therein contain'd, in the same Manner and to all Intents and purposes as other Our Governor or Commander in Chief of Our said province shou'd or ought to do, in Case of your Absence untill you return, or in all Cases untill Our further Pleasure be Known therein.

27. And We do hereby declare, ordain and appoint, that you the said Francis Bernard shall and may hold, execute and enjoy the office & Place of Our Captain General and Governor in Chief in and over Our province of Nova Cæsarea or New Jersey, together with all and Singular the Powers and Authorities hereby granted unto you for and during Our Will and Pleasure. In Witness whereof We have caused these our Letters to be made Patents. Witness Ourself at Westminster the ———— day of ———— 1758 in the thirty first year of Our Reign. And for so doing this shall be your Warrant. Given at our Court at St James's the ———— day of ———— 1758 in the thirty first year of Our Reign.[1]

---

[1] This draft of a commission was approved by an order of council dated January 27, 1758. See *Analytical Index to the Colonial Documents of New Jersey* (New Jersey Historical Society, *Collections*, V.), 344.

5. INSTRUCTIONS TO FRANCIS BERNARD AS GOVERNOR OF NEW JERSEY, 1758. [Draft.]

[From the Public Record Office, Board of Trade, New Jersey papers, vol. xvi. p. 64; printed in *New Jersey Documents*, ix. 40.]

INSTRUCTIONS to Our Trusty and Well beloved FRANCIS BERNARD ESQ^R. Our Captain General and Governor in Chief in and over Our province of Nova Cæsarea or New Jersey in America. Given at Our Court at St James's the ———— day of ———— 1758 in the thirty first day of Our Reign.

1st *With* these Our Instructions your [you] will receive Our Commission under Our Great Seal of Great-Britain, constituting You Our Captn General and Governor in Chief in and over Our province of New Jersey, You are therefore with all convenient Speed to repair to Our said Province, and being there arrived, You are to take upon you the Execution of the Peace [Place] and Trust We have reposed in You, and forthwith to call together the Members of our Council in and for that province, vizt. Jno Reading, Robert Hunter Morris, Edward Antill, James Hude, Andrew Johnston, Peter Kimbold, Thomas Leonard, Richd Salter, David Ogden, Lewis Ashfield, Samuel Woodruffe and Wm Alexander Esq^{rs}

2^d *And* you are with all due Solemnity to cause Our said Commission to be read and published at the said Meeting of our Council, which being done, You shall then take and also administer to each of the Members of Our said Council the Oaths mention'd in an Act pass'd in the first Year of His late Majesty Our Royal Father's Reign, entituled, *an Act for the further Security of His Majesty's Person and Government and the Succession of the Crown in the Heirs of the late princess Sophia being Protestants, and for extinguishing the hopes of the pretended prince of Wales and His open and secret Abettors :* as also make and subscribe and cause the Members of Our said Council to make and subscribe the Declaration mentioned in an Act of Parliament made in the 25th Year of the Reign of King Charles the second, entituled, *an Act for preventing Dangers which may happen by Popish Recusants ;* And you, and every of them, are likewise to take an Oath for the due Execution of your and their places and Trusts with Regard to your and their equal and impartial Administration ; of Justice ; and you are also to take the Oath required by an Act pass'd in the 7 & 8 years of the Reign of King William the 3^d to be taken by Governors of Plantations to do their utmost that the Acts of Parliament relating to the plantations be observed.

3. *You* shall administer or cause to be administered the Oaths mentioned in the aforesaid Act, entituled, an *Act for the further Security of His Majesty's Person and Government, and the Succession of the Crown in the Heirs of the late Princess Sophia being Protestants, and for extinguishing the Hopes of the pretended Prince of Wales, and his open and secret Abettors ;* to the Members and officers of the Council and Assembly, and to all Judges, Justices, and all other Persons, that hold any Office or Place of Trust or Profit in the said Province, whether by virtue of any patent under Our Great Seal of this Kingdom, or the Publick Seal of New Jersey, or otherwise ; And you shall also cause them to make and subscribe the aforesaid Declaration ; without the doing of all which you are not to admit any person whatsoever to any publick Office, nor suffer those who have been admitted formerly, to continue therein.

4. *You* are forthwith to communicate to Our said Council such and so many of these Our Instructions wherein their Advice and Consent are required, as likewise all such others from time to time as you shall find convenient for Our Service to be imparted to them.

5. *You* are to permit the Members of Our said Counb[c]il to have and enjoy Freedom of Debate and Vote in all Affairs of publick Concern, that may be debated in Council.

6. *And* although by Our Commission aforesaid We have thought fit to Direct, that any three of Our Councillors make a Quorum, it is nevertheless *Our Will and Pleasure,* that you do not act with a Quorum of less than five Members, unless upon extraordinary Emergencies, when a greater Number cannot be conveniently had.

7. *And* that we may be always informed of the Names and Characters of Persons fit to supply the Vacancies that shall happen in Our said Council, you are from time to time, when any Vacancies shall happen in Our said Council, forthwith to transmit unto Our Commissioners for Trade and Plantations, in order to be laid before Us, the Names of three persons, Inhabitants of the Eastern Division, and the Names of three other Persons Inhabitants of the Western Division, of Our said Province, whom you shall esteem the best qualifyed for that Trust.

8. *And* whereas by Our Commission You are impower'd, in Case of the Death or Absence of any of Our Council of the said Province, to fill up the Vacancies in Our said Council to the number of seven, and no more ; you are from time to time to send to Our Commissioners for Trade and Plantations, in order to be laid before Us, the Name or Names

and Qualities of any Member or Members by you put into Our said Council by the first conveniency after your so doing.

9. *And* in the Choice and nomination of the Members of Our said Council, as also of the Chief Officers, Judges, Assistant Justices and Sheriffs ; You are always to take Care, that they be men of good Life, well affected to Our Government, of good Estates, and of Abilities suitable to their Employments.

10. *You* are neither to augment nor diminish the Number of Our said Council, as it is already establish'd, nor to suspend any of the Members thereof without good and sufficient Cause, nor without the Consent of the Majority of the said Council signified in Council, after due Examination of the Charge against such Councillor and his answer thereunto. And in Case of Suspension of any of them, You are to cause your Reasons, for so doing, together with the Charges and proofs against the said Persons, and their Answers thereunto, to be duly entred upon the Council Books ; and forthwith to transmit Copies thereof, to Our Commissioners for Trade and Plantations, in Order to be laid before us. Nevertheless if it should happen, that you should have Reasons for suspending any Councillor not fit to be communicated to the Council, you may in that Case suspend such Person without their consent ; but you are thereupon immediately to send to Our Commissioners for Trade and Plantations, in Order to be laid before Us, an Account of your proceedings therein, with your Reasons at large for such Suspension, as also for not communicating the same to the Council, and Duplicates thereof by the next Opportunity.

11. *And* whereas We are sensible, that effectual Care ought to be taken to oblige the Members of Our Council to a due Attendance therein, in Order to prevent the many inconveniences that may happen for want of a Quorum of the Council to transact Business, as Occasion may require ; It is *Our Will & Pleasure*, that, if any of the Members of Our said Council residing in the said Province shall hereafter absent themselves, from Our Said Province, and continue absent above the Space of twelve months together, without leave from you or from Our Governor or Commander in Chief of the said Province for the time being, first obtain'd under your or his Hand and Seal, or shall remain absent for the Space of two Years successively, without Our Leave given them under Our Royal Sign Manual, their place or places in Our said Council shall immediately thereupon become void ; and that if any of the Members of Our said Council residing in our said Province shall hereafter willfully absent themselves from the Council Board when duly

summon'd without a just and lawfull Cause, and shall persist therein after Admonition, you suspend the said Councillors, so absenting themselves, till Our further pleasure be known, giving timely notice thereof to Our Commissioners for Trade and plantations, in Order to be laid before Us ; And We do hereby Will and require you, that this Our pleasure be signified to the several Members of Our Council aforesaid, and that it be enter'd in the Council Books of Our said Province as a standing Rule.

12. *And Our Will and Pleasure is,* that with all convenient Speed you call together one general Assembly for the enacting of Laws for the joint and mutual Good of the whole province ; that the first meeting of the said general Assembly be at Perth Amboy in East New Jersey, in case the last was at Burlington ; And that all future General Assemblies do meet and sit at one or the other of these Places alternately, or otherwise as You, with the Advice of Our foresaid Council, shall think fit in Case of extraordinary Necessity to appoint them.

13. *Our Will & Pleasure is,* and you are accordingly to make the same Known in the most publick Manner, that the Method of choosing Representatives for the future shall be, as follows ; Viz! two by the Inhabitants — Householders of the City or Town of Perth Amboy in East New Jersey, and two by the Freeholders of each of the Five Counties in the said Division of East New Jersey ; Two by the Inhabitants Householders of the city or Town of Burlington in West New Jersey, and two by the Freeholders of each of the five Counties in the said Division of West New Jersey ; which Persons, so to be chosen, make up together the Number of twenty four Representatives. And it is *Our further Will & Pleasure,* that no Person shall be capable of being elected a Representative by the Freeholders of either Division, as aforesaid, or afterwards of sitting in general Assembly, who shall not have one thousand Acres of Land an Estate of Freehold in his own Right within the Division for which he shall be chosen, or have a personal Estate in Money, Goods or Chattels to value of five hundred pounds sterling and all Inhabitants of Our said Province being so qualifyed, as aforesaid, are hereby declared capable of being elected accordingly.

14. *You* are to choose in the passing of Laws, that the Stile of enacting the same be by the Governor, Council and Assembly and no other ; You are also, as much as possible, to observe in the passing of all Laws, that whatever may be requisite upon each different matter be accordingly provided for by a different Law, without Intermixing in one and the same Act such things as have no proper relation to each other, and you

are more especially to take care, that no Clause or Clauses be inserted in or annexed to any Act, which shall be foreign to what the Title of such respective Act imports; and that no perpetual Clause be made part of any temporary Law; and that no Act whatsoever be suspended, altered, continued revived or repeated [repealed] by general Words, but that the Title and Date of such Act so suspended, alter'd, continued, revived or repealed be particularly mentioned and expressed in the enacting part.

15. *And* whereas several Laws have formerly been enacted in several of Our Plantations in America, for so short a time, that the Assent or refusal of Our Royal predecessors cou'd not be had thereupon before the time, for which such Laws were enacted, did expire; You shall not for the future give Your Assent to any Law; that shall be enacted for a less time than two Years, except in the Cases hereinafter mention'd. And you shall not reenact any Law to which the Assent of Us or Our Royal predecessors has once been refused, without express Leave for that purpose first obtained from Us, upon a full Representation by you to be made to Our Commissioners for Trade and Plantations, in order to be laid before Us, of the reason and necessity for passing such Law, nor give your Assent to any Law for repealing any other Act pass'd in Your Government, whether the same is [has] or has not received Our Royal Approbation, unless You take care that there be a Clause inserted therein suspending and deferring the Execution thereof until Our Pleasure be known concerning the same.

16. *And* whereas great Mischiefs do arise by the Frequent passing Bills of an unusual and extraordinary Nature and Importance in Our Plantations, which Bills remain in force there from the time of enacting until Our Pleasure be signified to the contrary; We do hereby Will and require you not to pass or give your Consent hereafter to any Bill or Bills in the Assembly of Our said Province of unusual and extraordinary Nature and importance, wherein Our Prerogative, or the Property of Our Subjects may be prejudiced, or the Trade or Shiping of this Kingdom any Ways affected, until you shall have first transmitted to Our Commissioners for Trade and Plantations, in order to be laid before Us, the Draught of such a Bill or Bills, and shall have receiv'd Our Royal Pleasure thereupon, unless you take care in the passing of any Bill of such Nature as beforementioned, that there be a Clause inserted therein, suspending and deferring the Execution thereof untill Our Pleasure shall be known concerning the same.

17. *You* are also to take Care, that no private Act, whereby the property of private Persons may be affected, be passed, in which there is not

a saving of the Right of Us, Our Heirs and Successors, all Bodies Politick or corporate, and of all other Persons, except such as are mentioned in the said Act and those claiming by, from and under them; And further you shall take Care, that no such private Act be passed without a Clause suspending the Execution thereof, until the same shall have Our Royal Approbation. It is likewise Our *Will and Pleasure,* that you do not give your Assent to any private Act, until Proof be made before you in Council (and entred in the Council Books,) that publick notification was made of the Parties Intention to apply for such Act in the several Parish Churches, where the premises in Question lye, for three Sundays at least successively, before any such Act shall be brought into the Assembly; and that a Certificate under your hand be transmitted with and annexed to every such private Act, signifying that the same has passed through all the forms above mention'd.

18. *You* are to take Care, that in all Acts or Orders to be passed within that Our said Province, in any Case for levying Money or imposing Fines and Penalties, express mention be made, that the same is granted or reserved to Us, Our Heirs or Successors for the Publick Uses of that Our Province and the support of the Government thereof, as by the said Act or Order shall be directed, and you are particularly not to pass any Law or do any Act by Grant, Settlement or otherwise, whereby Our Revenue may be Lessened or impaired without Our especial leave or Command therein.

19. *You* are not to suffer any publick Money whatsoever to be issued or disposed of, otherwise than by Warrant under your hand, by and with the Advice and Consent of Our said Council, but the Assembly may be nevertheless permitted from time to time to view and examine the Accounts of Money or Value of Money disposed of by Virtue of Laws made by them, which you are to signify unto them, as there shall be occasion.

20. *You* are not to permit any Clause whatsoever to be inserted in any Law for the Levying Money or the Value of Money, whereby the same shall not be made lyable to be accounted for unto Us, and to Our Commissioners of Our Treasury or Our High Treasurer for the time being, and audited by Our Auditor General of Our Plantations or his Deputy for the time being. And we do particularly require and enjoyn you, under the pain of Our highest Displeasure, to take Care, that fair Books of Accounts of all Receipts & payments of all publick Money be duly kept, and the Truth thereof attested upon Oath And that all such Accounts be audited and attested by the Auditor General of Our Plantations or his Deputy, who is to transmit Copies thereof to Our Commis-

sioners of Our Treasury or to Our High Treasurer for the time being, and that you do every half Year or oftener send another Copy thereof attested by yourself to Our Commissioners for Trade and Plantations, and Duplicates thereof by the next Conveyance ; In which Books shall be specified every particular Sum raised, and disposed of, together with the names of the Persons to whom any Payment shall be made, to the end We may be satisfied of the Right and due application of the Revenue of Our said province with the probability of the increase or Diminution of it under every head or Article thereof.

21st. *It is Our express Will and Pleasure*, that no Law for raising any imposition on Wines or other strong Liquors be made to continue for less than one whole Year, and that all other Laws made for the supply and Support of the Government shall be indefinite and without Limitation, except the same be for a temporary Service, and which shall expire and have their full effect within the time therein prefixt.

22. *Whereas* Acts have been passed in some of Our Plantations in America for striking Bills of Credit and issuing out the same in lieu of Money, and for declaring the said Bills to be legal Tenders in payment of all private Contracts, Debts, Dues and Demands whatsoever, in Order to discharge their publick Debts and for other purposes ; from whence several Inconveniences have arisen ; It is therefore *Our Will and Pleasure*, that you do not give your Assent to or pass any Act in the Province of New Jersey under your Government, whereby Bills of Credit may be struck or issued in lieu of Money, unless upon sudden and extraordinary Emergencies of Government, in Case of War or Invasion, and upon no other occasion whatever, and provided that in every such Act so to be passed by you, due care be taken to ascertain the real Value of such Bills of Credit, and that an ample and sufficient fund be provided, for calling in, sinking and discharging the

This Article was struck out by the Lords of the Council, & in lieu thereof was insert'd the 19th Article of the Instructions given to Jonathan Belcher Esqr the late Govr

Vide order in Council dated 1st of April 1758 Bundle^{le} 1

---

[1] The article substituted was the same as the 19th article in the instructions to Governor Lewis Morris in 1738, which was as follows : " Whereas Acts have been pass'd in some of Our Plantations in America for striking Bills of Credit and issuing out the same in lieu of Money in Order to discharge their publick Debts and for other purposes, from whence sev! Inconveniencies have arisen It is therefore *Our Will and Pleasure* that you do not give your Assent to, or pass any Act in Our said Province of New Jersey under your Government whereby Bills of Credit may be struck or issued in lieu of Money without a Clause be inserted in such Act declaring that the same shall not take Effect, until the said Act shall have been ap-

said Bills within a reasonable time, not exceeding five Years; and provided also, that such Bills of Credit shall not be declared to be a legal
Tender in payment of any private Contracts, Bargains, Debts, Dues or
Demands whatsoever within Our said Province; and it is Our further
Will & Pleasure, that you do not upon any pretence whatsoever give
your Assent to any Act or Acts, whereby the time limited or the Provision
made for the calling in, sinking and discharging such paper Bills of Credit,
as are already subsisting or passing in payment within Our said Province,
shall be protracted or postponed, or whereby any of them shall be depreciated in Value, or whereby they shall be re-issued, or obtain a new and
further Currency.

23. *Whereas* several Inconveniences have arisen to Our Governments
in the Plantations by Gifts and Presents made to Our Governors by the
general Assemblies; you are therefore to propose unto the Assembly at
their first meeting after your Arrival, and to use your utmost Endeavour
with them, that an Act be passed for raising and settling a publick Revenue for defraying the necessary Charge of the Government of Our said
Province, and that therein Provision be particularly made for a competent
Salary to yourself as Captain General and Governor in Chief of Our said
Province, and to other Our succeeding Captains General and Governors
in Chief for supporting the Dignity of the same Office, as likewise due
Provision for the Contingent Charges of Our Council and Assembly, and
for the Salaries of the respective Clerks and other Officers thereunto belonging, as likewise of all other Officers necessary for the Administration
of that Gover[n]ment, and particularly that such Salaries be enacted to be
paid in Sterling or Proclamation Money or in paper Bills of Credit current
in that Province in proportion to the Value such Bills shall pass at in Exchange for Silver, that thereby the respective Officers may depend on
some certain income, and not be lyable to have their Stipends varied by
the uncertain Value of Paper Money, and that in such Act all Officers
Salaries be fixed to some reasonable yearly Sum, except the Members of
the Council and Assembly and the Officers attending them, or others

proved & confirm'd by Us Our Heirs & Successors. And it is Our further *Will &
Pleasure* that you do not give your Assent to or pass any Act in Our said Province
of New Jersey under your Government, for payment of Money either to you the
Governor or to any Lieu^t Governor or Commander in chief or to any of the Members of Our Council or to any other Person whatsoever except to Us Our Heirs and
Successors without a Clause be like wise inserted in such Act declaring that the
same shall not take effect until the said Act shall have been approv'd and confirm'd by Us Our Heirs or Successors:" *New Jersey Documents,* vi. 15, § 19.
For Belcher's instructions, see *Ibid.,* vii. 5.

whose Attendance on the publick is uncertain, who may have a reasonable pay established per Diem during their Attendance only ; And when such Revenue shall have been so settled and Provision made as afore said, then Our express *Will & Pleasure is,* that neither you Our Governor, nor any Governor, Lieuten! Governor, Commander in Chief, or President of Our Council of Our said Province of New Jersey for the time being, do give your or their Consent to the passing of any Law or Act for any Gift or Present to be made to You or them by the Assembly ; and that neither you nor they do receive any Gift or Present from the Assembly or others on any Account or in any Manner whatsoever, upon pain of Our Highest Displeasure and of being recalled from that Our Government. And We do further direct and require that this Declaration of Our Royal Will and Pleasure be communicated to the Assembly at their first meeting after your Arrival in Our said Province, and entred in the Register of Our Council and Assembly, that all Persons, whom it may concern, may govern themselves accordingly.

24. *And* whereas an Act of Parliament was passed in the sixth Year of the Reign of Her late Majesty Queen Anne, intituled *an act for ascertaining the Rates of foreign Coins in Her Majesty's Plantations in America,* which Act the respective Governors of all Our Plantations in America have from time to time been instructed to observe and carry into execution ; And whereas notwithstanding the same, Complaints have been made, that the said Act has not been observed, as it ought to have been, in many of Our Colonies and Plantations in America, by means whereof many indirect Practices have grown up, and various and illegal Currencies have been introduced in several of the said Colonies and plantations, contrary to the true intent and meaning of the said Act, and to the prejudice of the Trade of Our Subjects ; It is therefore *Our Royal Will & Pleasure,* and you are hereby strictly required and commanded, under pain of Our highest Displeasure and of being removed from your Government, to take the most effectual care for the future, that the said Act be punctually and bona fide observed and put in execution, according to the true Intent and meaning thereof.

25. *And* whereas complaint has been made to Us by the Merchants of Our City of London in behalf of themselves and of several others of Our good Subjects of Great Britain trading to Our Plantations in America, that greater Duties and Impositions are laid on their Ships and Goods, than on the Ships and Goods of Persons who are Natives and Inhabitants of the said Plantations ; It is therefore *Our Will & Pleasure,* that you do not, on pain of Our Highest Displeasure give your Assent for the future

to any Law, wherein the Natives or Inhabitants of Our Province of New Jersey, under Your Government are put on a more advantageous footing, than those of this Kingdom, or whereby Duties shall be laid upon British Shipping, or upon the Product or Manufactures of Great Britain upon any Pretence whatsoever.

26. *Whereas* Acts have been passed in some of Our Plantations in America for laying Duties on the Importation and exportation of Negroes, to the great Discouragement of the Merchants trading thither from the Coast of Africa ; and whereas Acts have likewise been passed for laying Duties on Felons imported, in direct Opposition to an Act of Parliament passed in the fourth Year of His late Majesty's Reign, *for the further preventing Robbery, Burglary, and other Felonies, and for the more effectual Transportation of Felons;* it is Our Pleasure, that you do not give your assent to or pass any Act imposing Duties upon Negroes imported into the said province under your Government, payable by the importer, or upon any Slaves exported that have not been sold in the said Province, and continued there for the space of twelve Months : It is *Our further Will & Pleasure,* that you do not give your Assent to or pass any Act whatsoever for imposing Duties on the importation of any Felons from this Kingdom into the province under Your Government.

27. *You* are likewise to examine, what Rates and Duties are charged and payable upon any Goods imported or exported within Our Province of Nova Cæsarea or New Jersey, whether of the growth or Manufacture of Our said Province or otherwise ; and you are to suppress the engrossing of Commodities, as tending to the prejudice of that Freedom which Trade and Commerce ought to have : And to use your best Endeavours for the Improvement of Trade in those parts by settling such Orders and Regulations therein, with the advice of the Council, as may be most acceptable to the generality of the Inhabitants; and to send unto Our Commissioners for Trade and Plantations, in Order to be laid before Us, yearly or oftener as occasion may require, the best and most particular Account of any Laws that have at any time been made, Manufactures set up, or Trade carried on in the province under your Government, which may in any wise affect the Trade and Navigation of this Kingdom.

28. *You* are to transmit Authentick Copies of all Laws, Statutes and Ordinances that are now made and in Force which have not yet been sent, or which at any time hereafter shall be made or enacted within the said province, each of them separately under the Publick Seal unto Our said Commissioners for Trade and Plantations within three months or by the first Opportunity after their being enacted, together with Dupli-

cates thereof by the next Conveyance, upon pain of Our hig[h]est Displeasure and of the Forfeiture of that year's Salary, wherein you shall at any time or upon any pretence whatsoever, omit to send over the said Laws, Statutes and Ordinances, as aforesaid, within the time above limited, as also of such other penalty as We shall please to inflict; but if it shall happen, that no shipping shall come from the said Province within three Months after the making such Laws, Statutes and Ordinances, whereby the same may be transmitted, as aforesaid, then the said Laws, Statutes and Ordinances are to be transmitted, as aforesaid, by the next Conveyance after the making thereof, whenever it may happen, for Our Approbation or Disallowance of the same.

29. *And Our further Will & Pleasure is,* that the Copies and Duplicates of all Acts that shall be transmitted, as aforesaid, be fairly abstracted in the Margin, and that in every Act there be the several Dates or respective times when the same passed the Assembly and the Council and receiv'd Your Assent; and you are to be as particular as may be in your Observations (to be sent to Our Commissioners for Trade and Plantations) upon every Act, that is to say, whether the same is introductive of a New Law, declaratory of a former Law, or does repeal a law then before in being, And you are likewise to send to Our said Commissioners the reasons for the passing of such law, unless the same do fully appear in the preamble of the said Act.

30. *You* are to require the Secretary of Our said Province or his Deputy for the time being to furnish you with Transcripts of all such Acts and publick Orders as shall be made from time to time, together with a Copy of the Journals of the Council; and that all such transcripts and Copies be fairly abstracted in the Margins, to the end the same may be transmitted to Our Commissioners for Trade and Plantations, as above directed, in Order to be laid before Us; which he is duly to perform upon Pain of incurring the Forfeiture of his place.

31. *You* are also to require from the Clerk of the Assembly or other proper Officer transcripts of all the said Journals, and other proceedings of the said Assembly; and that all such transcripts be fairly abstracted in the Margins, to the end the same may in like manner be transmitted, as aforesaid.

32. *Whereas* it is necessary that Our Rights and Dues be preserved and recovered, and that speedy and effectual Justice be administred in all Cases relating to Our Revenue; you are to take Care that a Court of Exchequer be called and do meet at all such times as shall be needfull; and you are upon your Arrival to inform us by Our Commissioners for

Trade and Plantations, whether Our Service may require that a Constant Court of Exchequer be settled and established there.

33. *You* shall not erect any Court or Office of Judicature not before erected or established, nor dissolve any Court or Office already erected or establish'd without Our especial Order. But in regard We have been informed, that there is a great Want of a particular Court for determining of small Causes, you are to recommend it to the Assembly of Our said Province, that a Law be passed, if not already done, for the constituting such Court or Courts for the Ease of Our Subjects there.

34. *And* whereas frequent Complaints have been made to Us of great Delays and undue proceedings in the Courts of Justice in several of Our Plantations, whereby many of Our Subjects have very much suffered; and it being of the greatest importance to Our Service and to the Welfare of our Plantations, that Justice be every where speedily and duly administered, and that all Disorders, Delays and undue Practices in the Administration thereof be effectually prevented; We do particularly require you to take especial Care, that in all Courts, where you are authorized to preside, Justice be impartially administered, and that in all other Courts established within Our said province all Judges and other Persons therein concerned do likewise perform their several Duties without any Delay or partiality.

35. *You* are to take Care that no Man's Life, Member, Freehold or Goods be taken away or harmed in Our said province, otherwise than by established and Known Laws, not repugnant to, but as much as may be agreeable to, the Laws of this Kingdom.

36. It is Our further *Will & Pleasure*, that no persons be sent as Prisoners from [to] this Kingdom, from New Jersey without sufficient Proofs of their Crimes, and that Proof transmitted along with the said Prisoners.

37. *You* shall endeavour to get a Law passed (if not already done) for the restraining of any Inhuman Severity, which by ill Masters, or Overseers may be used toward their Christian Servants, and their Slaves; and that Provision be made therein, that the willfull killing of Indians and negroes may be punish'd with Death, and that a fit Penalty be imposed for the maiming of them.

38. *You* are to take Care that all Writs be issued in Our Name throughout Our said Province.

39. *Our Will & Pleasure* is, that you or the Commander in Chief of Our said province for the time being, do in all civil Causes, on Application being made to you or the Commander in Chief for the time being,

for that purpose, permit and allow Appeals from any of the Courts of common Law in Our said province unto You or the Commander in Chief or the Council of our said Province; and you are for that purpose to issue a Writ in the manner which has usually been accustomed, returnable before yourself and the Council of Our said Province, who are to proceed to hear and determine such Appeal, wherein such of Our Council [as] shall be at that time Judges of the Court, from whence such Appeal shall be so made to you Our Captain General or to the Commander in Chief for the time being, and to Our said Council, as aforesaid, shall not be permitted to vote upon the said Appeal; but they may nevertheless be present at the hearing thereof to give the Reasons of the Judgement given by them in the Causes wherein such Appeals shall be made; provided nevertheless that, in all such Appeals, the Sum or Value appealed for, do exceed the Sum of three hundred pounds Sterling, and that Security be first duly given by the Appellant to answer such Charges as shall be awarded, in Case the first Sentence be affirmed, and if either party shall not rest satisfyed with the judgment of you or the Commander in Chief for the time being and Council, as aforesaid, *Our Will & Pleasure* is, that they may then appeal unto Us in Our privy Council, provided the Sum or Value so appealed for unto Us exceed five hundred pounds Sterling, and that such Appeals be made within fourteen days after Sentence, & good Security given by the Appellant, that he will effectually prosecute the same, and answer the Condemnation, as also pay such Costs and Damages as shall be awarded by Us, in Case the Sentence of you or the Commander in Chief for the time being and Council be affirmed; provided nevertheless, where the matter in question relates to the taking or demanding any Duty payable to Us, or to any Fee of Office, or annual Rent or other such like matter or thing, where the Rights in future may be bound, in all such cases you are to admit an Appeal to Us in Our privy Council, though the immediate Sum or value appealed for be of a less Value; and it is Our further *Will & Pleasure*, that in all cases whereby [where by] your Instructions, you are to admit Appeals to Us in Our privy Council, execution be suspended until the final Determination of such Appeals, unless good and sufficient Security be given by the Appellee to make ample Restitution of all that the Appellant shall have lost by means of such judgment or Decree, in case upon the Determination of such Appeal such Decree or Judgment should be reversed, and Restitution awarded to the Appellant.

40. *You* are also to permit Appeals to Us in Council in all Cases of Fines imposed for Misdemeanors, provided the Fines so imposed amount

to or exceed the Value of £200 Sterling, the Appellant first giving good security, that he will effectually prosecute the same, and answer the Condemnation if the Sentence by which such Fine was imposed in Our said province of New Jersey, shall be confirmed.

41. *You* shall not appoint any person to be a Judge or Justice of the peace without the Advice and Consent of at least three of Our Council signified in Council; nor shall you execute yourself or by Deputy any of the said Offices; And it is Our further *Will & Pleasure*, that all Commissions to be granted by you to any person or persons to be Judges, Justices of the Peace, or other necessary Officers be granted during Pleasure only.

42. *You* shall not displace any of the Judges, Justices, Sheriffs or other Officers or Ministers within Our said Province without good and sufficient cause, which you shall signify in the fullest and most distinct manner to Our said Commissioners for Trade and Plantations, in order to be laid before Us, by the first Opportunity after such Removal.

43. *You* shall not suffer any Person to execute more Offices than one by Deputy.

44. *You* are, with the Advice and Consent of Our said Council, to take especial Care to regulate all Salaries and Fees belonging to places, or paid upon Emergencies, that they be within the Bounds of Moderation; and that no exaction be made on any Occasion whatsoever; as also that all Tables of Fees be publickly hung up in all places where such Fees are to be paid; and you are to transmit Copies of all such Tables of Fees to our Commissioners for Trade and Plantations, in order to be laid before Us, as aforesaid.

45. *Whereas* there are several Offices in Our Plantations, granted under Our great Seal of this Kingdom, and that Our Service may be very much prejudiced by reason of the absence of the Patentees, and by their appointing Deputies not fit to officiate in their stead, you are therefore, upon your Arrival, to inspect such of the said Offices as are in your Government, and to enquire into the Capacity and behaviour of the Persons now exercising them, and to report thereupon to Our Commissioners for Trade and Plantations, what you think fit to be done or altered in relation thereunto; and you are upon the misbehaviour of any of the said Patentees, or their Deputies, to suspend them from the Execution of their places, till you shall have represented the whole matter and receiv'd Our Directions therein; and in case of the Death of any such Deputy, It is Our express *Will & Pleasure*, that you take Care the Person appointed to execute the place, untill the Patentee can be informed thereof and

appoint another Deputy, do give sufficient Security to the Patentee, or in case of Suspension to the person suspended, to be answerable to him for the Profits accruing during such interval by Death or during suspension, in Case we shall think fit to restore him to his place again. It is nevertheless *Our Will & Pleasure,* that the person executing the place during such Suspension, shall, for his Encouragement receive the same profits as the Person dead or suspended did receive ; And it is Our further Will & Pleasure that in Case of the Suspension of a Patentee, the person appointed by you to execute the Office, during such Suspension, shall, for his encouragement, receive a Moiety of the Profits which would otherwise [have]* accrued and become due to such patentee, giving Security to such Patentee to be answerable to him for the other Moiety, in case We shall think fit to restore him to his place again: And it is Our further *Will & Pleasure* that you do countenance and give all due encouragement to all Our Patent Officers, in the enjoyment of their legal and accustomed Fees, Rights, Priviledges, and Emoluments, according to the true Intent and meaning of their Patents.

46. *You* shall not, by Colour of any Power or Authority hereby or otherwise granted or mention'd to be granted unto you, take upon you to give, grant or dispose of any Office or place within Our said Province, which now is or shall be granted under the great Seal of Great Britain or to which any person is or shall be appointed by Warrant under Our Signet or Sign Manual, any otherwise than that you may, upon the Vacancy of any such Office or Place, or Suspension of any such Officer by you, as aforesaid, put in any fit person to officiate in the interval, till you shall have represented the matter unto Our Commissioners for Trade and Plantations, in order to be laid before us, as aforesaid, which you are to do by the first Opportunity, and untill the said Office or Place be disposed of by Us, our Heirs or Successors, under the Great Seal of Great Britain, or until some Person shall be appointed thereto under Our Signet or Sign Manual, or that Our further Directions be given therein.

47. *And* whereas several Complaints have heretofore been by made [made by] the Surveyor General and other Officers of Our Customs in Our Plantations in America, that they have been frequently obliged to serve on Juries and personally to appear in Arms, whenever the Militia is drawn out, and thereby are much hindred in the Execution of their Employments, Our Will and Pleasure is, that you take effectual Care and give the necessary Directions, that the several Officers of Our Customs be excused and exempted from serving on any Juries.

48. *And* whereas the Surveyors General of Our Customs in the Plan-

tations are impower'd in case of the Vacancy of any our Offices of the Customs by Death, Removal or otherwise, to appoint other Persons to execute such Offices untill they receive further Directions from Our Commissioners of Our Treasury, or Our High Treasurer or Commissioners of Our Customs for the time being, but in regard the Districts of the said Surveyors General are very extensive, and that they are required at proper times to visit the Officers in the several Governments under their Inspection, and that it may happen, that some of the Officers of Our Customs in the Province of Nova Cæsarea or New Jersey, may dye at the time when the Surveyor is absent in some distant part of his District, so that he cannot receive Advice of such Officer's Death within a reasonable time and thereby make Provision for carrying on the Service, by appointing some other Person in the room of such Officer who may happen to die, therefore that there may be no delay given on such Occasion to the Masters of Ships or Merchants in their Dispatches, It is Our further *Will & Pleasure,* in case of such Absence of the Surveyor General, or if he should happen to die, and in such Cases only, that upon the Death of any Collector of Our Customs within that Our Province, you shall make choice of a Person of Known Loyalty, Experience, Diligence and Fidelity, to be imploy'd in such Collectors room for the purposes aforesaid, untill the Surveyor General of Our Customs shall be advised thereof, and appoint another to succeed in their places or that further Directions shall be given therein by Our Commissioners of Our Treasury, or Our High Treasurer, or by the Commissioners of Our Customs for the time being, which shall be first signified, taking Care that you do not under pretence of this Instruction, interfere with the Powers and Authorities given by the Commissioners of Our Customs to the said Surveyors General, when they are able to put the same in Execution.

49. *Whereas* it is convenient for Our Service, that all the Surveyors Gen! of Our Customs in America for the time being should be admitted to sitt and vote in the respective Councils of Our several Islands and Provinces within their Districts as Councillors extraordinary, during the time of their Residence there, We have therefore thought fit to constitute and appoint, and do hereby constitute and appoint the Surveyor General of Our Customs for the Northern District and the Surveyor General of Our Customs within the said District for the time being, to be Councillors extraordinary in Our said Province. And it is *Our Will & Pleasure,* that he and they be admitted to sit and vote in the said Council, as Councillors extraordinary, during the time of his or their Residence

there ; But it is Our Intention, if thro' length of time the said Surveyor General or any other Surveyor General should become the senior Councillor in Our said Province, that neither he nor they shall by virtue of such Seniority, be ever capable to take upon him or them the Administration of the Government there, upon the Death or Absence of Our Captains Gen! or Governors in chief for the time being ; but whenever such Death or Absence shall happen, the Government shall devolve upon the Councillor next in seniority to the Surveyor General, unless We should hereafter think it for Our Royal Service to nominate the said Surveyor General or any other of Our said Surveyors General Councillors in ordinary in any of Our Governments within their Survey, who shall not in the [that] Case be excluded any Benefit which attends the Seniority of their Rank in the Council.

50. It is Our further *Will & Pleasure,* and you are hereby required by the first Opportunity to move the Assembly of Our said Province under your Government, that they provide for the Expence of making Copies for the Surveyor General of Our Customs in the said District for the time being, of all Acts and Papers which bear any relation to the Duty of his Office ; and in the mean time you are to give Orders, that the said Surveyor General for the time being, as aforesaid, be allowed a free Inspection in the publick Offices within your Government of all such Acts and papers without paying any Fee or reward for the same.

51. *You* are to transmit unto Our Commissioners for Trade and Plantations, with all convenient speed, in Order to be laid before Us, a particular Account of all Establishments of Jurisdictions, Courts, Offices and Officers, Powers, Authorities, Fees and Privileges, granted or settled or which shall be granted or settled within Our said Province, together with an Account of all the Expences attending the Establishments of the said Courts, and of such Funds as are settled and appropriated for discharging such Expences.

52. *Our Will and Pleasure is,* that for the better quieting the Minds of Our good Subjects Inhabitants of Our said Province, and for settling the Properties and Possessions of all Persons concerned therein, either as General Proprietors of the Soil, under the first original Grant of the said Province made by the late King Charles the Second to the late Duke of York, or as particular Purchasers of any Parcels of Land from the general Proprietors, you shall propose to the General Assembly of Our said Province the passing of such Act or Acts whereby the Right or Property of the said General Proprietors to the soil of Our said Province may be confirmed to them according to their respective Rights and Titles together with

all such Quit Rents, as have been reserved or are or shall become due to the said General Proprietors from the Inhabitants of Our said Province and all such Priviledges as are expressed in the Conveyances, made by the said Duke of York excepting only the Right of Government which remains in Us, And you are further to take Care that by the said Act or Acts so to be passed the particular Titles and Estates of all the Inhabitants of that Province and other purchasers, claiming under the said General Proprietors be confirmed & settled, as of Right does appertain, under such Obligations as shall tend to the best and speedyest Improvement or Cultivation of the same provided always that you do not Consent to any Act or Acts to lay any Tax upon unprofitable Lands.

53. *You* shall not permit any other person or persons besides the said general Proprietors or Agents to purchase any Lands whatsoever from the Indians within the Limits of their Grants.

54. *You* are to permit the Surveyors and other Persons appointed by the forementioned General Proprietors of the Soil of that Province for surveying and recording the Surveys of Land granted by and held of them to execute accordingly their respective Trusts and you are likewise to permit and if need be aid and assist such other Agent or Agents as shall be appointed by the said Proprietors for that End to collect and receive the Quit Rents which are or shall be due unto them from the particular Possessors of any Parcels or Tracts of Land, from time to time, provided always that such surveyors Agents or other Officers appointed by the said General Proprietors do not only take proper Oaths for the due Execution and performance of their respective Offices or Employments And give good and sufficient Security for their so doing, but that they likewise take the oaths mentioned in the foresaid Act entituled, *an Act for the further Security of His Majesty's Person and Government and the Succession of the Crown in the Heirs of the late princess Sophia being protestants and for the extinguishing the Hopes of the Pretended Prince of Wales and his open and Secret Abettors:* as also make and subscribe the Declaration aforesaid and you are more particularly to take Care that all Lands purchased from the said Proprietors be cultivated and improved by the possessors thereof, And you are to take Care that no Fees be exacted or taken by any of the Officers under you, for the Grants of Lands made by the Agents of the Proprietors, which Agents are to deliver over to you in Council Duplicates of all such Grants to be registred in Our Council Books.

55. *Whereas* for some Years past the Governors of some of Our Plantations have seized and appropriated to their own use the produce of

Whales of several kinds taken upon those Coasts upon pretence that Whales are Royal Fishes, which tends greatly to discourage this Branch of Fishery in Our Plantations and prevent Persons from settling there, it is therefore Our Will & Pleasure that you do not pretend to any such Claim nor give any manner of discouragement to the fishery of Our Subjects upon the Coast of the Province under your Government but on the Contrary that you give all possible Encouragement thereto.

56. *You* shall not remit any fines or Forfeitures whatsoever above the Sum of ten pounds, nor dispose of any Forfeitures whatsoever, until upon signifying unto Our Commissioners of Our Treasury or Our High Treasurer for the [time?]* being, and to Our Commissioners for Trade and Plantations the Nature of the Offence, and the Occasion of such Fines and Forfeitures with the particular Sums or Value thereof (which you are to do with all speed) you shall have receiv'd Our Directions therein, but you may in the mean time suspend the payment of the said Fines and Forfeitures.

57. *Whereas* We have thought it necessary for Our Service to constitute and appoint a Receiver General of the Rights and Perquisites of the Admiralty. It is therefore *Our Will & Pleasure* that you be aiding and assisting to the said Receiver General; his Deputy or Deputies in the Execution of the said Office of Receiver General; And we do hereby require and enjoin you to make up your Accounts with him, his Deputy or Deputies of all Rights of Admiralty as you or your Officers have or shall or may receive, and to pay over to the said Receiver General, his Deputy or Deputies for Our Use all such Sum or Sums of Money, as shall appear upon the foot of such Accounts to be and remain in your hands, or in the Hands of any of your Officers; And whereas Our said Receiver General is directed, in case the Parties Chargeable with any part of such Our Revenue, refuse, neglect or delay payment thereof, by himself or suff.cient Deputy to apply to Our Governors, Judges, Atternies General or any other Our Officers or Magistrates to be aiding and assisting to him in recovering the same; it is therefore *Our Will & Pleasure* that you Our Governor, Our Judges, Our Attornies General and all other Our Officers whom the same may concern, do use all lawfull Authority for the recovering and levying thereof.

58. *You* are to permit a Liberty of Conscience to all Persons (except Papists) so they be contented with a quiet and peaceable enjoyment of the same, not giving Offence or Scandal to the Government.

59. *You* shall take especial Care that God Almighty be devoutly and duly served throughout your Government, the Book of Common

Prayer as by Law established, read each Sunday and Holy day and the blessed Sacrament administred according to the Rites of the Church of England.

60. *You* shall be carefull that the Churches already built there be well and orderly Kept, and that more be built, as the province shall by God's blessing be improved, and that besides a competent Maintenance to be assign'd to the Minister of each orthodox Church, a Convenient house be built at the common Charge for each Minister and a competent proportion of Land assigned to him for a Glebe and Exercise of His Industry, and you are to take Care that the parishes be bounded and settled as you shall find most convenient for the accomplishing this good Work.

61. *You* are not to prefer any Minister to any Ecclesiastical Benefice in that Our province without a Certificate from the Right Reverend Father in God the Lord Bishop of London of his being conformable to the Doctrine and Discipline of the Church of England and of a good Life and Conversation, and if any person already preferr'd to a Benefice shall appear to you to give Scandal either by his Doctrine or Manners you are to use the proper and usual means for the removal of him.

62. *You* are to give order that every Orthodox minister within your Government be one of the Vestry in his respective parish, and that no vestry be held without him except in Case of Sickness, or that after Notice of a Vestry summon'd he omit to Come.

63. *You* are to enquire whether there be any Minister within your Government who preaches and administers the Sacrament in any Orthodox Church or Chapel without being in due Orders & to give account thereof to the said Lord Bishop of London.

64. *And* to the End the Ecclesiastical Jurisdiction of the said Lord Bishop of London may take place in Our said Province so far as conveniently may be. We do think fit that you give all Countenance & Encouragement to the Exercise of the Same, except only the Collating to Benefices, Granting Licences for marriages, and probate of Wills, which we have reserved to you Our Governor and the Commissioner [Commander?] in Chief of Our said province for the time being.

65. *We* do further direct that no Schoolmaster be henceforth permitted to come from England and to keep School in the said province without the Licence of the said Bishop of London, and that no other person now there or that shall come from other parts, shall be admitted to keep School in that Our said province of New Jersey, without your Licence first obtained.

66. *And* you are to take especial Care, that a Table of Marriages established by the Canons of the Church of England be hung up in every Orthodox Church and duly observed And you are to endeavor to get a Law passed in the Assembly of Our said Province (if not already done) for the strict Observation of the said Table.

67. The Right Reverend Father in God Edmund late Lord Bishop of London having presented a pertition to his late Majesty Our Royal Father, humbly beseeching him to send Instructions to the Governors of all the several plantations in America, that they cause all Laws already made against Blasphemy, prophaneness, Adultry, Fornication, Polygamy, Incest, prophanation of the Lord's day, Swearing and Drunkeness in their respective Governments to be vigourously executed. And We thinking it highly just that all persons, who shall offend in any of the particulars aforesaid, should be prosecuted and punished for their said Offences. It is therefore *Our Will and Pleasure,* that you take due Care for the punishment of the forementioned Vices, and that you earnestly recommend it to the Assembly of New Jersey to provide effectual Laws for the Restraint and punishment of all such of the aforementioned Vices against which no Laws are as yet provided, and also you are to use your Endeavors to render the Laws in being more effectual by providing for the punishment of the aforementioned Vices by presentment upon Oath to be made to the temporal Courts by the Church Wardens of the several parishes, at proper times of the year to be appointed for that Purpose. And for the further discouragement of vice and Encouragement of Virtue and good Living (that by such Example the Infidels may be invited and desire to embrace the Christian Religion) you are not to admit any person to publick Trusts and Employments in the said Province under your Government whose ill Fame and Conversation may occasion Scandal. And it is Our further *Will and Pleasure* that you recommend to the Assembly to enter upon proper Methods for the erecting and maintaining of Schools, in Order to the training up of Youth to Reading and to a necessary Knowledge of the principals of Religion, and you are also with the Assistance of the Council and Assembly to find out the best means to facilitate and encourage the Conve[r]sion of Negroes and Indians to the Christian Religion.

68. *You* shall send unto Our Commissioners for Trade and Plantations by the first Conveyance in order to be laid before us, an Account of the present Number of Planters and Inhabitants, Men, Women, and Children, as well Masters as Servants free and unfree and of the Slaves in Our said

province as also an yearly Account of the increase or decrease of them and how many of them are fit to bear Arms in the Militia of Our said province. You shall also cause an exact Account to be kept of all Persons born and christned and buried, and you shall yearly send fair Abstracts thereof to Our Commissioners for Trade and Plantations as aforesaid.

69. *And We* do further expressly command and require you to give unto Our Commissioners for Trade & plantations once in every year the best Account you can procure of what number of Negroes Our said province is yearly supplied with.

70. *You* shall take Care that all planters and Christian Servants be well and fitly provided with Arms and that they [be] listed under good Officers and when and as often as shall be thought fit mustred and trained whereby they may be in a better readiness for the defence of Our said province under your Government.

71. *You* are to take especial care that neither the frequency nor unreasonableness of their Marches, Musters, and trainings be an unnecessary Impediment to the affairs of the Inhabitants.

72. *You* shall not upon any Occasion whatsoever establish or put in Execution any Articles of War or other Law Martial upon any of Our Subjects, Inhabitants of Our said province without the Advice and Consent of Our Council there.

73. *And* whereas there is no Power given you by your Commission to execute Martial Law in time of Peace upon Soldiers in pay and that nevertheless it may be necessary that some Care be taken for the keeping good Discipline amongst those that We may at any time think fit to send into Our said province (which may properly be provided for by the legislative power of the same) you are therefore to recommend to the general Assembly of Our said province that they prepare such Act or Law for the punishing of Mutiny, Desertion and false Musters and for the better preserving of good Discipline amongst the said Soldiers, as may best answer those Ends.

74. *You* are to encourage the Indians upon all Occasions so as to induce them to trade with Our Subjects rather than any others of Europe.

75. *And* for the greater Security of Our province of New Jersey you are to appoint fit Officers and Commanders in the several parts of the Country bordering upon the Indians who upon any Invasion may raise Men and Arms to oppose them till they shall receive your Directions therein.

76. *And* whereas you will receive from Our Commissioners for Executing the Office of High Admiral of Great Britain and of Our plantations a Commission of Vice Admiralty of Our said province of New Jersey, You are hereby required and directed carefully to put in execution the several powers thereby granted you.

77. *And* there having been great Irregularities in the Manner of granting Commissions in the plantations to private Ships of War. You are to govern yourself whenever there shall be occasion according to the Commissions and Instructions granted in this Kingdom, Copies whereof will herewith be delivered you. But you are not to grant Commissions of Marque or Reprizal against any Prince or State or their Subjects, in Amity with us to any Person whatsoever without Our Especial Command, and you are to oblige the Commanders of all Ships having private Commissions to wear no other Colours than such as are described in Our Order of Council of the 7th of Jan^{ry} 1730 in relation to Colours to be worn by all Ships and Vessels except Our own Ships of War. A Copy of which Order will be herewith be [*sic*] delivered to you.

78. *Whereas* we have been informed that during the time of War Our Enemies have frequently got Intelligence of the State of Our plantations by letters from private persons to their Correspondents in Great Britain taken on Board Ships coming from the plantations, which may be of dangerous Consequence if not prevented for the future. *Our Will and Pleasure is,* that you signify to all Merchants, planters and others that they be very Cautious in time of War, in giving any Account by Letters of the publick State and Condition of Our said province of New Jersey, and you are further to give Directions to all Masters of Ships or other persons to whom you may intrust your Letters, that they put such Letters in a Bag with a sufficient Weight to sink the same immediately, in Case of imminent danger from the Enemy. And you are also to let the Merchants and planters know how greatly it is for their Interest that their Letters should not fall into the Hands of the Enemy, and therefore that they should give the like Orders to the Masters of Ships in relation to their Letters. And you are further to advise all Masters of Ships that they do sink all Letters in Case of Danger in the manner before mentioned.

79. *And* whereas the Merchants and planters in America have in time of War corresponded and traded with Our Enemies and carried Intelligence to them, to the great prejudice and Hazard of the English plantations. You are therefore by all possible Methods to endeavour to hinder all such trade and Correspondence in time of War.

80. *And* whereas Commissions have been granted unto several persons in Our respective plantations in America, for the trying of pirates in those parts pursuant to the Acts for the more effectual Suppression of Piracy, and by a Commission already sent to Our province of New Jersey, you as Captain General and Governor in Chief of Our said province are impowered together with others mentioned, to proceed accordingly in reference to Our said province, *Our Will & Pleasure is*, that in all matters relating to pirates, you govern yourself according to the Intent of the Acts & Commission aforementioned.

81. *Whereas* it is absolutely necessary, that we be exactly informed of the State of Defence of all Our plantations in America, as well in relation to the Stores of War that are in each plantation, as to the forts and Fortifications there, and what more may be necessary to be built for the Defence and Security of the same. You are so soon as possible to prepare an Account thereof with relation to Our said province of Nova Cæsarea or New Jersey in the most particular manner, and you are therein to express the present State of the Arms, Ammunition and other Stores of War belonging to the province either in any publick Magazines or in the hands of private persons together with the State of all places either already fortified or that you judge necessary to be fortifyed for the Security of Our said province, and you are to transmit the said Accounts to Our Commissioners for Trade and plantations, in order to be laid before us, as also a Duplicate thereof to Our Master General or principal Officers of Our Ordnance, which Accounts are to express the particulars of Ordnance, Carriages, Ball, Powder, and all other sorts of Arms and Ammunition in Our publick Stores at your said Arrival, and so from time to time of what shall be sent to you b [or] bought with publick Money and to specify the time of the Disposal and the occasion thereof and other like Accounts half yearly in the same manner.

82. *Whereas* divers Acts have from time to time been passed in several of Our Colonies in America imposing a Duty of powder on every Vessel that enters and clears in the said Colonies, which has been of great Service in furnishing the Magazines with powder for the Defence of Our said Colonies in time of Danger: it is *Our Express Will & Pleasure*, and you are hereby required and directed to recommend to the Assembly of New Jersey to pass a Law for Collecting a powder Duty, and that the Law for that purpose be made perpetual, that a certain time in the said Act, not exceeding twelve months, be allowed for giving Notice thereof to the several masters of Vessels trading to New Jersey, and that for the more ample Notification thereof, a proclamation be also published in your said Gov-

ernment declaring that from and after the Expiration of the time limited by the said Act for such Notice, no Commutation shall be allow'd of but upon evident Necessity, which may some time happen, whereof you or Our Commander in Chief for the time being are to be the Judge; in which Case the said Master shall pay the full price Gunpowder sells for there, and the monies so collected shall be laid out as soon as may be in the purchase of Gunpowder; and you are also to transmit every six months to Our Commissioners for Trade and Plantations, an Account of the particular Quantities of Gunpowder collected under the said Act in your Government; and likewise a Duplicate thereof to the Master General or principal Officers of Our Ordnance.

83. *You* are to take especial Care, that fit Storehouses be settled throughout Our said province for receiving and keeping of Arms, Ammunition, and other publick Stores.

84. *And* in Case of any distress of any of Our plantations, you shall upon Application of the respective Governors to you, assist them with what Aid the Condition and safety of your Government will permit; and more particularly in Case Our province of New York be at any time attacked by an Enemy, the Assistance you are to contribute towards the Defence thereof, whether in Men or Money, is to be according to the Quota or Repartition which has already been signified to the Inhabitants of Our foresaid province under your Government, or according to such other Regulation as We shall hereafter make in that behalf, and shall signify to you or the Commander in Chief of Our said province for the time being.

85. *You* shall transmit unto Our Commissioners for Trade and plantations, by the first Opportunity, to be laid before us, a Map with the exact Description of Our whole Territory under your Government, and of the several plantations that are upon it.

86. *You* are from time to time to give an Account, as before directed, what Strength your bordering Neighbours have, be the[y] Indians or others, by Sea & Land & of the Condition of their plantations, & what Correspondence you do keep with them.

87. *You* are likewise from time to time to give unto Our Commissioners for Trade and Plantations, as aforesaid, in order to be laid before us, an Account of the Wants and Defects of Our said province; what are the Chief Products thereof, what new improvements are made therein by the Industry of the Inhabitants or planters; and what further Improvements you conceive may be made, or Advantages gained by trade, and in what manner We may best Advance the same.

88. If any thing shall happen that may be of Advantage and Security to Our said province, which is not herein by Our Commission provided for, *We* do hereby allow unto you, with the Advice and Consent of Our Council, to take order for the present therein, giving unto Our Commissioners for Trade and plantations speedy notice thereof, in order to be laid before Us, that so you may receive Our Ratification, if We shall approve of the same, provided always that you do not by Colour of any power or Authority given you, commence or declare War without Our Knowledge and particular Commands therein, except it be against Indians upon Emergencies, wherein the Consent of Our Council shall be had and speedy Notice given thereof unto Our Commissioners for Trade and plantations in Order to be laid before Us.

89. *And* whereas great Prejudice may happen to Our Service and the Security of Our said province under your Government by your Absence from those parts, you are not upon any pretence whatsoever, to come to Europe from your Government, without first having obtained leave for so doing under Our Signet and Sign Manual, or by Our Order in Our privy Council.

90. *And* whereas We have been pleased by Our Commission to direct [that], in Case of your Death or Absence from our said province, and in Case there be at that time no person upon the place commissioned or appointed by Us, to be Our Lieutenant Governor or Commander in Chief, the eldest Councillor whose name is first placed in these Instructions to you, and who shall be at the time of your Death or Absence residing within our said province, shall take upon him the Administration of the Government and execute Our said Commission and Instructions and the several powers and Authorities therein contained, in the manner therein directed; It is nevertheless Our express *Will and Pleasure*, that in such Case the said eldest Councillor, or President shall forbear to pass any Act or Acts [but] such as shall be immediately necessary for the peace and Wellfare of Our said province without Our particular Order for that purpose, and that he shall not take upon him to disolve the Assembly then in being, nor to remove or suspend any of the Members of Our said Council nor any Judges, Justices of the peace or other Officers civil or military without the Advice or [and] Consent of at least seven of the Council, and Our said President is to transmit to Our Commissioners for Trade and Plantations by the first Opportunity, the reasons of such Alterations, signed by himself and Our Council, in order to be laid before Us.

91. *And* whereas We are willing in the best manner to provide for the

support of the Government of Our said Province by setting a part sufficient Allowances to such as shall be Our Governor, Lieutenant Governor, Commander in Chief or President of Our Council, residing for the time being within the same ; Our *Will & Pleasure* therefore is, that when it shall happen that you shall be absent from the Territory of New Jersey of which We have appointed you Governor one full moi[e]ty of the Salary and of all perquisites and Emoluments whatsoever which would otherwise become due, unto you, shall during the time of your Absence, from the said Territory be paid and satisfyed unto such Governor, Lieutenant Governor, Commander in Chief or President of Our Council, who shall be resident upon the place for the time being, which We do hereby order and allot unto him, towards his maintenance, and for the better support of the Dignity of that Our Government.

92. *And* you are upon all Occasions to send unto Our Commissioners for Trade and plantations only, a particular Account of all your proceedings and of the Condition of Affairs within your Government, in order to be laid before Us, provided nevertheless whenever any Occurrence shall happen within your Government of such a Nature and importance as may require Our more immediate Direction by one of Our principal Secretaries of State, and also upon all Occasions & in all Affairs wherein you may receive Our Orders by one of the principal Secretaries of State, you shall in all such Cases transmit to the Secretary of State only, an Account of all such Occurrences & of your proceedings relative to such Orders.[1] *

[1] This draft of instructions was approved by an order of council dated April 1, 1758. The instructions were dated January 31, 1758. See *Analytical Index to the Colonial Documents of New Jersey* (New Jersey Historical Society, *Collections*, V.), 345.

* In the foregoing documents taken from the *New Jersey Documents*, the bracketed insertions marked with an asterisk are reproduced from the text as there printed. All others in the Appendices have been added by the present editor. With this exception and that noted on page 226, all the documents here given follow the previously printed text as indicated in the heading of each document.

6. COMMISSION TO JAMES HAMILTON AS PROPRIETARY GOVERNOR OF PENNSYLVANIA, 1759.

[From *Minutes of the Provincial Council of Pennsylvania* (*Pennsylvania Records*), viii. 409.]

THOMAS PENN and *RICHARD PENN, true and absolute Proprietaries and Governors-in-Chief of the Province of Pennsylvania, and Counties of Newcastle, Kent, and Suss[e]x, on Delaware,*

To James Hamilton, Esquire, Greeting :

WHEREAS, the late King Charles the second, by his Letters Patent, under the Great Seal of England, bearing date the fourth day of march, in the Thirty-third year of his Reign, was graciously pleased to grant unto William Penn, Esquire, (late Father of the said Thomas Penn and Richard Penn, since deceased), His Heirs and Assigns, The said Province of Pennsylvania, with large powers, Jurisdictions, and Authorities for the well-Governing, Safety, Defence, and preservation of the said Province and the People residing therein, and more particularly to do and perform sundry matters and things therein mentioned, either by himself and his Heirs, or his or their Deputies or Lieutenants, as by the said Letters patent, relation being thereunto had, may more fully appear : *And Whereas,* the late King James the second, before he came to the Crown, by the name of James Duke of York and Albany, being rightfully possessed of a Certain Tract of Land lying on the West side of the Bay and River of Delaware, more commonly called and known by the name or Names of the Counties of Newcastle, Kent, and Sussex, on Delaware ; and being likewise invested with Sundry Royalty's priviledges, Immunities, powers, Jurisdictions, and authorities, for the defence, safety, preservation, and well-Governing of the said Tract of Land and the Inhabitants thereof, did, by certain Deeds duly executed, and bearing date as therein mentioned, give and grant unto the said William Penn, his Heirs and Assigns, the said Tract of Land lying on the West side of the Bay and River of Delaware, with all and every the said Royalties, Privileges, Immunities, Powers, Jurisdictions, and Authorities which he the said Duke of York stood then invested with as aforesaid, as by such Deeds relation being thereunto had, may more fully appear : *And Whereas,* we did by our Commissions, under our Seals, bearing date the seventh day of May, in the year of our Lord, one thousand seven hundred and fifty-six, depute, constitute, and appoint William Denny, Esquire, to be Lieutenant Governor of the Said province and Counties, for and during the good pleasure of Us and the Survivor of us, and until further Order : *Now Know You*, that We have revoked and determined and by these presents Do revoke and determine our said recited Commission, and every Clause, article, and Thing therein contained : *And further Know You*, That we, reposing Special Trust and confidence in your Tryed and approved Loyalty to the King, and in your prudence, conduct and Integrity, Do, by Virtue of the said Letters patent and Deeds, depute, constitute, nominate, and appoint you, the said James Hamilton, to be Lieutenant Governor of the said province and Counties, Giving and hereby granting unto you full power and authority to exercise, execute, and put in practice, in ample manner, All and every the powers, Jurisdictions and Authorities, so granted unto the said William Penn, his Heirs and Assigns, by the said Letters patent and Deeds, as shall be necessary and convenient for the safety, well-being, defence, preservation, and well-Governing the said province and Counties and the people thereof, hereby comitted and entrusted to your care and charge ; And generally, at all Times, and upon all Occasions, when proper and convenient, to exercise, do, execute, act and perform all, and all manner of powers, authorities, acts, military, and all other matters and things whatsoever, requisite and necessary for the good order of Government, for the administering, maintaining, and executing of Justice, and for the safety, peace, defence, and preservation of the said province and Counties, and the people under your Government and Direction, as fully and amply, to all Intents, Constructions, and purposes, as We ourselves might or cou[l]d do by Virtue of the said Letters Patent and Deeds or any otherwise howsoever, were we personally present ; You following and observing such Orders, Instructions, and Directions as you now have, or hereafter, from time to time, shall receive from us or our Heirs, To have, hold, execute, exercise, and enjoy the said Office or post of Lieutenant Governor of the said Province, Jurisdictions and authorities hereinbefore Granted, and all Titles, privileges, pre-eminences, profits, and advantages to a Lieutenant Governor and Commander [in] Chief of the said province and Counties belonging and therewith usually held and enjoyed, unto you, the said JAMES HAMILTON, for and during the good pleasure of Us and the Survivor of Us, and until further Order : *Provided Always*, that nothing herein contained shall extend or be construed to extend to give you any power or Authority to sett, lett, lease out, Grant, Demise, receive, posess, Occupy, or dispose of any Manors, Messages, Lands, Tenements, Houses, Gardens, Royalties, Rent, Issues, or profits arising, belonging, or accruing unto us or either of Us, in the province and Counties aforesaid, or otherwise ; Nor to

intermeddle or concern yourself therewith, or with any part of the property thereof, or with any Officer or Officers appointed for the management thereof, e[i]ther by placing, displacing, interrupting, or hindering
any of them in the just Execution of their Offices; But in Case your
aid and assistance shall be wanted by them, and desired for our Service,
Then, and in such Case, You are hereby required to assist them by all
lawful ways and means to the utmost of your power, any thing hereinbefore contained to the contrary thereof in anywise, notwithstanding.
And we do hereby strictly Command, charge, and require all persons
within the said province and Counties, of what degree, quality, state or
Condition soever, To yield, give, and pay unto you, all Respect, sub-
mission, and Obedience as Lieutenant Governor of the said province
and Counties so appointed as aforesaid, as they will answer the contrary
at their peril. Given under our Hands and Seals at Arms, the Nine-
teenth day of July, in the Thirty-Third year of the Reign of Our Sovereign Lord George the Second, by the Grace of God, of Great Britain,
France, and Ireland, King, Defender of the Faith, and so forth, and in
the Year of our Lord, One thousand seven hundred and fifty-nine.

THOS. PENN, [L. s.]

RICH^{D.} PENN, [L. s.]

7. COMMISSION TO JOHN WENTWORTH AS LIEUTENANT-GOVERNOR OF NEW HAMPSHIRE, 1717.

[From a copy in the Secretary's Office; printed in *New Hampshire Provincial Papers*, ii. 712.]

GEORGE R.

GEORGE, by the Grace of God, King of Great Britain, France and Ireland, Defender of the Faith, &c.

To our Trusty and Well-beloved JOHN WENTWORTH, Esq. Greeting: Whereas, by our Commission, under our Great Seal of Great Britain, bearing date Fifteenth day of June, 1716, We have constituted and appointed Samuel Shute, Esq. our Captain General and Governor in Chief in and over our Province of New Hampshire, in New England, in America; and we reposing especial Trust and Confidence in your Loyalty, Courage and Circumspection, do, by these presents, constitute and appoint you, the said John Wentworth, to be our Lieutenant Governor, to hold, exercise and enjoy the said Place and office for and during our Pleasure, with all Rights, Privileges, Profits, Perquisites and Advantages, to the same belonging or appertaining : And further, in case of the Death or absence of the said Samuel Shute, We do hereby authorize and empower you to execute and perform all and singular the Powers and Directions contained in our said Commission to the said Samuel Shute, and such Instructions as are already or hereafter shall, from time to time, be sent unto him ; so nevertheless, that you observe and follow such orders and Directions as you shall receive from Us, and from the said Samuel Shute, or any Chief Governor of our said Province of New Hampshire, for the time being. And all and singular our officers and ministers and loving subjects of our said Province, and others whom it may concern, are hereby commanded to take due Notice hereof, and to give their ready obedience accordingly.

Given at our Court at Hampton Court, the 12th day of September, 1717, in the Fourth year of our Reign.

By his Majesty's Command,

J. ADDISON.

John Wentworth, Esq.
Lieutenant Governor of New Hampshire
in America.

APPENDIX B.

LIST OF COMMISSIONS AND INSTRUCTIONS.*

THIS list includes only documents which are printed in full, excluding summaries and extracts. The term "instructions" also requires explanation. As used here, it means the formal document which, together with the commission, was given to each governor on his appointment to his province. Single articles or so-called additional instructions which appear from time to time in the records of nearly every province are not recorded here. Letters from the home government, or from proprietors, are excluded even though they may contain more or less formal instructions on many matters connected with the government of the province. It should be said further that all the British colonies are not included in this list, but only those which afterwards became part of the United States.

For form of royal commission, see Stokes, *Constitution of the Colonies*, 150. [No names; arbitrary dates.]

1610. Proprietary commission to Lord La Warr, governor of Virginia: Brown, *Genesis of the United States*, i. 375.

1618. Proprietary instructions to George Yeardley, governor of Virginia: *Virginia Magazine of History and Biography*, ii. 154.

1624. Royal commission to Sir Francis Wyatt, governor, and to the council of Virginia: Rymer, *Fœdera*, xvii. 618.

1626. Royal commission to Sir George Yeardley, governor, and to the council of Virginia: Rymer, *Fœdera*, xviii. 311.

1626. Royal instructions to Sir George Yeardley, governor, and to the council of Virginia: *Virginia Magazine of History and Biography*, ii. 393.

1627. Royal commission to John Harvey, governor, and to the council of Virginia: Rymer, *Fœdera*, xviii. 980.

1635. Proprietary commission to John Winthrop, the younger, governor of the Connecticut River: Trumbull, *History of Connecticut*, i. 497.

1636. Royal commission to John Harvey, governor, and to the council of Virginia: Rymer, *Fœdera*, xx. 3.

1637. Proprietary commission to Leonard Calvert, governor, and to the council of Maryland: Bozman, *History of Maryland*, ii. 572; *Maryland Archives*, iii. 49.

1641. Royal commission to Sir William Berkeley, governor, and to the council of Virginia: Rymer, *Fœdera*, xx. 484.

* This list is reprinted with some revision from the *American Historical Review* for October, 1897.

[1641.] Royal instructions to Sir William Berkeley, governor of Virginia: *Virginia Magazine of History and Biography*, ii. 281.

1642. Proprietary commission to Leonard Calvert, governor of Maryland: Bozman, *History of Maryland*, ii. 621 ; *Maryland Archives*, iii. 108.

1644. Proprietary commission to Leonard Calvert, governor of Maryland: Bozman, *History of Maryland*, ii. 631 ; *Maryland Archives*, iii. 151.

1648. Proprietary commission to William Stone, governor of Maryland: Bozman, *History of Maryland*, ii. 642 ; *Maryland Archives*, iii. 201.

1656. Proprietary commission to Josias Fendall, governor of Maryland: Bozman, *History of Maryland*, ii. 689; *Maryland Archives*, iii. 323.

1660. Proprietary commission to Philip Calvert, governor of Maryland: *Maryland Archives*, iii. 391.

1661. Proprietary commission to Charles Calvert, governor of Maryland: *Maryland Archives*, iii. 439.

1662. Royal instructions to Sir William Berkeley, governor of Virginia: *Virginia Magazine of History and Biography*, iii. 15.

1664. Proprietary commission to Richard Nicolls, governor of New York: *Pennsylvania Archives*, 2nd Series, v. 509.

1665. Proprietary commission to Sir John Yeamans, governor of Clarendon County: *North Carolina Records*, i. 97.

[1665.] Proprietary instructions to Sir John Yeamans, governor, and to the council of Clarendon County : *North Carolina Records*, i. 95; Rivers, *Sketch of the History of South Carolina*, 338.

1665. Proprietary commission to Philip Carteret, governor of New Jersey: *New Jersey Documents*, i. 20.

1665. Proprietary instructions to Philip Carteret, governor of New Jersey: *New Jersey Documents*, i. 21.

1666. Proprietary commission to Charles Calvert, governor of Maryland: *Maryland Archives*, iii. 542.

1667. Proprietary commission to Samuell Stephens, governor of Albemarle County: *North Carolina Records*, i. 162.

1667. Proprietary instructions to Samuell Stephens, governor of Albemarle County : *North Carolina Records*, i. 162.

1669. Proprietary commission to William Sayle, governor of Carolina south and west of Cape Carteret: Rivers, *Sketch of the History of South Carolina*, 340.

1669. Proprietary instructions to the governor and council at Port Royal, Carolina: Rivers, *Sketch of the History of South Carolina*, 347.

1670. Proprietary instructions to the governor and council of Albemarle County : *North Carolina Records*, i. 181.

1671. Proprietary instructions to the governor and council of Ashley River: Rivers, *Sketch of the History of South Carolina*, 366.

1674. Proprietary instructions to Andrew Percivall, governor of a new plantation on the Edisto River: Rivers, *Sketch of the History of South Carolina*, 387.

1674. Proprietary commission to Philip Carteret, governor, and to the council of New Jersey: Leaming and Spicer, *Grants, Concessions*, etc., 58.

1674. Proprietary instructions to Philip Carteret, governor, and to the council of New Jersey: *New Jersey Documents*, i. 167.

1674. Proprietary commission to Edmund Andros, governor of New York: *New York Documents*, iii. 215 ; *New Jersey Documents*, i. 156.

1674. Proprietary instructions to Edmund Andros, governor of New York: *New York Documents*, iii. 216.

1675. Royal commission to Thomas, Lord Culpeper, governor of Virginia: Hening, *Statutes*, ii. 565.

1676. Proprietary commission to Thomas Eastchurch, governor of Albemarle County: *North Carolina Records*, i. 232.

[1676.] Proprietary instructions to the governor and council of Albemarle County: *North Carolina Records*, i. 230.

1679. Proprietary instructions to John Harvey, president, and to the council of Albemarle County: *North Carolina Records*, i. 235.

1679. Royal commission to John Cutt [or Cutts], president, and to the council of New Hampshire: *New Hampshire Provincial Papers*, i. 373 ; also prefixed to *Acts and Laws of New Hampshire* (1771).

[1681.] Proprietary instructions to Henry Wilkinson, governor, and to the council of Albemarle County: *North Carolina Records*, i. 333.

1681. Proprietary commission to William Markham, governor of Pennsylvania: *Charter and Laws of Pennsylvania*, 470.

1682. Royal commission to Edward Cranfield, governor of New Hampshire: *New Hampshire Provincial Papers*, i. 433.

[1682.] Royal instructions to Edward Cranfield, governor of New Hampshire: *New Hampshire Provincial Papers*, i. 443.

1682. Proprietary commission to Thomas Dongan, governor of New York: *New York Documents*, iii. 328.

1683. Proprietary commission to Robert Barclay, governor of East New Jersey: Smith, *History of New Jersey*, 166.

1683. Proprietary commission to Gawen Lawrie, deputy-governor of East New Jersey: *New Jersey Documents*, i. 423.

1683. Proprietary instructions to Gawen Lawrie, deputy-governor of East New Jersey: *New Jersey Documents*, i. 426.

1683. Proprietary instructions to Thomas Dongan, governor of New York: *New York Documents*, iii. 331.

[1684.] Royal commission to Thomas, Lord Culpeper, governor of Virginia: *Calendar of Virginia State Papers*, i. 14.

1686. Royal commission to Thomas Dongan, governor of New York: *New York Documents*, iii. 377.

1686. Royal instructions to Thomas Dongan, governor of New York: *New York Documents*, iii. 369.

1686. Royal commission to Sir Edmund Andros, governor of New England: Force, *Tracts*, iv. No. 8.

1688. Royal commission to Sir Edmund Andros, governor of New England: *New York Documents*, iii. 537.

1688. Royal instructions to Sir Edmund Andros, governor of New England: *New York Documents*, iii. 543.

1689. Proprietary commission to Philip Ludwell, governor of Carolina north and east of Cape Fear: *North Carolina Records*, i. 360.

1689. Proprietary instructions to Philip Ludwell, governor of Carolina north and east of Cape Fear: *North Carolina Records*, i. 362.

1689. Proprietary instructions to John Blackwell, governor of Pennsylvania: *Pennsylvania Records*, i. 318.

1690. Proprietary commission to Lionel Copley, governor of Maryland: *Maryland Archives*, viii. 200. [Draft.]

[1690.] Royal commission to Henry Sloughter, governor of New York: *New York Documents*, iii. 623. [Draft.]

1690. Royal instructions to Henry Sloughter, governor of New York: *New York Documents*, iii. 685.

1691. Proprietary commission to Philip Ludwell, governor of Carolina: *North Carolina Records*, i. 373.

1691. Proprietary instructions to Philip Ludwell, governor of Carolina: *North Carolina Records*, i. 373; Rivers, *Chapter in the History of South Carolina*, 59.

1691. Royal commission to Lionel Copley, governor of Maryland: *Maryland Archives*, viii. 263.

1691. Royal instructions to Lionel Copley, governor of Maryland: *Maryland Archives*, viii. 271.

1692. Royal commission to Samuel Allen, governor of New Hampshire: *New Hampshire Provincial Papers*, ii. 57.

1692. Royal instructions to Samuel Allen, governor of New Hampshire: *New Hampshire Provincial Papers*, ii. 63.

1692. Proprietary commission to Andrew Hamilton, governor of West New Jersey: *New Jersey Documents*, ii. 87.

1692. Royal commission to Benjamin Fletcher, governor of New York: *New York Documents*, iii. 827; *Pennsylvania Records*, i. 357.

1692. Royal instructions to Benjamin Fletcher, governor of New York: *New York Documents*, iii. 818.

1692. Royal commission to Benjamin Fletcher, governor of Pennsylvania: *Pennsylvania Records*, i. 352; also drafts in *New York Documents*, iii. 856, and *Charter and Laws of Pennsylvania*, 539.

1692. Royal instructions to Benjamin Fletcher, governor of Pennsylvania: *New York Documents*, iii. 861.

1694. Proprietary commission to John Archdale, governor of Carolina: *North Carolina Records*, i. 380.

1694. Proprietary commission to William Markham, governor of Pennsylvania: *Pennsylvania Records*, i. 474; *Charter and Laws of Pennsylvania*, 558.

1697. Proprietary commission to Jeremiah Basse, governor of West New Jersey: *New Jersey Documents*, ii. 143. [Draft.]

1697. Royal commission to Richard, Earl of Bellomont, governor of New Hampshire: *New Hampshire Provincial Papers*, ii. 305.

1697. Royal commission to Richard, Earl of Bellomont, governor of New York: *New York Documents*, iv. 266.

1697. Royal instructions to Richard, Earl of Bellomont, governor of New York: *New York Documents*, iv. 284.

[1698 ?] Royal instructions to Francis Nicholson, governor of Virginia: *Virginia Magazine of History and Biography*, iv. 49.

1698. Proprietary instructions to Jeremiah Basse, governor of East New Jersey: *New Jersey Documents*, ii. 209.

1699. Proprietary commission to Andrew Hamilton, governor of West New Jersey: *New Jersey Documents*, ii. 301.

1702. Royal instructions to Joseph Dudley, governor of Massachusetts: Massachusetts Historical Society, *Collections*, 3rd Series, ix. 101.

1702. Royal commission to Joseph Dudley, governor of New Hampshire: *New Hampshire Provincial Papers*, ii. 366.

1702. Royal commission to Edward, Lord Cornbury, governor of New Jersey: Leaming and Spicer, *Grants, Concessions, etc.*, 647; *New Jersey Documents*, ii. 489; Smith, *History of New Jersey*, 220; Field, *Provincial Courts of New Jersey*, Appendix B.

1702. Royal instructions to Edward, Lord Cornbury, governor of New Jersey: Leaming and Spicer, *Grants, Concessions, etc.*, 619; *New Jersey Documents*, ii. 506; Smith, *History of New Jersey*, 230; Field, *Provincial Courts of New Jersey*, Appendix B.

1702. Proprietary commission to Sir Nathaniell Johnson, governor of South and North Carolina: *North Carolina Records*, i. 554.

1702. Proprietary instructions to Sir Nathaniell Johnson, governor of South and North Carolina: *North Carolina Records*, i. 555.

1708. Proprietary commission to Edward Tynte, governor of North and South Carolina: *North Carolina Records*, i. 694.

1709. Royal commission to Robert Hunter, governor of New York: *New York Documents*, v. 92. [Draft.]

1709. Royal instructions to Robert Hunter, governor of New York: *New York Documents*, v. 124. [Draft.]

1712. Proprietary instructions to Edward Hyde, governor of North Carolina: *North Carolina Records*, i. 844.

1715. Royal commission to Robert Hunter, governor of New York: *New York Documents*, v. 391. [Draft.]

1717. Royal commission to John Wentworth, lieutenant-governor of New Hampshire: *New Hampshire Provincial Papers*, ii. 712.

1719. Proprietary instructions to William Keith, governor of Pennsylvania: *Pennsylvania Records*, iii. 63.

1720. Royal instructions to Francis Nicholson, governor of South Carolina: Rivers, *Chapter in the History of South Carolina*, 68.

1727. Royal commission to John Montgomery, governor of New York: *New York Documents*, v. 834. [Draft.]

1730. Royal commission to George Burrington, governor of North Carolina: *North Carolina Records*, iii. 66. [Draft.]

1730. Royal instructions to George Burrington, governor of North Carolina: *North Carolina Records*, iii. 90. [Draft.]

1738. Royal commission to Lewis Morris, governor of New Jersey: *New Jersey Documents*, vi. 2. [Draft.]

1738. Royal instructions to Lewis Morris, governor of New Jersey: *New Jersey Documents*, vi. 15. [Draft.]

1741. Royal commission to George Clinton, governor of New York: *New York Documents*, vi. 189. [Draft.]

1753. Royal commission to Sir Danvers Osborn, governor of New York: Smith, *History of New York*, 297.

1754. Royal instructions to Arthur Dobbs, governor of North Carolina: *North Carolina Records*, v. 1107. [Draft.]

1758. Royal commission to Francis Bernard, governor of New Jersey: *New Jersey Documents*, ix. 23. [Draft.]

1758. Royal instructions to Francis Bernard, governor of New Jersey: *New Jersey Documents*, ix. 40. [Draft.]

1759. Proprietary commission to James Hamilton, governor of Pennsylvania: *Pennsylvania Records*, viii. 409.

1760. Royal commission to Benning Wentworth, governor of New Hampshire: *New Hampshire Provincial Papers*, vi. 908.

1761. Royal commission to Arthur Dobbs, governor of North Carolina: *North Carolina Records*, vi. 524. [Draft.]

1766. Royal commission to John Wentworth, governor of New Hampshire: prefixed to *Acts and Laws of New Hampshire* (1771).

1771. Royal instructions to John, Earl of Dunmore, governor of Virginia: *Aspinwall Papers* (Massachusetts Historical Society, *Collections*, 4th Series, x.), 630.

APPENDIX C.

LIST OF AUTHORITIES CITED.

[ALMON, JOHN.] A Collection of Interesting, Authentic Papers, relative to the Dispute between Great Britain and America; shewing the Causes and Progress of that Misunderstanding, from 1764 to 1775. London, 1777.

ASPINWALL PAPERS [1617–1817]. 2 vols. (Massachusetts Historical Society, *Collections*, 4th Series, ix.–x.). Boston, 1871.

BANCROFT, GEORGE. History of the United States. The Author's Last Revision. New York, 1883–1885.

BELKNAP, JEREMY. The History of New Hampshire. 3 vols. Philadelphia and Boston, 1784–1792.

[BEVERLEY, ROBERT.] The History of Virginia, in Four Parts. By a Native and Inhabitant of the Place. 2nd edition. London, 1722. [1st edition, 1705.]

BLACKSTONE, WILLIAM. Commentaries on the Laws of England. 4 vols. Oxford, 1768–1769.

BOZMAN, JOHN LEEDS. The History of Maryland, from its first Settlement, in 1633, to the Restoration, in 1660, with a copious Introduction, and Notes and Illustrations. 2 vols. Baltimore, 1837.

BRODHEAD, JOHN ROMEYN. History of the State of New York. 2 vols. New York, 1853, 1871.

BROWN, ALEXANDER. The Genesis of the United States. A narrative of the movement in England, 1605–1616, which resulted in the plantation of North America by Englishmen, disclosing the contest between England and Spain for the possession of the soil now occupied by the United States of America; set forth through a Series of Historical Manuscripts now first printed together with a reissue of rare contemporaneous tracts, accompanied by bibliographical memoranda, notes, and brief biographies. 2 vols. Boston and New York, 1891.

BURNABY, ANDREW. Travels through the Middle Settlements of North-America. In the years 1759 and 1760. With Observations upon the State of the Colonies. London, 1775.

CALVERT PAPERS. No. 1 [1624–1682] (Maryland Historical Society, *Fund Publications*, No. 28). Baltimore, 1889.

CAMPBELL, CHARLES. History of the Colony and Ancient Dominion of Virginia. Philadelphia, 1860.

CAROLINA. The Case of Protestant Dissenters in Carolina, shewing How a Law to prevent Occasional Conformity There, has ended in the Total Subversion of the Constitution in Church and State. London, 1706.

CAROLINA. Party-Tyranny: or, An Occasional Bill in Miniature; as now Practised in Carolina. London, 1705.

CAROLINA. The Two Charters granted by King Charles IId. to the Proprietors of Carolina. With the First and Last Fundamental Constitutions of that Colony. London, [1705?].

CARROLL, B. R. Historical Collections of South Carolina. 2 vols. New York, 1836.

CHALMERS, GEORGE. An Introduction to the History of the Revolt of the American Colonies. 2 vols. Boston, 1845,

CHALMERS, GEORGE. Opinions of Eminent Lawyers on various points of English Jurisprudence, chiefly concerning the Colonies, Fisheries and Commerce of Great Britain. Burlington, 1858.

CHALMERS, GEORGE. Political Annals of the Present United Colonies, from their Settlement to the Peace of 1763: compiled chiefly from Records, and authorized often by the insertion of State-Papers. Book i. London, 1780.

DELAWARE. Laws of the State of Delaware, [Oct. 14, 1700 — Aug. 18, 1797]. 2 vols. Newcastle, 1797.

DINWIDDIE, ROBERT. Official Records . . . 1751–1758. Edited by R. A. Brock. 2 vols. (Virginia Historical Society, *Collections*, New Series, iii.–iv.). Richmond, 1883–1884.

DOUGLASS, WILLIAM. A Summary, Historical and Political of the first Planting, progressive Improvements, and present State of the British Settlements in North America. 2 vols. Boston, 1749, 1751.

DOYLE, J. A. The English in America. 3 vols. London, 1882–1887.

DUMMER, JEREMIAH. A Defence of the New-England Charters. Boston, 1765. [1st edition, 1721. See Winsor, *Narrative and Critical History*, v. 121.]

EGERTON, HUGH EDWARD. A Short History of British Colonial Policy. London, 1897.

FIELD, RICHARD S. The Provincial Courts of New Jersey, with Sketches of the Bench and Bar. (New Jersey Historical Society, *Collections*, iii.) New York, 1849.

FORCE, PETER, editor. Tracts and other Papers, relating principally to the Origin, Settlement, and Progress of the Colonies in North America, from the Discovery of the Country to the Year 1776. 4 vols. Washington, 1836–1846.

FRANKLIN, BENJAMIN. Complete Works. Edited by John Bigelow. 10 vols. New York and London, 1887–1888.

GEORGIA. Acts passed by the General Assembly of the Colony of Georgia. 1755 to 1774. Edited by Charles Colcock Jones, Jr. Wormsloe, 1881.

GREAT BRITAIN. Journals of the House of Lords, beginning Anno Quarto Annæ Reginæ, 1705. Vol. xviii.

GREAT BRITAIN. The Statutes at Large, from Magna Charta, to the Twenty-fifth Year of the Reign of King George the Third, inclusive. . . . By Owen Ruffhead, Esq. . . . Revised, corrected, and continued, by Charles Runnington. 10 vols. London, 1786. [Each volume has a distinct title-page. Continued to the present time.]

HARTWELL, BLAIR, AND CHILTON. The present State of Virginia, and the College. London, 1727.

HAWKS, FRANCIS L. History of North Carolina: with Maps and Illustrations. 2 vols. Fayetteville, 1857-1858.

HAZARD, EBENEZER. Historical Collections; consisting of State Papers, and other authentic documents; intended as materials for an history of the United States of America. 2 vols. Philadelphia, 1792-1794.

HENING, WILLIAM WALLER. The Statutes at Large; being a Collection of all the Laws of Virginia, from the first Session of the Legislature, in the year 1619. 13 vols. Richmond, etc., 1819-1823.

HISTORY of the British Dominions in North America: from the first Discovery of that vast Continent by Sebastian Cabot in 1497, to its present glorious Establishment as confirmed by the late Treaty of Peace in 1763. 2 vols. London, 1773.

HOWELL, T. B. A Complete Collection of State Trials and Proceedings for High Treason and other Crimes and Misdemeanors from the earliest Period to the Year 1783, with Notes and other Illustrations. 21 vols. London, 1816. [Continued to 1820 in 12 additional volumes; also an index volume.]

HUTCHINSON, THOMAS. The History of Massachusetts, from the first Settlement thereof in 1628, until the Year 1750. 2 vols. Boston, 1795. — The History of the Province of Massachusetts Bay, from the Year 1750, until June, 1774. Vol. iii. London, 1828.

JEFFERSON, THOMAS. Writings. Edited by Paul Leicester Ford. Vol. iii. New York and London, 1894.

JONES, CHARLES COLCOCK, JR. The History of Georgia. 2 vols. Boston, 1883.

JONES, HUGH. The Present State of Virginia. London, 1724.

LEAMING, AARON, and SPICER, JACOB. The Grants, Concessions, and Original Constitutions of the Province of New-Jersey. The Acts passed during the Proprietary Governments, and other material Transactions before the Surrender thereof to Queen Anne. The Instrument of Surrender, and Her formal Acceptance thereof. Lord Cornbury's Commission and Instructions consequent thereon. Philadelphia, [1752?].

McCRADY, EDWARD. The History of South Carolina under the Proprietary Government 1670-1719. New York, 1897.

McMAHON, JOHN V. L. An Historical View of the Government of Maryland, from its Colonization to the Present Day. Vol. i. Baltimore, 1831.

MARYLAND. Laws of Maryland at Large [1637–1763]. . . . Collected into One Compleat Body. . . . Together with Notes and other Matters, relative to the Constitution thereof. . . . To which is prefixed The Charter, with an English Translation. By Thomas Bacon. Annapolis, 1765.

MARYLAND. Votes and Proceedings of the Lower House of Assembly of the Province of Maryland [1753–1759]. Annapolis, 1759.

MARYLAND ARCHIVES. Edited by William Hand Browne. 16 vols. Baltimore, 1883–1897.

MASSACHUSETTS. The Acts and Resolves, Public and Private, of the Province of the Massachusetts Bay: to which are prefixed the Charters of the Province. With historical and explanatory Notes. 8 vols. Boston, 1869–1895.

MASSACHUSETTS. Journal of the Honourable House of Representatives, of His Majesty's Province of the Massachusetts-Bay in New-England, begun and held at Boston, on Wednesday the Twenty-Ninth Day of May, Anno Domini, 1723. Boston, 1723.

MASSACHUSETTS. Records of the Governor and Company of the Massachusetts Bay in New England. Edited by Nathaniel B. Shurtleff. 5 vols. Boston, 1853–1854.

MASSACHUSETTS HISTORICAL SOCIETY. Collections. 4th Series, ii. Boston, 1854.

MORRIS, LEWIS. Papers . . . from 1738 to 1746. (New Jersey Historical Society, *Collections*, iv.) New York, 1852.

NEILL, EDWARD D. Virginia Carolorum: the Colony under the rule of Charles the First and Second [1625–1685]. Albany, 1886.

NEW ENGLAND. The Deplorable State of New England, by Reason of a Covetous and Treacherous Governour, and Pusillanimous Counsellors. London, 1708. [Reprinted in Massachusetts Historical Society, *Collections*, 5th Series, vi.]

NEW HAMPSHIRE. Acts and Laws of His Majesty's Province of New-Hampshire in New-England. With sundry Acts of Parliament [1696–1771]. By Order of the General Assembly. Portsmouth, 1771.

NEW HAMPSHIRE. Provincial Papers. Documents and Records relating to the Province of New-Hampshire from the earliest period of its Settlement [1623–1776]. Edited by Nathaniel Bouton. 7 vols. Concord, etc., 1867–1873. [Continued.]

NEW JERSEY. Acts of the General Assembly of the Province of New-Jersey, from the Surrender of the Government to Queen Anne, on the 17ᵗʰ Day of April, in the Year of our Lord 1702, to the 14ᵗʰ Day of January 1776. Compiled by Samuel Allinson. Burlington, 1776.

NEW JERSEY. An Analytical Index to the Colonial Documents of New Jersey, in the State Paper offices of England. Compiled by Henry Stevens. Edited by William A. Whitehead. (New Jersey Historical Society, *Collections*, v.) New York, 1858.

NEW JERSEY. Documents relating to the Colonial History of the State of New Jersey. Edited by William A. Whitehead, W. Nelson, and F. W. Ricord. 19 vols. (also index volume). Newark, etc., 1880–1897. [Called also " New Jersey Archives."]

NEW JERSEY HISTORICAL SOCIETY. Proceedings. 1st Series. 10 vols. Newark, 1847–1867.

NEW YORK. Acts of Assembly, passed in the Province of New York, from 1691 to 1718. London, 1719.

NEW YORK. Documents relative to the Colonial History of the State of New York; procured in Holland, England and France, by John Romeyn Brodhead, Esq. Edited by E. B. O'Callaghan. 14 vols. (also index volume). Albany, 1853–1883.

NEW YORK. Journal of the Votes and Proceedings of the General Assembly of the Colony of New York [1691–1765]. 2 vols. New York, 1764–1766.

NEW YORK. Laws of New York, from the Year 1691, to 1773 inclusive. Vol. i. New York, 1774.

NORTH CAROLINA. The Colonial Records of North Carolina. Edited by William L. Saunders. 10 vols. Raleigh, 1886–1890.

NORTH CAROLINA. Laws of the State of North Carolina [1715–1790]. Published according to Act of Assembly by James Iredell. Edenton, 1791. [With additions to 1800.]

NORTH CAROLINA. The Public Acts of the General Assembly of North Carolina. Vol. i. Containing the Acts from 1715 to 1790; revised and published . . . by the Honorable James Iredell, Esq. And now revised by Francois-Xavier Martin. 2 vols. Newbern, 1804. [Vol. ii., 1790–1803.]

O'CALLAGHAN, E. B. The Documentary History of the State of New-York; arranged under direction of the Hon. Christopher Morgan, Secretary of State. 4 vols. Albany, 1849–1851.

[OLDMIXON, JOHN.] The British Empire in America, containing the History of the Discovery, Settlement, Progress and State of the British Colonies on the Continent and Islands of America. 2 vols. London, 1741.

PENNSYLVANIA. Charter to William Penn, and Laws of the Province of Pennsylvania, passed between the years 1682 and 1700, preceded by Duke of York's Laws in force from the year 1676 to the year 1682, with an Appendix containing Laws relating to the organization of the Provincial Courts and Historical matter. Edited by Staughton George, Benjamin M. Nead, and Thomas McCamant. Harrisburg, 1879.

PENNSYLVANIA. An Historical Review of the Constitution and Government of Pennsylvania, from its Origin . . . . London, 1759. [Reprinted in Franklin's *Works*, Sparks edition, 1809, Vol. ii.]

PENNSYLVANIA. Minutes of the Provincial Council of Pennsylvania, from the Organization to the Termination of the Proprietary Government [1683–1776]. Published by the State. 10 vols. Philadelphia and Harrisburg, 1851–1852. [Continued in 6 additional volumes as "Minutes of the Supreme Executive Council of Pennsylvania, from its Organization to the

Termination of the Revolution " (1776-1790). — Called also " Colonial Records." — Index volume.]

PENNSYLVANIA. The Statutes at Large of Pennsylvania from 1682 to 1801. Compiled under the authority of the Act of May 19 1887 by James T. Mitchell and Henry Flanders. Vols. ii., iii., iv. [Harrisburg], 1896-1897.

PENNSYLVANIA. Votes and Proceedings of the House of Representatives of the Province of Pennsylvania [1682-1776]. 6 vols. Philadelphia, 1752-1776.

PENNSYLVANIA ARCHIVES [1664-1790]. Selected and arranged from original documents in the office of the Secretary of the Commonwealth. . . . By Samuel Hazard. 12 vols. Philadelphia, 1852-1856. — Second Series. Edited by John B. Linn and William H. Egle. 19 vols. Harrisburg, 1874-1893.

PERRY, WILLIAM STEVENS. The History of the American Episcopal Church, 1587-1883. 2 vols. Boston, 1885.

PERRY, WILLIAM STEVENS. Papers relating to the History of the Church in Virginia, A. D. 1650-1776. [Hartford?] 1870.

POORE, BEN: PERLEY. The Federal and State Constitutions, Colonial Charters, and other Organic Laws of the United States. 2 vols. Washington, 1878.

POWNALL, THOMAS. The Administration of the Colonies. London, 1765.

PROUD, ROBERT. The History of Pennsylvania, in North America, from the original Institution and Settlement of that Province under the first Proprietor and Governor William Penn, in 1681, till after the year 1742; with an Introduction. 2 vols. Philadelphia, 1797-1798.

QUINCY, JOSIAH, JR. Reports of Cases argued and Adjudged in the Superior Court of Judicature of the Province of Massachusetts Bay, between 1761 and 1772. Boston, 1865.

RHODE ISLAND. Records of the Colony of Rhode Island and Providence Plantations, in New England [1636-1792]. Edited by John Russell Bartlett. 10 vols. Providence, 1856-1865.

RIVERS, WILLIAM JAMES. A Chapter in the Early History of South Carolina. Charleston, 1874.

[RIVERS, WILLIAM JAMES.] A Sketch of the History of South Carolina to the Close of the Proprietary Government by the Revolution of 1719. Charleston, 1856.

ROGERS, ROBERT. A Concise Account of North America. London, 1765.

RYMER, THOMAS. Fœdera, Conventiones, Litteræ, et Cujuscunque Generis Acta Publica, inter Reges Angliæ, et Alios quosvis Imperatores, Reges, Pontifices, Principes, vel Communitates, ab ineunte Sæculo Duodecimo, viz. ab Anno 1101 ad nostra usque Tempora, Habita aut Tractata. 20 vols. London, 1727-1735.

SAINSBURY, W. NOEL, editor. Calendar of State Papers, Colonial Series [America and West Indies], 1574–1660. London, 1860. — Continuation, 1661–1668, London, 1880; 1669–1674, London, 1889; 1675–1676, London, 1893; 1677–1680, London, 1896.

SEWALL, SAMUEL. Diary [1674–1729]. 3 vols. (Massachusetts Historical Society, *Collections*, 5th Series, v–vii.). Boston, 1878–1882.

SMITH, SAMUEL. The History of the Colony of Nova-Cæsaria, or New-Jersey: containing, an Account of its first Settlement, progressive Improvements, the original and present Constitution, and other events, to the Year 1721. With some particulars since; and a short view of its present state. Burlington, 1765.

SMITH, WILLIAM. The History of the Province of New-York, from the first Discovery. To which is annexed a Description of the Country, an Account of the Inhabitants, their Trade, Religious, and Political State, and the Constitution of the Courts of Justice in that Colony. London, 1776.

SOUTH CAROLINA. Statutes at Large. Edited by Thomas Cooper and David J. McCord. 10 vols. Columbia, 1836–1841.

SOUTH CAROLINA HISTORICAL SOCIETY. Collections. 3 vols. Charleston, 1857–1859.

SPOTSWOOD, ALEXANDER. Official Letters . . . 1710–1722. Edited by R. A. Brock. 2 vols. (Virginia Historical Society, *Collections*, New Series, i.–ii.). Richmond, 1882, 1885.

STILLÉ, CHARLES J. The Life and Times of John Dickinson. Philadelphia, 1891.

STITH, WILLIAM. The History of the First Discovery and Settlement of Virginia. New York, 1865.

STOKES, ANTHONY. A View of the Constitution of the British Colonies, in North-America and the West Indies, at the time the Civil War broke out on the Continent of America. London, 1783.

TOWNSHEND. The Manuscripts of the Marquess Townshend. (Historical Manuscripts Commission, *Eleventh Report*, Appendix, Part iv.) London, 1887.

TROTT, NICHOLAS. The Laws of the British Plantations in America, relating to the Church and the Clergy, Religion and Learning. London, 1721.

TRUMBULL, BENJAMIN. A Complete History of Connecticut, Civil and Ecclesiastical, from the Emigration of its first Planters, from England, in the Year 1630 to the Year 1764; and to the close of the Indian Wars. 2 vols. New Haven, 1818.

VIRGINIA. Calendar of Virginia State Papers and other Manuscripts, 1652–1781, preserved in the Capitol at Richmond. Arranged and edited by William P. Palmer, M. D. Vol. i. Richmond, 1875. [Continued.]

VIRGINIA. Colonial Records. [Edited by Thomas H. Wynne, and W. S. Gilman.] Richmond, 1874.

VIRGINIA. Statutes at Large. See HENING, W. W

VIRGINIA COMPANY. Abstract of the Proceedings . . . 1619–1624, prepared from the records in the Library of Congress by Conway Robinson, and edited with an introduction and notes by R. A. Brock. 2 vols. (Virginia Historical Society, *Collections*, New Series, vii.–viii.). Richmond, 1888–1889.

VIRGINIA HISTORICAL SOCIETY. Collections. New Series. 11 vols. Richmond, 1882–1892.

VIRGINIA HISTORICAL SOCIETY. The Virginia Magazine of History and Biography. 4 vols. Richmond, 1894–1897.

WINSOR, JUSTIN. Narrative and Critical History of America. 8 vols. Boston and New York. 1886–1889.

WINTHROP PAPERS [1630–1659]. (Massachusetts Historical Society, *Collections*, 4th Series, vi.) Boston, 1863.

WOOD, SILAS. A Sketch of the first Settlement of the several Towns on Long-Island; with their Political Condition to the end of the American Revolution. Brooklyn, 1828.

WRIGHT, ROBERT. A Memoir of General James Oglethorpe. London, 1867.

INDEX.

284 *INDIAN — MAINE.*

Indian commissioners, appointment of, 187–188, 193.

Indians, invasions in South Carolina, 15, 20; Shirley's service with, 62; relations of colonies with, 107–110; governors' proclamations concerning, 160. See also French and Indian Wars.

Instructions to governors, bond for observance of, in proprietary governments, 14, 196; features, 93–97; violation, 94–95, 163–165, 173–175; restricting colonial legislation, 162–165. See also Provincial Governor (powers), and governors by name.

Intercolonial relations, 109, 192. See also Indians, Provincial Governor (powers).

JAMAICA assembly, resolutions of, on financial powers of the assembly, 182.

James I. inaugurates royal government in Virginia, 3.

James II., effect upon New York of his accession to the throne, 15; organizes royal government in Massachusetts, 16; Penn's relation with, 18; opposes representation in New York, 38; policy of, 52. See also York, Duke of.

Jefferson, Thomas, on the salary of the executive, 175–176.

Jennings, Samuel, deputy-governor of West Jersey, 8; speaker of New Jersey assembly, 150.

Jerseys. See East Jersey, New Jersey, West Jersey.

Johnson, Robert, governor of South Carolina, adherence to instructions, 187.

Johnston, Gabriel, governor of North Carolina, dissolves assembly, 154; approves paper-money bill, 164.

Judges. See Judiciary.

Judiciary, consent of council required in appointment of officers, 81, 111–112, 134; governor's relation to, 133–144; English, 133; tenure of office, 134–137; erection of courts, 137–139; prosecution, 139; governor's criminal jurisdiction, 140; appeal cases, 140–141; equity cases, 141–142; minor functions, 142; governor's abuse of power, 143, 144; jurisdiction of King's Bench over colonial governors, 196–197. See also Courts, Provincial Governor (powers).

KEITH, Sir William, governor of Pennsylvania, insubordination, 83–84; alliance with assembly, 87; salary obtained by system of bargain and sale, 174.

King's Bench, colonial governors subject to jurisdiction of, 196–197. See also Courts, Judiciary.

King's Province, included in royal government of Massachusetts, 16.

LAND, grants of, in the colonies, 126.

Leeward Islands, suit against governor of, 197.

Legislation, consent of freemen required in Maryland, Carolina, and Pennsylvania, 32, 34; power at first exercised by executive, 34–36; ordinances and proclamations, 34–39, 159–161; power transferred to assembly, 36–39; initiative claimed by governor, 39–41, 161; advice of council asked, 82–84; governor's indirect influence, 145–159; governor's right of recommendation, 161; governor's veto, 162; veto reserved by the crown, 162; certain acts not to be approved by the governor, 162–163; "legislative riders," 164; influence of salary grants on, 167–176. See also Assembly, Governor and Council, Provincial Governor (powers), and colonies by name.

Leisler rebellion, 38.

Libel cases, 143–144, 200–201.

Liberty of speech and press. See Press, Speech.

Lieutenant-governor, office sought as source of profit, 47; temporary successor of governor, 53, 55–58; power in Virginia, 58; sometimes member of council, 58, 78.

Lloyd, John, asks appointment as lieutenant-governor of South Carolina, 47.

London Company, 2, 3; Bishop of, see Bishop of London.

Lovelace, John, Lord, governor of New York and New Jersey, 139.

Lowther, governor of Barbadoes, 197.

MAINE, province of, included in royal government of Massachusetts, 16; representation in Massachusetts council, 76.